School-Based Interventions for Students with Behavior Problems

School-Based Interventions for Students with Behavior Problems

Julie M. Bowen

Jordan School District,
University of Utah

William R. Jenson

University of Utah,
Salt Lake City, UT

and

Elaine Clark

University of Utah,
Salt Lake City, UT

 Springer

Library of Congress Cataloging-in-Publication Data

Bowen, Julie M.
    School-based interventions for students with behavior problems / by Julie M. Bowen,
    William R. Jenson, and Elaine Clark.
        p. cm.
    Includes bibliographical references (p.) and index.
    ISBN 0-306-48114-6
    1. Problem children–Education–United States. 2. Behavior disorders in children–United
    States. 3. Behavior modification–United States. I. Jenson, William R. II. Clark, Elaine.
    III. Title.

LC4802.B69 2004
371.93—dc22   2003062062

ISBN 0-306-48114-6

Printed in the United States of America.   (IBT)

9 8 7 6 5 4 3

springer.com

In memory of my mother, Irene McDermaid, a caring, dedicated teacher who made a difference in children's lives—J. B.

In memory of Dr. Ken Reavis, the founder of the Utah BEST Project and the "connector" between best practice interventions and tough kids who were successful because of them—W. R. J.

In memory of Grayson Jenson, who reminded us all that some tough kids aren't so tough after all—E. C.

Preface

Children, by their nature, are active, impulsive, easily distracted, and sometimes irritable. Most children do not begin school with the skills to handle problems without conflict, think through the consequences of their actions, and listen attentively to uninteresting topics—these are skills that develop throughout childhood, adolescence and even into adulthood. Some students, however, will exhibit behavior problems so severe that they consistently disrupt the learning of the entire classroom, frequently engage in conflicts with peers and adults, and fail to comply with rules and requests. Although these students only comprise about 7% of the student population, their actions affect everyone else in the school. These students are the focus of this book.

School-Based Interventions for Students with Behavior Problems is a book about helping children and adolescents who engage in severe behaviors to behave appropriately in the school setting. The emphasis of this book is on the prevention of behavior problems through structuring the instructional environment and teaching appropriate skills—and intervention to reduce problems with practical, proven, and positive procedures. This book is designed for teachers faced with the daily challenge of instructing students with behavior problems, as well as others who work with teachers and students; school administrators, counselors, special educators, and school psychologists.

The orientation and contents of this book represent the authors' experience and professional training in teaching, clinical work, and research involving students with behavior problems over the last 25 years. In searching for effective behavioral and academic strategies, the authors have reviewed hundreds of research-validated studies to select techniques applicable to varied instructional settings within the school.

It is our hope that this volume will provide educational professionals with a useful set of ideas and strategies that are a combination of research-supported interventions and practical guidelines, one that will help them with the critical task of helping at-risk students and those with behavior disorders to develop the competencies needed for academic and social success.

Contents

Chapter 1

Introduction

Scene One

Seven-year-old Cody never seemed to listen to the teacher's directions. As soon as the students went to their desks to begin working independently on daily assignments, Cody was up and down out of his seat, playing with small objects in his desk, or bothering the other students around him. He never seemed to complete any of the worksheets, without constant teacher prompts and reminders. Staying in for recess, taking the work home, and conferences with his parents did not seem change this behavior.

Scene Two

Twelve-year-old Britten, a 6th grade girl was constantly making rude comments to students around her, calling them names, pushing and shoving when in line, or poking them with her pencil. She often talked loudly or laughed inappropriately in the middle of instruction. She was disliked by her peers and frequently complained of problems with other students. Britten seemed to have a quick temper and became easily irritated or annoyed by others, even when their behaviors were unintentional. Her schoolwork was sloppy and often incomplete. When corrected by her teacher, Britten would argue and shout back, ignoring teacher directions.

Scene Three

Alex, a 15-year-old student had received special education services since the 4th grade because of severe behavior problems. He attended resource for reading, and math classes, however, was in regular education classes the rest of the school day. Alex was extremely disruptive in most of his classes, particularly the mainstream classes, made verbally aggressive comments to other students, refused to follow class and school rules, used foul language, and had been in several physical fights. He was referred to the assistant principal frequently for disciplinary action and in-school suspension. In fact, most of his teachers just wanted him out of their classroom!

Do any of these scenarios sound familiar? What behaviors do educators describe as the most problematic? Children may exhibit behaviors ranging from

1

Table 1.1. Teacher Top
Ten Problem Behaviors

1. Talking Out
2. Not Following Directions
3. Not Respecting Others
4. Not Finishing Work
5. Fighting
6. Disruptive/acting out
7. Arguing
8. Out of Seat
9. Tattletale
10. Interrupting

whining, complaining, and refusal to follow directions or complete tasks, to more aggressive behaviors such as hurting other children, name-calling, kicking, screaming or physical assaults or threats. Some teachers report annoying behaviors such as nose-picking, making noises, or playing with objects. Based on a recent survey of the most problematic behaviors that teachers report, we have developed a *Top Ten List of Problem Behaviors* (Nicholas, 1998). Table 1.1 lists these top ten problem behaviors. You may identify many of these common problems as interfering with your teaching effectiveness and impeding student success.

If you are a new teacher or school practitioner just beginning the daunting task of educating children, or if you have several years of teaching experience, one of the major challenges you will encounter in your career is working with students with behavior problems. The prevalence of behavioral problems in the classroom is increasing considerably, with about 5–10% of the school-aged population meeting criteria for diagnosis of a serious emotional disturbance, an Attention Deficit Hyperactivity Disorder, or another behavior disorder (Barkley, 1990; Walker, Colvin, Ramsey, 1995). Many teachers can identify at least two or three students in each class who exhibit severe disruptive behaviors. Most teachers will also identify several other students in their class with social problems, off-task behaviors, poor work completion, and difficulty learning. In special education settings, the incidence of disruptive behavior problems, attentional problems, learning difficulties, and peer-relationship problems may be much higher. In fact, teachers rate disruptive classroom behavior as one of the most critical issues affecting classroom climate and impeding instruction. Often, the misbehavior of one student or a few students will interrupt established routines and spread to other students, jeopardizing an otherwise well-planned lesson.

The purpose of this volume is, therefore, to assist you in working more effectively with these difficult students—while creating a positive classroom climate for all students. *School-Based Interventions for Students with Behavior Problems* is your guide to handling many common behavior problems exhibited by school-aged children. In the following chapters you will find strategies for improving a variety of problem behaviors in the classroom, problems getting along with other students, problems at recess or transition periods, as well as strategies for improving the academic deficiencies that often accompany behavior problems.

For many students with behavior problems, school quickly becomes an unpleasant, negative experience. A pattern of undesirable behaviors combined with academic difficulties and social problems may lead to a cycle of school failure that could eventually contribute to school avoidance, school dropout, and/or severe psychosocial problems. It is critical that children who are at high risk for behavior problems receive early intervention. There is substantial data that show that early intervention for learning and behavior problems increases the likelihood of a successful school experience (Serna, Nielsen, Lambros, & Forness, 2000). By structuring the classroom environment to facilitate positive social interactions and productive study skills, those of you who work with these students will have a significant impact on their long-term outcome.

WHO CAN BENEFIT FROM THIS BOOK

This book is designed to provide school practitioners and educational professionals with a handbook of researched-based, practical interventions for use with school-aged students with behavior and learning problems. *School-Based Interventions for Students with Behavior Problems* is a compilation of usable, practical, creative ideas that teachers, parents, and school administrators can implement in the classroom or school-wide, to improve classroom management and student learning. This book is primarily intended for educational practitioners who work with school-age children from preschool to secondary levels, including classroom teachers, special education teachers, paraeducators, administrators, school psychologists, social workers, and school counselors. Parents may also use many of the interventions in the home setting with some simple modifications. College students enrolled in teacher training programs, as well as graduate students in education, special education, and educational psychology programs will find these research-based interventions a useful addition to their personal library. This book will be a valuable reference source in public libraries, university libraries, or school district libraries that provide materials for educators.

THE 4 PS—PROVEN, PRACTICAL, POSITIVE, PREVENTATIVE

In this book we have combined new research information and adaptations of previous research to create a helpful reference and instructional guide to over 100 interventions for managing and reducing behavior and learning problems in children and adolescents. Specific, successful techniques for use with individual students, on a class-wide basis, or with an entire school are designed and written in a format that is teacher-friendly and easy to implement. We believe successful interventions must include the 4 Ps—**Proven, Practical, Positive, and Preventative.** The interventions that are included are research proven—meaning they are empirically based, up-to date, and have been tried and proven to be effective. These interventions are based on time-tested principals of behavior management techniques. Interventions must also be practical and time efficient—which means they do not take excessive time or effort to implement, are inexpensive, and do not interfere with valuable instructional time. An effort has been made to combine these research-based ideas with practical suggestions and adaptations for use with larger groups or in a variety of settings. These interventions focus primarily on positive, not punitive strategies to increase appropriate behaviors and create cooperative interactions in the classroom. Many of the interventions utilize reinforcement and positive group contingencies to encourage desirable behaviors. And finally, they are preventative, focusing on proactive programs that educators may use to prevent the misbehavior of one student from spreading to other students or to prevent misbehaviors from escalating into more severe problems. Proactive programs are an effective means to structure the classroom environment to allow all students to succeed. Rather than rely on reactive consequences, a proactive behavior management plan focuses on instructional techniques and promoting a positive climate to motivate students.

HOW TO USE THIS BOOK

This book differs from other intervention manuals that are available on the market, in that it provides a variety of proven classroom strategies in a step-by-step format that you can easily implement and incorporate into your classroom routine and curriculum. The contents of this book include a review of effective schools' research and proactive strategies, a framework to help you understand what makes a good intervention, the key characteristics of students with behavior and learning disorders, and specific, proven classroom strategies collected from the education and psychology literature. This book is a practical reference guide that you can refer to when faced with a challenging student or when you simply want to improve or add variety to your current classroom management plan.

Although you may choose to turn directly to the interventions section (Chapters 5–8) to select specific interventions for immediate problems, we encourage you to review the first section (Chapters 2–4), which includes the following:

- What is a good intervention—the definition, the variables that make interventions effective and acceptable, and the controversies associated with intervention use.

- Students with behavior problems—the prevalence of behavior disorders, the risk factors, and understanding the substantial deficits in basic academic, social, and self-management skills that students with behavior disorders often exhibit.
- Classroom basics—the proactive classroom management skills that effective teachers use to minimize the occurrence of misbehavior and create positive classrooms.

The second section, which is the "hands-on" section, is divided into four major areas of intervention:

- Interventions for Behavior Problems.
- Interventions for Academic Problems.
- Interventions for Social Skills.
- School-wide Interventions.

Each of these chapters includes research proven interventions and how to implement them correctly. The interventions were selected for this collection based on the following criteria, which we refer to as the **Effectiveness Rating Scale**. This rating scale is comprised of eight variables and a total effectiveness rating score. The following code was developed to provide an indication of acceptability and to assist with intervention selection: **EFECTIV+ T**, where **E** = Expense, **F** = Hassle-Free Index, **E** = Effectiveness. **C** = Complexity, **T** = Time, **I** = Student Interest, **V** = Social Validity, **+** = Positive (vs. negative), and **T** = Total Rating of overall effectiveness. Ratings for each code are based on a scale of 1–10 (1 = low value of acceptability and 10 = high value of acceptability). For example, a rating of **Expense = 9** indicates the cost or expense to implement the intervention is relatively minor and highly acceptable based on the expense factor.

Each intervention is written in an easy-to-follow format, which includes, the targeted behavior, age group, goal, materials needed, implementation steps, and troubleshooting ideas. Although each intervention includes complete step-by-step instructions for implementation we encourage you to change or supplement the steps to meet specific needs of your students. Many of these interventions can be adapted for use with other age groups or can target a variety of behavior problems. Most, if not all of the classroom activities, strategies, and environmental modifications described in this book will benefit most students, not just those with behavioral or academic impairments. To use these interventions, simply identify the behavior or academic problem you wish to target. The subject index will be useful in quickly locating interventions for specific problems. The index lists frequently occurring behaviors, along with the page number for each intervention that is designed for that behavior. You may select interventions based on age or developmental level, setting, and/or severity of the problem. Most interventions need few materials to implement. We have included examples of student organizers, student contracts, self-management forms, and handouts in Appendix A, as well as a list of behavioral intervention terms and examples in Appendix B.

We appreciate the tremendous effort and complex task it is working with and teaching today's children and adolescents. As the prevalence of children with behavioral and learning problems increases, the need for excellent school practitioners increases. Educating children can be a challenging, sometimes frustrating, but rewarding task. It is our hope that the tools presented here will help you find success in this endeavor.

Chapter 2

What is a Good Intervention?

What makes a good school-based intervention for students with behavioral, academic, or social difficulties? First, it is important to understand what an intervention is and what it is not. For the purposes of this book, interventions are not counseling or non-directive psychotherapies. There are places for these approaches in a school setting, however, their overall effectiveness for behavior problems, social skills deficits, and academic problems are less robust (Stage & Quiroz, 1997; Weiss, Catron, Harris, & Phung, 1999; Weisz, Weiss, Alicke, & Klotz, 1987). Our definition of an intervention is: *the systematic application of research-validated procedures to change behaviors through either teaching new skills or through the manipulation of antecedents and consequences*. It is important that any procedure implemented with students has been research-validated and published in a peer reviewed professional journal. This process insures that the intervention has been implemented with integrity and its' effectiveness has been demonstrated using an acceptable research design and outcome measures. Most of the interventions reviewed in this book are either single subject or group research designs. Having the procedure "peer reviewed", means that objective experts in the field have reviewed the intervention research study and found its' methodology to be acceptable and the procedure effective in changing behaviors.

The second part of our intervention definition involves teaching a new skill or the manipulation of antecedents or consequences. Often, problematic behaviors result from a student's deficit and his or her inability to perform a needed skill that is required in the school environment. These required skills can include academic, social, and even self-management skills. If the student can be taught the needed skill, then sometimes the problematic behavior will be replaced by a new and more

7

appropriate behavior. Teaching new skills that are adaptive and serve the student's needs is an effective intervention.

At other times, antecedent and consequence manipulation are also needed to effectively change a behavior. An antecedent is anything that comes just before a behavior and sets the occasion for that behavior to occur. Antecedents can be persons, places, times, events, or other behaviors. If the antecedent is changed or altered, then sometimes the behavior can also be changed. For example, if thumb-sucking behavior is a problem for a young child, then tracking and changing the event that happens just before the thumb-sucking occurs can change the behavior. For example, the child may pick up his favorite baby blanket and rub it between his fingers just before the thumb sucking starts. The blanket sets the occasion for the thumb-sucking to begin. If the blanket is removed, then the sucking may stop. People, places, and other behaviors are common antecedents to behavior problems in the school setting. There might be one person such as a peer who teases and upsets another student that sets the occasion for a tantrum or outburst. Problematic places for misbehaviors might be unsupervised bathrooms, hallways, or stairwells. Other behaviors that are antecedents to common problem behaviors can be as simple as how an adult makes a request of the student. If the adult yells, gives the request many times without waiting for compliance (nagging), or makes the request from across the room rather than up close, then this ineffective request sets the occasion for noncompliance (Rhode, Jenson, & Reavis, 1992). By changing or altering the antecedent, the behavior can frequently be changed.

Frequently, when we think of interventions we think of consequence-based interventions. These can be consequence rewards like gold stars, candies, or social approval. Or, these consequences can be mildly aversive such as a verbal reprimand or taking a privilege away when the child misbehaves. Consequences fall into three broad categories that sometimes change behaviors. These include positive reinforcement, negative reinforcement, and punishment. A **positive reinforcement** is anything that increases or maintains a behavior by gaining access to that stimulus. For example, if you work harder to get a grade of an A—then the stimulus of an A on an assignment is a positive reinforcement to you. Positive reinforcements can be a tangible object (money), an activity (going dancing), sensory (a massage), or social (attention from peers). If the behavior increases or is maintained to get access to the stimulus (tangible, activity, sensory, or social), then by definition it is a positive reinforcer. Ironically, if a student's misbehavior is increased or maintained by a teacher's yelling and negative comments, then the yelling and negative comments are reinforcing to the student by our definition.

A more difficult concept to understand is the concept of **negative reinforcement**. Like positive reinforcement, negative reinforcement involves increasing or maintaining a behavior. But unlike positive reinforcement in which access to a stimulus is sought, with **negative reinforcement** the behavior is increased or maintained to avoid or escape a stimulus. For example, a student may increase his misbehavior to escape (get to leave) an algebra class that he dislikes. The coercive cycle explained in Chapter 3 is a negatively reinforced cycle. The student increases his problem behaviors of arguing, temper tantrums, and aggression to escape a command given by an adult. Many of the problem behaviors experienced by educators from their students have a long history of negative reinforcement.

Punishment is any consequence that suppresses or decreases a behavior when the stimulus is applied. Punishment and negative reinforcement are commonly confused but they are very different. Negative reinforcement increases or maintains a behavior to escape or avoid a stimulus. Punishment suppresses or decreases a behavior when a stimulus is applied. Common punishers that are used by educators include verbal reprimands, withdrawal of privileges such as recess, time-out from a rewarding environment, or suspension from school (if being in school is rewarding). There are several problems with using too much punishment. If the behavior that is being punished is rewarding to the student (talking out in class), then the behavior will continue after the punishing stimulus is withdrawn. To permanently decrease most punished behaviors, a replacement appropriate behavior must also be taught. An example of a replacement behavior is learning to raise your hand and ask for permission to speak in class. Too much punishment can also result in emotional side effects such as when a student becomes anxious or tries to avoid the school environment. Or, the student may become resentful and learn to dislike the adult who applies the punishment procedures resulting in even more problem behaviors.

We have used the word "sometimes" in reference to interventions changing behaviors. No intervention is 100% effective and always changes behavior. There is frequently a need to combine interventions to effectively manage behaviors over time. An educator might need to change an antecedent and combine it with an effective consequence and even teach an appropriate replacement behavior to manage a problem behavior. For instance, one of the most common problem behaviors encountered by teachers in the classroom is noncompliance. The student simply will not follow the teacher's requests. To manage noncompliance, the teacher could be taught to give effective precision requests (the antecedent). If the student complies with the request, this behavior would consistently be followed by teacher praise (the positive consequence). If the student fails to comply, then the student would lose privileges such as recess time (the punishment consequence). To enhance the behavior change, the student could be taught a replacement social skill to noncompliance such as the "Sure I Will" program (refer to Chapter 5). All of these interventions such as making "precision requests" and the "Sure I Will" social skills program are described later in this book. But first, it is important to understand what makes an effective intervention.

EFFECTIVE INTERVENTIONS

An intervention may be designed to teach a new skill, alter an antecedent, or apply a consequence, however, still be ineffective. It can even be demonstrated to effectively manage a behavior in the published research literature and still be ineffective in the real world of schools. There are several variables of an intervention that are critically important if a teacher under the real-life educational stresses of everyday will implement and continue to use that intervention. These variables include amount of teacher time required, expenses and costs associated with implementation, complexity, hassles and risks involved, positive versus negative, degree of effectiveness, social validity, and student interest.

Time

One of the most important aspects of any intervention is the time it takes to implement that intervention (Elliott, 1988). Teachers have too little time to attend to all the demands and tasks that are required of them each day. Adding one more "thing" to a teacher's workday is like adding the proverbial straw that breaks the back. Intervention time can be viewed in two basic ways. First, how much time does it take to design, gather the necessary materials, and implement the intervention? This is called **start time**. The more start time required, the less likely the intervention will be used by a teacher. The second time component is called **run time**. Once the intervention is designed, how much time does it take to actually implement the intervention in practice each day? The more time it simply takes to run an intervention each day, the less likely the intervention will be incorporated into the classroom or school routine and used consistently.

Start time is less important than the running time of the intervention. In reality, it only takes one instance to design, put together the materials, and start an intervention. Start time is important but it is usually a one-time investment. Run time is critically important because it is done each time the intervention is used. If the intervention is required each day, then run time cuts into the teacher's instructional time each day and should be kept to a minimum. Effective interventions have small investments in actual running time.

Complexity

The more complex an intervention is, the less likely it will be used. Complexity involves such issues as how many steps does it take to do the intervention? Does the intervention come with difficult to understand instructions for implementation? Are there lots of materials needed before the intervention can be started? Does the intervention add more activities that are outside of the normal classroom or school schedule? Is special training required before the intervention can be mastered?

Does the intervention require additional staff to use the intervention effectively in the classroom? Even the name of the intervention can add a dimension of complexity. For example, the phrase "Mystery Motivator" is far less complex and more easily understood than the phrase "variable schedule-intermittent reinforcement" which both refer to the same intervention.

It should be noted that there is also an interaction between the variable time and complexity. The more complex an intervention, then generally the more start and run time is required. Keeping an intervention simple without sacrificing its' usefulness is a key element in determining effective interventions.

Cost

By cost we mean how many resources, especially money does it take to implement the intervention. The more costly an intervention, the less likely it will be used consistently. It has been estimated that teachers in states such as Utah invest as much as $245 of their own money on materials for their classrooms. Many attractive interventions require very expensive rewards, materials, and even instruments (such as computers) for their implementation. Extra training in the use of the intervention, hiring extra staff to implement the intervention, or continuously having to re-stock a classroom reward store can be hidden costs. Economical interventions are some of the most effective interventions.

Positive

It is frequently reported in the research literature on intervention acceptability that educators prefer positive interventions to aversive interventions (Elliott, 1988). This can be an important variable in designing any type of intervention for behavior problems. Aversive or punishing consequences are problematic when new behaviors are being taught. They can cause anxiety or fears that interfere with learning. However, it is important to realize that although educators report in surveys that they prefer positive interventions, in practice they frequently overuse aversive procedures. A verbal reprimand is the most frequently used intervention by teachers in their classrooms followed by withdrawal of privileges, and referrals to the office. Suspension is the most frequently used intervention for severe problematic behaviors in secondary schools (Raffaele, 2000; Morgan-D'Atrio, Northrup, LaFleur, & Sepra, 1986).

A priority should be placed on positive interventions. However, it is unrealistic to assume that educators will use totally positive approaches. A better fit to the reality of the classroom is to insure the vast majority of interventions used in schools are positive. When any aversive procedure is used, it should be used with the least intense but effective application. Also, teachers should be taught the most efficient manner in which to apply any aversive technique. For example, if reprimands are the most common aversive procedure used by teachers, they should be given effectively rather than making hollow threats, yelling, or repeatedly nagging. Precision requests or commands that are described in Chapter 4 are a research-based effective way for educators to give effective requests or reprimands (Rhode, et al., 1993). In this book, an effectiveness premium is given to positive interventions as opposed to aversive procedures.

Effectiveness

The more effective an intervention is, the more likely teachers will use it. However, effectiveness can be a difficult concept to define. When we think of intervention effectiveness, we often think that once an intervention is successfully implemented the behavior will be permanently changed. This "one shot" permanent behavior change is the exception rather than the rule for interventions. More often, we manage behaviors through interventions. This means that the intervention must be in place for a long period of time. Some of the best interventions are permanently integrated in the teaching practices of teachers and routinely used each day. For example, the use of social praise for appropriate behavior and the differential reinforcement of behaviors are second nature to master teachers. They never stop using them.

If interventions are used in the long-term management of behaviors, then they must be adjusted from time to time. It is not uncommon to hear an educator complain, "I used that intervention and it worked for awhile and then was ineffective." There are no perpetual motion machine interventions. What we mean by perpetual motion is—once an intervention is started and running, it will not run forever without some adjustments and changes. For instance, if a particular reinforcer is used over and over again without change with a student, sooner or later the student is going to tire of it and become satiated. The type of reinforcement and the way it is implemented must be periodically varied to keep the procedure effective.

Another major advance in the way interventions are judged to be effective has been the introduction of statistical techniques called meta-analyses (Stage & Quiroz, 1997). Instead of relying on an expert's judgment or one or two research papers, meta-analyses compares hundreds of studies to determine what are the most effective and least effective interventions in changing behaviors. Meta-analyses have frequently been used in educational research to determine best practice approaches for changing behaviors (Forness, Kavale, Blum, & Lloyd, 19xx). They have been used to review social skills programs (Quinn, Kavale, Mathur, Rutherford, & Forness, 1999), reading programs (Forness, et al., 19xx), and classroom behavior interventions (Stage & Quiroz, 1997). With a meta-analysis, comparisons are made across studies between baseline behaviors and then compared to the same behaviors after interventions have been implemented. These comparisons are then statistically transformed to z-scores. With z-scores, direct comparisons can be made across interventions to assess which are the most effective. Z-scores have an average of 0 (the baseline) and with a standard deviation change of 1 (indicating an improvement in the behavior) the students who receive the intervention are approximately 84% more improved than comparison control students who did not receive the intervention (Maughan, 2003). As a general rule of thumb, an "effect size" of 1 (one standard deviation improvement) indicates the intervention students are 84% improved over control students who did not receive the intervention.

Stage and Quiroz (1997) conducted a meta-analysis across 99 studies comparing 223 effect sizes to assess which were the most effective classroom interventions to decrease disruptive behaviors in public education settings. The following were the most effective interventions; group contingencies with an effect size of 1.02, self-management with an effect size of .97; differential reinforcement with an effect size of .95; and token economies with an effect size of .90. Less effective interventions of those measured include; individual counseling with an effect size of .31, cognitive behavioral techniques with an effect size of .36, functional assessment with an effect size of .51, and response cost with an effect size of .53. Interventions that focused on talking with a student about their behaviors or using punishment consequences were the least effective. Clearly, for reducing disruptive behaviors, interventions that focus on managing group behavior with positive consequences and teaching self-management skills or self-control skills were the most effective and should be utilized first.

Social Validity

The term social validity has a long history in applied behavior analysis and the use of interventions (Wolf, 1978; Kazdin, 1977; Schwartz & Baer, 1991). Social validity has two important parts to its' definition. First, will the intervention be accepted and viable if implemented in a community setting? For this book, the "community setting" is the school and specifically the classroom. Second, does the intervention make meaningful and important changes in the student's life?

Community acceptance by teachers, principals, other students, staff, and parents revolves around several of the issues already discussed such as time involvement, cost, positive, and effectiveness. Interventions need to be also balanced with the regional, ethnic, and cultural values represented in the school. For instance, making eye contact with a student when giving a precision request is an important effectiveness variable. However, some Native American cultures consider making direct eye contact in social interactions disrespectful. In these situations, eye contact should be eliminated from the procedure. For the mainstream culture, eye contact is not considered insulting and can be included in the intervention. Other regional community values may make some interventions such as overt reinforcement programs, time out procedures, or social skills training not acceptable and too intrusive.

Interventions that result in meaningful behavior change for students are an important aspect of social validity. In many instances, interventions are done for the school's benefit with little thought given to the student's benefit. Interventions that require students "to be quiet, to be docile, and to be still" generally do not benefit a student's adjustment and learning. Similarly, interventions such as in school and out of school suspensions do not improve a student's behavioral adjustment. Suspension merely removes students from the instructional environment, usually without assessing causes of the problematic behaviors or teaching replacement behaviors. Socially valid interventions focus on the student's positive behavioral adjustment, social acceptance, and enhance learning.

Student Interest

This effectiveness variable is rarely addressed when interventions are implemented in school settings. Students' interest in interventions is difficult to measure but when you see it you know it is operating. Simply defined, student interest is how much the student enjoys the intervention. Is it fun? Do they request the intervention? Do they show disappointment when it is stopped?

Interventions that are high on student interest require a little bit of "kid" in the designer of the intervention to make it effective. Interventions that students actually request because they are fun and interesting are techniques such as Mystery Motivators, the Dots for motivation program, reward spinners, chart moves, and many more discussed in this book.

Hassle Index

The "hassle index" is just how much difficulty is involved to implement and maintain the intervention. Even if the intervention is effective and would make a valuable contribution to the school or classroom there can be substantial "hassles" that impede its' implementation. There can be district or school policy that prohibits using certain interventions. Similarly, state law can preclude the use of certain techniques. These laws can be general and vague and make it very problematic for an educator to ascertain if they can actually use a particular intervention. Some state laws broadly restrict the use of aversive procedures with students, making it difficult for a teacher to assess what exactly can or cannot be used in a classroom. Other states very specifically restrict some procedures such as the use of time-out and manual-restraint procedures.

Related to legal issues and interventions is the risk of injury for the student or staff. Even if the state does not restrict the use of a particular intervention, if there is a substantial risk of injury, then it is difficult to use the intervention. For instance, manually restraining a student, chasing after a student who bolts into traffic, or trying to manually escort a student to the principal's office or a time-out room can be very problematic.

Table 2.1. EFECTIV + T

E	F	E	C	T	I	V	+	T
Expense	Hassle-Free	Effective	Complexity	Time	Student Interest	Social Validity	Positive	Total Score

Other hassles that educators face are, lack of staff or parent support, and/or conflicts with the values or philosophy of other staff or parents when some interventions are used. For example, other staff members in a school may disagree with the use of edible rewards in classrooms. Parents can object to the use of response cost procedures such as losing recess time or being excluded from a field trip because of the student's inappropriate behavior. If the building principal does not support a teacher's use of an intervention because of values or philosophical issues, then the teacher is taking a large job security risk in implementing the intervention. It is also important to assess if the intervention affects other students adversely. Some students may become upset observing the intervention being used, it may interfere with the overall learning environment in the classroom, or the students may feel it is unfair if one student gets the intervention and others do not.

All of these hassle variables are important in the selection and effective implementation of an intervention. They are serious concerns. In a survey of approximately 100 experienced teachers, Nicholas (1999) reported the percentage of teachers who did not use an intervention because of one of these hassle variables. Forty-one percent indicated they were prevented from using an intervention if it was risky (injury or legal problems), 33% if it conflicted with school district policy, 29% if it did not fit school or classroom values or philosophy, 25% if it affected other students adversely, 19% if parents did not find it acceptable, and 8% if other staff found it unacceptable. Interventions that are effective minimize these hassle variables for a better fit in classrooms and schools.

Intervention Effectiveness Rating Scale

All types of services and consumer articles are rated in our society to better inform the person who uses them. We have taken a similar approach in this book for the interventions we have included. Each intervention selected in this book has been rated on the Interventions Effectiveness Rating Scale. The scale variables and how they are defined is given in Table 2.1.

Each intervention presented in this book has a code at the beginning of the intervention. This code represents an average rating for cost (expense), hassle, effectiveness, complexity, time, student interest, social validity, and positiveness (vs. negative) rated on a scale from 1 (low) to 10 (high). Each intervention was reviewed and rated using the definitions from Table 2.1 by a group of advanced graduate students, educators, and faculty with extensive intervention experience in the school setting. The independent ratings were then averaged across the eight effectiveness variables, yielding a total score for effectiveness. The eight EFECTIV+ variable scores and the Total score are intended as a general guide for practitioners in selecting the interventions presented in this book. Although the raters were experienced educators or advanced graduate students, the ratings are based on subjective judgments and are intended only as a general guideline.

CONTROVERSIES AND ISSUES ASSOCIATED WITH SCHOOL-BASED INTERVENTIONS

There are many controversies and issues that abound in educational practice, and the use of interventions is no exception. These issues focus on the use of rewards, reinforcers, aversive procedures, functional behavior assessment, the effects of grouping students for interventions and many more. Each controversy and issue has to be weighed against the best research evidence and the benefits that a well-designed intervention can bring to a student's adjustment. In a sense, interventions are much like the use of medications. There is a *risk benefit ratio* when they are used and there may be *side effects* when they are used. It is important to understand the risk benefit ratio and which side effects accompany which interventions.

Rewards, Reinforcers, and Aversive Procedures

There are two basic controversial areas when rewards, reinforcers, and aversive procedures are used in educational settings. The first controversy involves the simple use of rewards and reinforcers and their side effects or long-term effects. The second controversy involves the issue of whether behavior management techniques should be purely positive or whether there is a need to have a combination of reinforcement-based interventions with some aversive procedures.

Do External Rewards Reduce Internal Motivation?

As simple and as appropriate as using rewards-based interventions seem, some researchers and writers question their overall effectiveness and their possible damaging side effects (Kohn, 1993; Sansome & Harackiewicz, 2000). The most controversial publication concerning the detrimental effects of positive interventions is Kohn's (1999) book, *Punished by Rewards: The trouble with gold stars, incentive plans, A's, praise, and other bribes.* Kohn references approximately 70 studies to bolster his argument that positive reward techniques reduce student interest in the rewarded tasks, cause a diminished quality of performance, and reduce risk taking and creativity. He indicates that students become overly dependent upon praise, which further decreases their intrinsic spontaneous motivation. He suggests instead the "Three Cs". The first C is making sure the school's academic "content" is interesting and useful. The second C suggests that the school should evolve into a "community" of cooperative learning that fosters the sense of feeling safe, caring for one another, and the freedom to ask for help. The third C is "choice", in which students think about what they are doing and are taught to make good choices.

Other researchers have found the use of rewards and particularly positive verbal feedback to have a positive effect on motivation. A meta-analysis on 100 studies involving use of rewards conducted by Cameron and Pierce (1994) concluded that students who received rewards demonstrated significantly improved behavior and that these students reported higher intrinsic motivation than the non-rewarded students.

Much has been written about this debate (as reviewed by Jenson, Olympia, Farley, & Clark, in press). There have been several conflicting meta-analyses conducted and editorial comments made in trying to resolve the issue (Cameron & Pierce, 1994; Deci, Koestner, & Ryan, 1999; Eisenberger & Cameron, 1996; Eisenberger, Pierce, & Cameron, 1999; Lepper, Henderlong, & Gingras, 1999). In trying to sort out the issues, several conclusions become evident (Jenson et al., in press). First, most of research supporting the detrimental effects of rewards on internal motivation are laboratory-based and their harmful effects appear exaggerated when examined in more applied clinical and educational settings (Reitman, 1997). Second, it may be less the absolute negative effects of rewards (i.e., reward use or reward not used) and more the nature of the contingency between the reward and the behavior (Chance, 1992; Dickenson, 1989, Eisenberger & Cameron, 1996). If the reward is given to a student for participating in an activity *without regard to the quality of the student's performance*, then the student appears to lose interest over time in the rewarded activity such as with "busy work", where students are rewarded for filling out worksheets. Or the opposite extreme, if the reward is available for *performance standards that are too high* and the student frequently fails, the student will also lose interest. In such a situation, a student might be placed in a mathematics class where he cannot do the work because of a lack of prerequisite math skills. However, if the rewards are given for improving performance and the student is successfully challenged into moving towards an attainable goal, then motivation appears to be enhanced (Chance, 1992; Dickenson, 1989; Eisnberger & Cameron, 1996).

For this book, positive rewards are considered a viable and necessary intervention when used correctly—particularly with difficult students who have failed repeatedly. While Kohn's three Cs of content, community, and choice are important—for many struggling students, particularly those with disabilities, we feel they are not enough. In fact, there is good evidence to indicate that students with behavioral, social, and academic problems receive far fewer rewards and praise in schools than other students (Jenson et al., in press). The lesson appears clear when using rewards as an intervention with students. If rewards are given for low performance-based tasks (busy work), then motivation will be compromised. If rewards are only given for exceeding high performance tasks with unrealistic goals resulting in frequent student failure, then motivation will be compromised. If the rewards are given for improving performance that is successful, then motivation will be enhanced.

Are Rewards, Positives, and Praise Enough?

On the other end of the controversy continuum, is the argument that only positive incentive with no aversives should be used in educational settings. Some authors (Donnellan & La Vigna, 1990) have suggested that positive approaches such as differential reinforcement can be used as effectively as punishment techniques to reduce problematic behaviors. The argument is made that punishment is not necessary and that punishment is no more effective in changing behavior than positive approaches. In addition, when aversives are used they can result in negative side effects such as fear, avoidance of persons who deliver the aversive intervention, and overuse or abuse of the techniques (Donnellan & La Vigna, 1990; Maag, 2001).

At the other end of this continuum are those who argue that reasonable use of restrictive procedures in applied settings is sometimes warranted (Axelrod, 1990; Jenson et al., in press). These authors highlight that positive reinforcement does not have superior modification characteristics to punishment (Axelrod, 1990). Some researchers (Rosen, O'Leary, Joyce, Conway, & Pfiffner, 1984) found that teachers who completely stopped providing negative feedback to their students resulted in deterioration of their students' academic and behavioral performance. Similarly, Pfiffner, Rosen, & O'Leary (1985) found that when they removed all verbal reprimands and privilege losses from the classroom, behavior worsened and positive praise became ineffective. Using only positive procedures commonly fails in applied settings because they are time intensive, produce slower behavior change, and are less effective than a combination of positive mild and aversive procedures. When aversive procedures are totally banned they are often used surreptitiously by staff (Axelrod, 1990; Jenson et al., in press). Surreptitious and unsupervised use of aversive interventions is especially problematic because it frequently leads to excessive and abusive use of these procedures.

Least Restrictive Behavior Interventions (LRBI)

A best practice approach is that a mix of supervised and regulated positive and negative procedures should be used as interventions. The ratio of this mix should place a heavy emphasis on positive consequences and a leaner emphasis on aversive procedures (Jenson et al., in press). Least restrictive forms of aversive interventions should be tried first when changing behavior and objective data should be collected to document the effectiveness of the interventions. It is also important for practitioners to assure that both positive and negative interventions are applied consistently, with integrity, and with an awareness of associated side effects. Evans, Jenson, Rhode, and Striefel (1990) published a guide titled *Least Restrictive Behavior Intervention (LRBI)*, a portion of which is included in Appendix B of this book. The *LRBI* guide was adopted by the Utah State Office of Education, as a policy to help educators select the least restrictive and most effective interventions for use with students with disabilities. The *LRBI* guide lists preliminary interventions to be used before any other more intrusive interventions are used. A list of interventions is divided into four levels from the least to the most intrusive and aversive. The *LRBI* guide also gives objective definitions for each intervention, examples of their use, cautions that should be noted, and common side effects associated with the various interventions. Approaches such as *LRBI* help ensure that the least intrusive and most effective intervention will be used with students with disabilities.

FUNCTIONAL BEHAVIOR ASSESSMENT AND INTERVENTIONS

Functional behavior assessment procedures have become very popular in determining interventions for students and have even been incorporated into the federal law, the *Individuals with Disabilities Education Act* (IDEA), Amendments of 1997. It is important to understand the basic definition of functional behavior assessment and when the federal law requires its' use. As the name implies, *functional* behavior assessment strives to understand the relationship between the behavior being assessed and the function it serves in the environment. This functional relationship is generally between the antecedents that precede the behavior and set the occasion for the behavior to occur and the consequences that follow the behavior. Consequences either motivate behavior by increasing the frequency of the behavior through positive or negative reinforcement, or decrease the frequency of a behavior with a punishing stimulus. We discussed the concepts and gave examples of antecedents and consequences at the beginning of this chapter.

Functional behavior assessment uses multiple approaches to collect information about antecedents and consequences (Gresham, Watson, & Skinner, 2001). These methods can include interviews with people who are familiar with the student such as teachers or parents, review of records such as school discipline reports, and multiple observations of the student's behavior—recording what happens just before (antecedents) the behavior and what immediately follows the behavior (consequences). Good functional behavior assessment generally combines these data collection approaches and results in a convergence of information about the function of the behavior.

One very practical approach to conducting a functional behavior assessment is to collect information on each occurrence or behavioral event when the behavior occurs. This approach is referred to as an ABC event recording procedure where *A* stands for antecedents, *B* is the behavior, and *C* is the consequences that follow the behavior. Generally ABC event recording requires filling out an ABC sheet (an example is listed in Appendix A), every time a behavior occurs. For example, ten or more ABC sheets can be copied, with the behavior filled in the B-section of each sheet. Each time the behavior occurs across several days the antecedent events (people, places, time, or other behaviors) are filled in the A-section of the sheets. Then, any consequence events are also filled in on the C-section of the sheet. After several occurrences of the behavior (5 or 10 times) the sheets are collected and reviewed to see if there are common antecedents and consequences that could be causing the behavior. For example, if the behavior that is defined is tantrumming, then each time a student tantrums an ABC sheet is filled out. After ten tantrums have occurred, all the sheets are reviewed to look for common antecedents and consequences. In our example, we might find that 8 out of 10 tantrums occurred when one particular staff member (the antecedent) asked the student to start doing their assignment. In 7 out of the 10 tantrums, the student was allowed to avoid doing the work and instead rest and collect himself by doing a game on the computer (the consequence). Most examples are not as obvious as this example. But collecting multiple ABC event sheets, interviewing the teachers, and observing the student engaging in the behavior can provide an assessment picture of the behavior and its function. A reasonable intervention that could be designed in this example would be to train the staff member to give an effective request for the student to begin the assignment. In addition, an intervention that provides consequences for finishing the assignment and privilege loss (actually losing computer time) for not doing the assignment could be implemented.

Functional assessment includes a whole range of procedures (interviews, observations, record reviews, etc.) that can be used to identify the antecedents and consequences associated with the occurrence of a behavior. However, it is important to understand another assessment technique that is also part of the broader assessment procedure of functional behavior assessment. This technique is called *functional behavior analysis*. Functional behavior analysis is different than most of the other functional behavior assessment techniques in that it involves the active manipulation of antecedents and consequences in highly controlled setting to determine their controlling functions (Gresham et al., 2001). With other functional behavior assessment techniques questions are asked in interviews, records are reviewed, and observations are taken. With functional behavior analysis, different antecedents and consequences are systematically introduced one at a time to determine their effects on the behavior. In a sense, functional behavior analysis is a systematic experiment to determine what controls the function of a behavior. For example, with the functional behavior analysis of self-injurious (head banging) behavior in an autistic child, different antecedents or consequences could be introduced one at a time in a clinical setting to see if head banging increased. Although functional behavior analysis is one type of functional behavior assessment technique, it is not used extensively in school settings because of the intensive time and controlled conditions requirements involved. Functional behavior analysis is generally reserved for the most severe behaviors under the most controlled conditions.

FUNCTIONAL BEHAVIOR ASSESSMENT AND CONTROVERSIES

There are two basic controversies associated with functional behavior assessments and interventions. The first controversy involves the legal requirements of when a functional behavior assessment is mandated for a student with a disability. The second controversy involves how important are functional behavior assessments in making interventions more effective. Does the information obtained from a functional behavior assessment improve the selection and effectiveness of an intervention?

The Individuals with Disabilities Education Act (IDEA), Amendments of 1997 (P.L. 105–17) includes as part of its' legislation, the intent of Congress to make schools safer environments that are conducive to learning. IDEA included provisions whereby students with disabilities can be disciplined for behavior problems. School administrators can suspend students with disabilities for up to 10 days without providing educational services (Drasgow & Yell, 2001). However, if the suspension time exceeds 10 days and the behavior for which the student is suspended is a *manifestation* of his or her disability, then the student may be placed in an interim alternative educational setting (which provides educational services) for up to 45 days. During this time, the student's Individual Education Program (IEP) team members must conduct a functional behavior assessment on the problematic behavior and develop a Behavior Intervention Plan (BIP) to remediate the problem behavior and allow the student to return to school. Generally, students with disabilities are suspended for safe schools violations that often include weapons, drugs, or dangerous behavior offenses.

The critical elements to understand under IDEA are the time limits involved, what constitutes an adequate functional behavior assessment, and the meaning of the term *manifestation*. First, the time limits are more than 10 days of suspension. The 11th day triggers the law's requirements. Second, the IEP team has only 45 days to conduct the functional behavior assessment and develop a viable behavior intervention plan. There is confusion as to what constitutes an "adequate functional behavior assessment" under the law. Clearly, an adequate functional behavior assessment is not simply a checklist but involves multiple techniques that we have already discussed. It is interesting to note that IDEA and its' regulations purposefully does not define what makes up an adequate functional behavior assessment in the hopes that it would be defined in the field by best practice standards. The two areas in which school districts have lost most legal challenges involve not completing a functional behavior assessment in a timely manner as required by the law, or doing an inadequate functional behavior assessment (Drasgow & Yell, 2001).

If the behavior for which the student is suspended is not a manifestation of their disability, then the legal requirements listed above do not apply and the student with disabilities can be disciplined the same as a non-disabled student. Understanding the standards for manifestation determination is critical if the conditions of the law are to be followed. The three critical questions that should be asked in determining if the behavior is a manifestation of the student's disability are first, is the student's IEP well designed to confer educational benefit for the student and was the **IEP implemented**? If not, then there is a good chance that whatever behavior resulted in the student being suspended was a manifestation of their disability. Second, is the student able to **control** his or her behavior? For example, if the student is very impulsive and that impulsivity has been well documented in the student's school records, then the behavior might be a manifestation of his or her disability. And third, was the student able to **understand the consequences** for his or her behavior? If the student could not understand what would happen if they engaged in the problematic behavior, then the behavior is probably a manifestation of their disability.

School districts and school personnel may have legal problems if they do not understand when a functional behavior assessment is required, the time limits required, what constitutes an adequate functional behavior assessment, and when a behavior is a manifestation of a disability. IDEA, is currently under review and Congress may change these requirements in future regulations.

The last controversy involving functional behavior assessment and interventions is the effectiveness question. There has been a major explosion in the research on functional behavior assessment and the selection of the most effective and proper intervention since the mid 1980s. It is a common standard of practice that functional behavior assessment information is essential in tailoring the most effective interventions for students. However, functional behavior assessment has recently come under scrutiny on two fronts (Gresham, 2002). First, the basic psychometric properties of functional behavior assessment techniques such as basic reliability and validity measures have not been well established. To date, no one knows the technical assessment adequacy of most functional behavior assessment techniques (Gresham, 2002). Second, does a functional behavior assessment prior to the selection and design of an intervention enhance the effectiveness of that intervention?

Gresham, McIntyre, Olson-Tinker, Dolstra, McLaughlin, & Van (2002) reviewed 150 school based intervention studies from the *Journal of Applied Behavior Analysis* from 1991–1999. They compared interventions that incorporated functional behavior assessments and interventions that did not. Using effect size comparisons and one type of statistical comparison, interventions that *did not* utilize functional behavior assessment techniques were more effective than those that did incorporate functional behavior assessment techniques.

This is a difficult finding to explain. It is only one study, but it is an important study. If functional behavior assessment delays the implementation of an intervention or emphasizes the wrong type of interventions, then it may in fact impede the overall effectiveness of an intervention. However, the authors of this book feel that more research is needed in this area and that a well-conducted functional behavior assessment generally enhances the effects of an intervention. This enhancement may be especially significant for severe behaviors or chronic problem behaviors where several interventions have been tried and failed.

GROUPING AND INTERVENTIONS

It is hard to imagine that grouping students together for the purpose of implementing an intervention would have negative side effects. Classroom settings themselves are groupings of students so that teaching can be done more economically. Frequently, grouping is used for the same reason, the economy of providing interventions such as social skills instruction, aggression replacement training, and many other types of interventions. However, there is good evidence that suggests if disruptive students who display noncompliance, aggression, arguing, and other types of externalizing behavior are put into groups for interventions, some harm may be done (Arnold & Hughes, 1999; Dishion, McCord, & Poulin, 1999). Dishion et al., (1999) found that when at-risk, anti-social youth were grouped with peers for interventions there was an actual increase in problem behavior over time that could result in negative life outcomes in adulthood. These students actually engaged in "deviancy training" for each other that was facilitated by grouping them with other at-risk peers. The authors indicated that the peer reinforcement for deviant behaviors was "quite subtle and potentially powerful." They cite one study (Buehler, Patterson, & Furniess, 1966) showing that in youth groups in institutional settings the ratio of peer provided reinforcement was 9-to-1 when compared to adult staff. In another study that reviewed the literature on the effects of grouping students to teach skill-based interventions the effects were clear—grouping increased problem behaviors (Arnold & Hughes, 1999).

It should be noted that the harmful effects of grouping occurred with externalizing students. These are students whose problem behaviors are directed towards adults and peers external to themselves. These problem behaviors generally include noncompliance, arguing, aggression, impulsivity, off-task, and disruptive behaviors (Rhode. et al., 1993). This is in contrast to internalizing students whose behaviors are directed inward, such as anxiety, fear, and depression. However, the evidence appears unmistakable that when externalizing students are exclusively grouped they tend to teach each other new and more disruptive behaviors and reinforce each other for these behaviors. The peer reinforcement for these problematic behaviors is generally subtle but at much higher rates than adult reinforcement. It also appears not to make too much difference which particular interventions or subjects are being used or taught. These grouped instruction interventions could include social skills, problem solving strategies, or remedial academic skills.

However, grouping is generally considered essential for some types of interventions both for economic reasons and assumed teaching effectiveness. There appears to be some approaches that can reduce the adverse effects of grouping for interventions. First, if the group is a mixture of externalizing and prosocial students, then there is a dampening effect for the subtle reinforcement of problematic behavior (Dishion, et al., 1999). Mixing prosocial students into the group who do not respond to inappropriate social reinforcement from peers, will reduce the overall harmful effects of group.

The second approach to reducing the harmful effects of grouping is to utilize *group contingencies* with the group (Litow & Pumroy, 1975; Rhode, et al., 1993). Group contingencies involve a system of delivery of reinforcement for the group dependent on the behaviors of the individuals within the group (Jenson & Reavis, 1996). There are three basic types of group contingencies: Individual group contingencies are when reinforcement for the whole group is dependent upon the performance of one individual. This is a severe form and is rarely used because of placing too much pressure upon a single student. Independent group contingencies are when each member of the group meeting an appropriate criterion gets reinforced. Students not meeting the criteria are excluded from reinforcement. Finally, interdependent group contingencies are where the whole group is interdependent upon each other and must reach a pre-set appropriate criterion before the group is reinforced. There can be several variations of group contingencies such as, randomly selecting an unidentified student to determine if a criterion has been met (Jenson & Reavis, 1996). It is important when using group contingencies that they are positive, with no undue pressure on one individual student, and to recognize that there may be group "saboteurs" who set the whole group up for failure.

Group contingencies have been shown in one meta-analytic study to be the most effective in reducing disruptive behaviors in classroom settings (Stage & Quiroz, 1997) and they are highlighted in several interventions in this book. With group contingencies, if the members of the group teach, model, and reinforce disruptive behaviors in each other, they will lose a valuable reinforcer for the group as a whole. When externalizing students are grouped for the purpose of providing an intervention, the practitioner should consider the use of a positively oriented group contingency. Once behavioral control is lost in a group setting, it can be very difficult to recover that control and use an intervention effectively.

SUMMARY

Interventions are the *systematic applications of research-validated procedures to change behaviors through either teaching new skills or through the manipulation of antecedents and consequences.* From this definition, it is important to understand that interventions used with students should be research-validated procedures that have had their effectiveness validated in published research studies. All too frequently in education, dubious techniques that have face validity or a marketing campaign but have no research behind them are used with students—wasting valuable opportunities, resources, and time. Validated interventions change behavior in two basic ways. First, new behaviors are taught to students who are deficient in a specific skill area. Second, behavior can be changed by manipulating either antecedents or consequences.

Even if an intervention has been proven effective under laboratory or research conditions it still may not be effective in field use. Several aspects of an intervention must be taken into account if it is to be used in the field in everyday practice. Some of these important aspects include time, cost, complexity, positiveness, effectiveness, social validity, the student's interest in the intervention, and the overall hassles of implementing the intervention. Possibly the most important component is time. If it takes too much time to start the intervention and then to run the intervention each day, then the intervention will not be used. Similarly, if the complexity and cost of the intervention are too high, then it is unlikely the intervention will be used. The overall effectiveness of the intervention is important but so is the social validity of the intervention. Are the behaviors being changed meaningful to the community and student? The student's interest in the intervention is an important factor. If the student likes the intervention and wants to participate, then the task of implementing the intervention is much easier for the educator. There is also an overall hassle index associated with interventions. These hassles include school district policies, state, and federal laws that prohibit some types of interventions. Also included in the hassle index are the values and philosophies of other co-workers, parents, students, and administrators that can limit whether an intervention will be used in a particular setting.

The intervention research has its' share of controversies which surround its' use. Some of the common controversies include the assumed undermining of student's internal motivation through the use of positive procedures. Similarly, whether only positive interventions should be used with students as opposed to a mix of positive and mild aversive procedures. Should functional behavior assessments always be used before an intervention is implemented? Or, do functional behavior assessments actually decrease the effectiveness of interventions? The hidden negative effects of grouping students for the purpose of effectively implementing an intervention is a new and troubling controversy. Does grouping actually make behaviors worse and what can be done to ameliorate the negative effects of grouping?

Interventions are powerful and effective ways to manage behavior and teach new skills to students. An insistence of research proven techniques, understanding the variables which impact the effectiveness of intervention, and being aware of intervention controversies are all essential components to the best practice implementation of interventions.

Chapter 3

Students with Behavior Problems
Who, Why, and What

This book is about interventions for students with behavior problems—problems that are pervasive and present a considerable challenge to educators in preschool, elementary, and secondary classrooms across the United States. It is not necessary for educators to have extensive training in psychology or psychiatry to identify and experience the impact of a student with a behavior disorder in their classrooms. In fact, educators are often the first to recognize and seek assistance for children with significant behavior problems (which is typically a phone call home or referral to the school psychologist). These students usually stand out in class after the first few days of school! Acquiring a knowledge base and understanding of the causes and development of behavioral problems will assist educators and parents in intervening more effectively with these difficult students.

PREVALENCE OF BEHAVIOR PROBLEMS

Who are students with behavior problems? One way to determine this is to picture a child's behavior as falling at some point on a continuum. All children exhibit occasional behavior problems—fighting, crying, arguing, noncompliance, or over-activity that can be considered normal for their developmental level or a particular situation. However, students who present persistent school problems exhibit these behaviors to a much greater degree than most children, with more frequency, more severity, and more consistency over time. When viewed on a behavior problem continuum or scale of 0 to 100—students with behavior problems usually fall above the 90th percentile, in frequency, severity, and consistency of inappropriate behaviors.

The prevalence of severe behavior problems in the United States is somewhere between 5 and 16% for children identified with a specific behavior or mental disorder, depending on the nature of the population sampled and methods of assessment. Many other children exhibit significant behavior problems that may be undiagnosed and the occurrence of these problems has dramatically increased over the past few decades. During childhood, the number of boys referred and identified as having psychological and behavioral problems is much higher than girls, particularly for problems with aggression, attention-deficit hyperactivity disorder, or other conduct problems. After puberty, however, rates for females with conduct problems are more equal to that of males. Behavioral disorders are found to occur in various cultures, most geographical regions, and socio-economic levels, however, a higher prevalence may occur within some populations, such as children exposed to severe environmental or psychosocial stressors.

Most of the time, behavior problems that are difficult to manage in school can be described as externalizing behaviors. Externalizing behaviors are highly observable, directed towards others, and are extremely distressing to teachers. Externalizing behaviors usually consist of excessive amounts of disruptive behaviors, including noncompliance, arguing, fighting, tantrums, excessive talking or noises, hyperactivity, impulsive actions, and conduct problems. Some students, however, also exhibit internalizing behavior problems or behavioral deficits that are frequent, severe, and consistent over time. Internalizing behaviors are inner-directed and typically don't impact other students. Students with internalizing behavior problems may have difficulties with inattention and poor concentration, social withdrawal, excessive worries and fears, or persistent feelings of sadness. They are also of great concern to educators and parents, as these behaviors may greatly impede successful school adjustment and progress.

Although not all students with behavior problems exhibit academic deficits, a strong relationship between behavior problems and low academic achievement has been documented. For example, the prevalence of a learning disability in at least one area (reading, math, or spelling) among children with ADHD is somewhere between 19–25% (Barkley, 1990). Because academic difficulties often contribute to avoidance of academic tasks, students with poor academic skills are more likely to disrupt the classroom or refuse to comply with teachers' demands in order to escape from aversive academic tasks. These behaviors can, in turn, lead to increased academic deficits, increased negative interactions with teachers, increased association with delinquent peers, and increased removal from the instructional setting (e.g., time-out, office referral, in-school suspension, out-of-school suspension, etc.).

The Triangle and the Seven Percent Student

We have discussed students with behavior problems as primarily external-
izers who make up between 5 to 16% of all students. However, another popular
approach of conceptualizing problematic students in a school is to visualize a triangle consisting of students that make up the whole student population of a particular
school (Lewis & Sugai, 1999; Sprick, Sprick, & Garrison, 1992). This approach
termed "positive behavior supports" emphasizes viewing problem behaviors in a
school in a positive, proactive manner. The positive behavior support movement
highlights prevention first, with group and individual intervention as second and
third stage treatments.

Included in the broad base of the positive behavior supports triangle, are 80%
to 90% of the student body, those students who are not generally problematic.
These are the average students who only need the prevention stage with well-
defined school rules and explicit behavioral expectations to do well. A little further
up in the middle section of the triangle are approximately 5% to 15% of the
student body, students who are at-risk for behavior problems. These students may
need specialized group intervention, such as social skills training and study skills
instruction to prevent more serious behavior problems. At the top of the triangle are
the 1% to 7% of students who exhibit chronic and intense behavior problems. These
students need specialized individual interventions and consistent supervision and
long-term monitoring to prevent more serious problems that will affect the climate
of the whole school.

The interventions in this book fit all aspects of the positive behavior supports
model. Some of the interventions presented are clearly preventative and proactive
and will benefit all students. Others interventions are group oriented and will
benefit both at-risk students and those with chronic problems—still others are
more intensive individualized interventions for the most serious problems.

RISK FACTORS FOR BEHAVIOR PROBLEMS

Why do some children adjust easily to school experiences and routines while
other children seem to have considerable difficulty throughout their school years
and beyond? Most students with severe disruptive behavior problems present with
symptoms during early childhood, unless problems arise following an acquired
injury to the brain, or result following a trauma or adjustment to a significant
life change (death, illness, new baby, divorce, etc.). Disruptive behavior patterns
may be established early in a child's school career or be present long before
they begin their formal schooling. Once they begin school, children with behavior
problems often quickly establish a reputation with their teachers and their peers

that can follow them from one year to the next and from one teacher to another. Furthermore, research has shown that such well-established patterns of disruptive behavior early in life are predictive of later antisocial behavior, lower grades, and poor school performance (Reid, Patterson, & Snyder, 2002; Stage & Quiroz, 1997).

There are a number of factors inside and outside the child, the family, and the school environment that have been found to contribute to the development and maintenance of behavior problems in children and adolescents. These include child temperament, genetic influences, neurobiological factors, parent-child interactions, family characteristics, and observational learning, as well as school characteristics (teaching style, classroom variables, and school-wide management and discipline plans). Any or all of these factors can interact to put children at greater risk for the development of troublesome behaviors. While educators and other professionals may not be able to change or eliminate all of the potential causes of misbehavior and psychological disorders, gaining an understanding of the factors impacting students with behavior problems is an important key in understanding these students and developing and selecting effective school-based interventions to help them be successful.

Temperament

As most parents will agree, children begin life with a unique personality or temperament. Temperament, or a child's intrinsic nature or disposition, will affect their adaptability, activity levels, sociability, responsiveness, persistence, and distractibility. Soon after birth, some infants will show easy temperaments—smooth eating and sleeping patterns, calm dispositions, and sociability with caretakers. Other infants may be quite difficult—poor eating and sleeping habits, oversensitive to stimulation, frequently irritable, and have difficulty adapting to changes. In Thomas and Chess's (1977) longitudinal study of infants they identified nine basic temperament characteristics (Activity, Rhythmicity, Approach-Withdrawal, Adaptability, Intensity, Mood, Persistence-Attention Span, Distractibility, and Sensory Threshold). The infants in the study were scored on the nine characteristics (high, medium, and low) and later grouped into three basic temperament categories; difficult, slow to warm up, and easy. There has been some research linking these temperamental factors with later behavior problems. Seventy percent of children identified as "difficult" by Chess and Thomas (1983) later developed behavior disorders, while 18 percent of children identified as "easy" later developed behavior disorders. It may be that a child's temperament contributes to coping styles or that a temperament trait (i.e., fearfulness or irritability), over time leads to a pattern of interaction characterized by peer rejection or other interpersonal problems. In addition, children with difficult temperaments are much more stressful for parents to manage, possibly resulting in more negative parent-child interactional patterns throughout childhood and continuing into the school setting. While all temperament traits are regarded as normal variations in behavioral style, behavioral problems may be more likely if there exists a "poor fit" between a child's temperament and the teaching style or parenting style of the adult (Carey, 1998).

Genetic Contributions

Although researchers have been unable to identify a genetic basis or group of genes that causes disorders to be genetically transmitted for the vast majority of behavioral disorders, there are some known medical disorders that do seem to run in some families. These include specific genetic syndromes such as fragile X syndrome, William's syndrome, Huntington's Disease, Tuberous Sclerosis, etc. that are associated with specific behavioral and cognitive impairments. Other psychological disorders including, schizophrenia, autism, attention deficit disorders, conduct disorders, and Tourette's syndrome are suspected to have a possible genetic component or familial resemblance. Geneticists conclude, however, that many genes, rather than a single gene most likely contribute to these disorders. As the search to identify genes that cause some disorders to be genetically transmitted continues, research can hopefully provide educators with more information to assist with early identification and intervention. For the present, we can assume that most if not all behavioral disorders are extremely complex with both genetic and environmental factors interacting and contributing to their development.

Neurobiological Contributions

Behavioral problems may occur as a consequence of disturbance in neural functioning (e.g., seizures), or neurological insult (e.g., brain damage). Neurobiological factors can include changes in brain structure due to brain injury either prior to birth, during the birth process, or at some time following birth. The effects of prenatal exposure to some drugs, toxins, or excessive amounts of alcohol, for example cause neurological damage to the developing fetus and result in cognitive and behavioral impairments, including severe attentional problems, hyperactivity, and agitation. Children with fetal alcohol syndrome (FAS), have been found to have a range of structural brain abnormalities and a behavioral profile that includes increased activity and reactivity, attention and inhibitory deficits, mental retardation, and poor motor skills (Mattson & Riley, 1995). Complications resulting from neonatal hemorrhage, which occurs in about 25% of low birth weight preterm infants (born prior to 32 weeks gestation), may also be predictive of adverse neurodevelopmental outcome (Walker, 1993). Vascular diseases (strokes) occasionally occur during childhood, causing disruption of the supply of oxygen and glucose to the brain, resulting in cognitive as well as behavioral impairments. Epilepsy or seizure disorder is relatively common among children, affecting about 1% of the population. Although many children with seizure disorders have minimal difficulties in social or cognitive development, recent evidence indicates that seizure disorders are associated with an increased risk for a variety of behavior and learning problems. Several studies have linked childhood seizure activity with poor school performance and increased occurrence of behavioral problems (Seidenberg & Berent, 1992). A traumatic brain injury, caused by falls, non-accidental trauma (abuse or assault), or motor vehicle accidents can result in an increase in newly acquired behavioral problems, such as low frustration tolerance, poor anger control, aggression, disinhibition (verbal or physical responses that one would ordinarily inhibit), poor impulse control, mood swings, and social inappropriateness (Deaton, 1990).

Parent-Child Interactions

Some parenting behaviors actually reinforce children who are aggressive and noncompliant. Ineffective parent management skills play a critical role in the escalation of these behaviors. This parent-child interaction pattern was investigated by Gerald Patterson (1976) and found to contribute to the development of deviant child behavior and noncompliance. This process, referred to as *coercion*, begins when a parent or adult makes a request or gives a direction to the child. Coercion occurs when a child learns to repeat or intensify behaviors such as whining, crying, or tantrumming in order to terminate parent directives. Parents respond by either withdrawing the direction (giving in to the child's tantrum) or with intensifying parental coercive behaviors (yelling or threatening). If the parent responds by withdrawing, the child's noncompliance is rewarded through negative reinforcement and the child's behaviors will increase. If the parent responds with coercive behaviors of his or her own, the parent behavior is negatively reinforced and will likely occur again in the future. If the parent response is inconsistent, the child learns that sometimes noncompliance, crying, or tantrumming "pays off", and the parent will terminate the command.

Family Characteristics

In addition to parenting styles, there are clearly documented family characteristics and demographic variables that are associated with behavior problems. Longitudinal research conducted with preschoolers has found that several family stressors such as marital conflict, maternal depression, and lower educational levels are predictive of behavior problems in children (Stormont, 2002). Other family stressors; poverty, drug and alcohol problems, divorce, physical, sexual, or emotional abuse, and lack of outside social support disrupt effective parenting practices and can lead to the development of externalizing behavior problems and school dropout. Parental supervision, which may be related to parent stress and income, also contributes to children's behavior, as children who are not well-supervised will have more opportunity to misbehave.

Observational Learning

Some children learn aggressive behaviors through observing the behavior of others and observing the consequences of aggression on others. Children who see older siblings, peers, or parents successfully use aggression and intimidation to get what they want, are more likely to model such behaviors themselves. Extensive research conducted by Bandura (1977) and colleagues, has demonstrated that exposure to socially deviant modeling, such as excessive viewing of violent television will increase the likelihood of a child's engaging in aggressive behaviors. It is also clear from the research that parental aggression and harsh management towards children significantly affects children's aggression at school (Stormont, 2002).

School Characteristics

Children who enter school with noncompliant, aggressive, or negative behavior patterns, have an elevated risk for continued behavior problems. Classrooms where these students receive low rates of positive interactions with teachers and low rates of positive reinforcement for appropriate behavior will increase the probability of their eventual school failure and peer rejection (Jenson, Olympia, Farley, & Clark, in press). Punitive disciplinary strategies, unclear rules and expectations, and failure to consider individual differences contribute to increasing rates of problematic behaviors. Children who experience repeated academic failure and social isolation early on, often seek out other children with similar behavioral problems and become involved with a deviant peer group by early adolescence.

Given that some children begin school with a history that puts them at risk for severe behavioral problems, it is clearly evident that teachers alone cannot provide the support necessary to develop school climates that will alter this deviant pathway. Schools that fail to monitor school-wide discipline, lack adequate staff support, disregard individual differences and diversity, fail to collaborate with families, and repeatedly remove disruptive students from the instructional setting will only exacerbate the problem. School-wide models of prevention that maximize the probability of academic and social success are critical to the reduction of risk factors in students with behavior problems (Lewis & Sugai, 1999).

BEHAVIORAL DISORDERS—DIAGNOSIS AND DEFINING CHARACTERISTICS

What are the defining characteristics of students with behavior problems? Students with severe behavior problems will eventually be referred to the attention of school service providers as well as mental health providers in the community. When behavior problems are frequent, severe, and persistent—those students who exceed the 90th percentile, teachers and/or parents generally seek outside help. Although a specific diagnosis or educational classification is not required or necessary before implementing school-based interventions in the classroom, understanding the characteristics associated with a specific disorder is helpful in determining which interventions may be the most effective with a particular student. Formal classification or diagnosis of behavior problems in school-aged children or youth can be conceptualized by looking at two different, but overlapping sets of criteria. In the school system, students with severe behavioral problems can be eligible for special education services under the Individuals with Disabilities Education Act (IDEA), a law passed by congress in 1975, requiring states to provide full educational opportunities to all handicapped children. Under IDEA, students may be identified as having a disability in one of thirteen categories. Most of the time, students with severe behavior problems who receive special education services, do so under the classification of "Emotional Disturbance", although they may also qualify under one of several other categories, including; Autism, Intellectual Disability, Other Health Impairment, Specific Learning Disabilities, or Traumatic Brain Injury. Students with an "emotional disturbance" need not be diagnosed with a specific medical or psychiatric diagnosis, but must be found to exhibit behavior difficulties, either externalizing or internalizing, that have occurred for a long period of time, to a marked degree, that adversely affect their educational performance—and require special education services to succeed in the school setting.

The other set of criteria used to describe some students with behavioral problems are found in the *Diagnostic and Statistical Manual of Mental Disorders— Fourth Edition* (DSM-IV) (American Psychiatric Association, 1994). The DSM-IV delineates the criteria by which clinicians, psychiatrists, other physicians, psychologists, social workers, and other mental health professionals use to diagnose a variety of mental disorders. A mental disorder as defined in the DSM-IV is a "clinically significant behavioral or psychological syndrome or pattern" that impairs one or more areas of life functioning. There are several disorders described in the DSM-IV, that are diagnosed in infancy, childhood, or adolescence that are often applied to students who have behavior problems, including Attention-Deficit and Disruptive Behavior Disorders, Pervasive Developmental Disorders, Tic Disorders, Mood and Anxiety Disorders, and Learning Disabilities. Although many children, particularly those served in special education have a diagnosis from both systems, a DSM-IV diagnosis is not necessary to qualify for special education services. A brief explanation listing the essential features and associated characteristics of some specific disorders found in school-age children is presented in the following section.

DISORDERS FOUND IN SCHOOL-AGE CHILDREN

Attention-Deficit/Hyperactivity Disorder (ADHD)

Perhaps the most frequently diagnosed childhood disorder is Attention-Deficit/Hyperactivity Disorder (ADHD). ADHD is quite well known to most educators, because they often have at least one or two students in their classroom with this diagnosis or who display symptoms characteristic of ADHD. Children with ADHD symptoms usually enter the school system and are quickly identified in Kindergarten or first grade by their teachers as inattentive, impulsive, and overactive when compared to same aged peers. The prevalence of ADHD ranges from 3% to 5% in the school-age population (American Psychiatric Association, 1994). Rates of occurrence fluctuate to some degree depending on the population sampled (socioeconomic status), with poorer regions associated with higher rates of ADHD. Boys are much more likely than girls to manifest with symptoms of ADHD, with the ratio anywhere from 2:1 to 6:1 for clinic-referred samples.

The defining characteristics of ADHD include marked inattention, inability to inhibit responses or regulate behavior, and excessive levels of physical activity (Barkley, 1990). A child with severe ADHD will often fidget or squirm or have difficulty remaining seated while in class, will be easily distracted and unable to concentrate, will blurt out, interrupt others or talk excessively, will shift from activity to activity and fail to finish tasks, and may engage in dangerous or risky behaviors. To receive a clinical diagnosis of ADHD-Combined Type, a child must exhibit six or more symptoms of inattention, and six or more symptoms of hyperactivity-impulsivity. According to the DSM-IV criteria, children who exhibit fewer than six symptoms in one of these two categories (inattentive or hyperactive-impulsive) are diagnosed as having ADHD, Predominantly Inattentive Type, or ADHD, Predominantly Hyperactive-Impulsive Type. In addition, to meet criteria for diagnosis, these symptoms must be present prior to age 7, and must be present in more than one setting (e.g., school and home).

Children with ADHD present a challenge to teachers because their behaviors are disruptive during instruction, they annoy other students, they need frequent prompts, they don't comply with rules, and their work is unorganized and usually incomplete. Severe disruptive behaviors also likely impede a child's learning and mastering new material, resulting in underachievement in at least some academic areas. By adolescence, these children may be less hyperactive or fidgety, however, they usually continue to be unorganized, fail to complete assigned schoolwork, and have difficulty sustaining attention to repetitive or unexciting tasks that require concentration and focus such as independent school assignments, homework, and chores. Adolescence, in fact, can be quite difficult for students with ADHD, because of the increasing expectations by adults of independence and responsibility.

Because of their impulsivity, children with ADHD are much more likely to be accident-prone, sustain a head injury, or engage in risk-taking activities. Children with ADHD are also more likely to exhibit other behavioral and learning disorders, with over 40% having at least one other disorder. Many children with ADHD also meet criteria for Oppositional Defiant Disorder, Conduct Disorder, or a Learning Disability. Comorbid anxiety or mood disorders and somatic complaints are also quite common. Many of the interventions described in Chapter 5 to reduce disruptive behaviors will be helpful to use with students with attentional problems (e.g., Homenotes, Self-management) as well as Organizational Strategies and Social Skills interventions described in Chapter 6 and Chapter 7.

Oppositional Defiant Disorder (ODD)

School-age children who are stubborn, defiant, and angry are another group of students easily identified by teachers and parents as frustrating and difficult to manage. These are students who actively refuse to comply with requests, often lose their temper, argue with teachers, parents, and peers, and usually blame other students when there are problems. In fact, teacher or parent requests for the student to engage in a less enjoyable task (e.g., clean room or do schoolwork) are often the triggers to these oppositional behaviors.

The prevalence of youth diagnosed with Oppositional Defiant Disorder (ODD) is between 2% to 16% (American Psychiatric Association, 1994). There is a higher rate among boys during childhood, however, in adolescence, female rates are similar to that of males. A large percentage of children with ODD will eventually present with a Conduct Disorder. There is some evidence that oppositional features are more prevalent in males who exhibit difficult temperaments as preschoolers (Patterson, Reid, & Dishion, 1992). ODD is also more common in families with marital discord, or with a family history of a conduct disorder.

While some oppositional behavior is common in young children and adolescents, a diagnosis of ODD requires that these behaviors occur much more frequently than would occur in children of similar age or developmental level, and that these behaviors significantly impair functioning at home or school. The defining characteristics of ODD according to DSM-IV (1994) criteria, include a persistent pattern of negative, defiant behavior, with four or more oppositional symptoms such as, frequent temper loss, arguments with adults, noncompliance, deliberate annoyance of others, blames others, easily annoyed, angry, or vindictive. Noncompliance, in particular is a behavior that is most distressing to adults who work or live with these students. Noncompliance refers to behaviors including failure to respond to adult requests within a reasonable time (10–15 seconds), failure to sustain or complete the requested task, and failure to follow rules previously established. Defiant behavior refers to behaviors that include active verbal or physical refusal to comply.

Oppositional behavior is different from inattentive or hyperactive behavior. Oppositional children are actively defiant, aggressive, and argumentative to adults, whereas children with ADHD symptoms do poorly at school as a result of their inattentive and restless behaviors. Although ODD and ADHD are distinct disorders, as many as 35% to 45% of children and adolescents with ADHD meet criteria for both disorders (Mash & Wolfe, 1999). Children with both attentional and oppositional problems will undoubtedly present with more physical aggression, greater peer relationship problems, greater academic underachievement, and present a greater challenge to their classroom teachers. In Chapter 5, interventions such as Precision Commands, and "Sure I Will", are effective in helping children with ADHD and ODD. Teens with ODD often have high levels of family conflict, poor homework completion, and frequent disciplinary referrals at school. Interventions that work well with this age group include individual Behavior Contracts, Behavior Checkbooks, and group contingencies as well as several of the organizational and study skills strategies listed in Chapter 6.

Conduct Disorder (CD)

Children or adolescents that exhibit some of the features of Oppositional Defiant Disorder, but in a more severe form that violates the basic rights of others and violates societal rules, may be diagnosed as having a Conduct Disorder (CD). The prevalence of CD in the school-age population appears to be increasing. Rates for males under age 18 vary from 6% to 16%, and for females, from 2% to 9% (American Psychiatric Association, 1994). Conduct disorders are one of the most frequently diagnosed disorders, sometimes as early as age 5, but more typically in late childhood or adolescence. The risk for CD is higher in children with a family history of conduct problems.

The diagnosis of CD requires that an individual exhibit a persistent pattern of rule-breaking behavior, causing significant impairment in life functioning in a variety of settings. The criteria include three or more specific behaviors falling under four groupings: aggression to people or animals (fights, use of weapons, animal cruelty, etc.), property destruction (sets fires, vandalism), theft or deceitfulness (lies, stealing), and serious rule violations (runs away from home, truancy, etc.).

Children with CD may initially present with oppositional or defiant behaviors, however, these behaviors increase in severity and often include aggression towards other people, property destruction or illegal activities. In the school setting, these are students that are physically aggressive, bully or threaten other students, frequently get into fights on the playground, vandalize property, and steal money or property. By adolescence they may engage in overt delinquent behaviors such as, use of weapons, school vandalism, or stealing from stores. Some adolescents with CD become involved in the juvenile justice system before they enter high school, however, only about 50% of children with early delinquent patterns continue on a life-course path of criminal behavior in adulthood. Many of the behavioral interventions discussed in Chapter 5, particularly Behavioral Contracts, Sit and Watch, Structured Recess, and Other Class Time-out are effective in reducing acting out and rule-breaking behaviors in the school setting.

Pervasive Developmental Disorders

Children with a Pervasive Developmental Disorder (PDD) exhibit severe and pervasive impairments in three areas of development: social relationships, language and communication skills, and stereotypic behaviors or activities. The symptoms of a pervasive developmental disorder range across a spectrum in severity and form of expression. Autistic Disorder is the most commonly diagnosed PDD. Other PDDs include Asperger's Disorder, Rett's Disorder, and Pervasive Developmental Disorder Not Otherwise Specified. These disorders are usually evident and diagnosed in early childhood, although some children with milder impairments may not be diagnosed until later in childhood or even adolescence. Children with Autism and Asperger's Disorder have recently seen increased attention and classification in the school setting. Autistic Disorder occurs in less than 1% of the population, however, recent studies suggest rates are much higher. Rates for both Autism and Asperger's are higher in males than females. Students with PDDs such as Autism or Asperger's may not necessarily exhibit severe externalizing behavior problems as primary features of the disorder; however, these students may present challenging behaviors as a result of their social and language impairments. These students may have significant difficulty making friends, lack empathy skills, and in severe cases may be unable to communicate their needs appropriately, resulting in temper tantrums or self-injurious behaviors (head banging, hand biting). Children with PDDs may also exhibit behavior symptoms of hyperactivity, inattention, impulsivity, and aggressiveness.

The onset of Autism, the most commonly diagnosed PDD, is prior to age 3 years, although symptoms in some children may be milder and more difficult to diagnose in infancy. The diagnostic criteria include significant impairments in three areas, 1) social interaction skills including, nonverbal skills such as, eye gaze, facial expression, body gestures, and peer relationships such as, sharing interests, social reciprocity, 2) communication skills such as development of language, sustaining a conversation, repetitive use of language, or social language, and 3) repetitive and/or stereotyped behaviors or interests, such as intense preoccupation with an interest or activity, inflexibility in routines, repetitive motor actions (e.g., hand flapping, moving fingers in front of the eyes, body rocking), and abnormal preoccupation with objects (lining up objects, spinning pencils or toy parts). Although some children with Autism have normal intelligence, about 75% of children with Autism also have mental retardation.

In higher functioning children with Autism, expressive language skills are better developed than receptive language skills (American Psychiatric Association, 1994).

Asperger's Disorder is another PDD that is similar to Autism; however, it can be distinguished from Autism by normal language development. Children with Asperger's Disorder exhibit severe impairments in social interaction and repetitive or restricted behaviors or interests, however, there are no significant delays in language or self-help skills. Asperger's Disorder is often identified later in childhood than Autism, although difficulties with motor skills, and social interactions may be noticed in preschool or after entry into the school setting. Children with Asperger's Disorder have difficulty forming friendships, unusual preoccupation with topics or facts, and often ramble on in conversation with poor awareness of social reciprocity.

Tourette's Disorder

Tourette's Disorder or Syndrome (TS) is a type of tic disorder that is characterized by motor and vocal tics that occur many times a day and cause significant impairment in daily functioning. A tic is a recurrent, stereotyped motor movement or vocalization. Most motor tics usually occur in the face or shoulder muscles and can range from large muscle movements (e.g., jumping, shoulder shrugging) to milder tics (e.g., eye blinking, facial grimacing). Common vocal tics include throat clearing, grunting, sniffing, barking, and less frequently, repetition of words or phrases out of context. Although tics are uncontrollable and irresistible, they can sometimes be suppressed for a period of time. Tics may also increase during periods of stress.

TS is a neurological disorder affecting the central nervous system. The vulnerability for developing a tic disorder is genetically transmitted. Because TS symptoms begin during childhood, they may significantly impact the school age years. The first symptoms are usually facial tics such as eye blinking or nose twitching. A particular tic may disappear and then another tic will emerge. Over time other motor and vocal tics develop, although over the course of the disorder periods of remission may occur. In many cases the severity and frequency of symptoms diminish in adulthood. Although simple tics are fairly common in normal children (about 12% of the population), the incidence of TS in the general population is estimated to be between 1–2% (Comings, 1990). The rate is higher among males than females.

Children with milder tic disorders such as Transient Tic Disorder or Chronic Tic Disorder may experience single or multiple tics but to a lesser degree and duration than TS. Children who meet criteria for TS experience both motor and one or more vocal tics that occur daily, over a period of more than one year. The onset must be prior to age 18 and not due to other medical conditions or effects of a substance. The disturbance must significantly affect functioning at home or school (American Psychiatric Association, 1994).

Some children with TS or other tic disorders do not exhibit behavior problems, however, about 50% of individuals with TS also have ADHD. The tics per se are usually not as problematic in the classroom as the difficulties associated with hyperactivity, distractibility, poor concentration, and impulsivity related to the ADHD. Children with TS may also have difficulty with poor handwriting and academic performance. Behaviors may be inconsistent and vary from day to day, causing the teacher to attribute problem behaviors to poor motivation or noncompliance. Obsessions and compulsions commonly co-occur in children with TS and may exacerbate behavioral problems at school. Persistent tic behavior and excessive compulsions such as touching other students, along with self-consciousness and social discomfort may lead to problems with peer relationships. Because of the frequency and severity of social and behavioral problems in many children with TS, several of the behavioral strategies and procedures described in the interventions chapters, particularly those that address social skills, can be utilized to help meet their unique educational needs.

Traumatic Brain Injury

The term Traumatic Brain Injury (TBI) refers to individuals who have sustained brain damage as a result of a traumatic open or closed head injury or secondary damage due to oxygen deprivation, brain swelling, infection, hemorrhage, etc. Children with TBIs may have a variety of long-term physical, intellectual, or behavioral difficulties. Depending on the cause of the injury, site of injury, and degree and nature of brain damage, the problems these students present in the classroom can range from mild to severe. Some students may exhibit only temporary problems with headaches, irritability, and fatigue, while other students will experience persistent intellectual and academic impairments, and life-long psychosocial difficulties.

Incidence rates indicate that over 150 per 100,000 school-aged children in the United States sustain a brain injury each year. While up to 10% of these injuries are fatal, most of those who survive will return to the school setting (Begali, 1992). Many of these children will require special education services—or accommodations and individualized strategies in their regular education classrooms. Students with a brain injury may be classified in special education under the category of TBI. To receive this classification there must be prior documentation by a physician that a student has an acquired brain injury and the injury must adversely affect their educational functioning. Children with brain injuries present with a wide range of cognitive and behavioral problems, however, impairments in attention, impulse control, problem solving, social judgment, mood fluctuation, and memory loss are quite common. In addition, deficits in communication skills, motor skills, and ability to learn new information frequently affect school performance. Students with TBI are just as likely to benefit from good classroom management and individualized strategies as other students with behavior or learning problems. Although there is no set program or list of interventions that apply to all students with brain injuries, many of the interventions presented in this manual can be used to support the student with a brain injury who has difficulty with attention, organization, and following directions.

Mood and Anxiety Disorders

Although mood disorders do not always impact classroom behavior, many school-age children do experience significant problems with depression, anxiety, or exhibit other emotional symptoms in response to psychosocial stressors (e.g., recent death or divorce), therefore, educators should be alerted to symptoms associated with these internalizing disorders.

Depression in children occurs equally in boys and girls and frequently co-occurs with other disorders, particularly disruptive disorders and ADHD. Large research studies indicate that over 2% of children, and 8% of adolescents suffer from depression (National Institute of Mental Health, 2000). Children with depression and other mood disorders may exhibit symptoms such as somatic complaints, irritability, and social withdrawal—resulting in low self-esteem, impaired school performance and poor social skills. The research on depression in children lags behind the research on adult depression. Diagnosing depression in children is difficult, because many of these symptoms resemble acting-out behaviors and may be attributed to other causes. The number of children, particularly adolescents, diagnosed with a mood or anxiety disorder, and receiving medication treatment has increased dramatically over the last decade. Furthermore, depression that emerges early in life may persist and continue into adulthood.

The symptoms of depression include depressed mood much of the time, poor appetite or overeating, disturbed sleep, lack of energy or enthusiasm, low self-esteem, poor concentration, and feelings of hopelessness. In children, increased irritability is quite common. Adolescents with depression may show a decline in school performance and engage in drug and/or alcohol abuse. Children and adolescents with depression are at increased risk for suicide attempts. Suicide rates for children between the ages of 10–14 have increased, with rates of mortality from suicide steadily increasing through adolescence. Suicide is the third leading cause of death for youth aged 15–19 years old. Although completed suicides are relatively uncommon, suicidal thoughts and attempts are quite common, especially among secondary level students. There are likely 2–3 students in every high school classroom who have considered suicide or made some type of suicide attempt.

In younger children, symptoms of anxiety are often indistinguishable from those of depression. Although all children experience short-term fears and worries in their normal development, those with excessive, persistent, exaggerated or unrealistic worries, which begin to interfere with normal daily living, may be diagnosed with an Anxiety Disorder. Anxiety is defined as a mood state that includes a negative affect and physical symptoms of apprehension and fear. Anxiety Disorders occur in about 3–6% of the childhood population and are equally common in boys and girls (Mash & Wolfe, 1999). Anxiety Disorders are listed by different categories that reflect the cause of the extreme fear and apprehension, such as separation from parent (Separation Anxiety Disorder) or a fear of specific situations (school reluctance, Social Phobia). The features of an Anxiety Disorder that are observed in the school setting can include frequent physical complaints, avoidance of school, crying and tantrums in anticipation of separation, difficulty paying attention, and social problems. School-based interventions to assist students with mood or anxiety disorders can include reinforcement programs to encourage school attendance (Behavior Contracts), Self-Management procedures, Bibliotherapy to address worries and fears, teaching problem solving skills (Think Aloud) and social skills interventions to target skills deficits.

Learning Disabilities

The term Learning Disability or Learning Disorder (LD) is used to describe a disorder in learning—in one or more of the essential processes involved in using or understanding language. Students with LD may have difficulty in reading, writing, spelling, mathematics, listening, thinking, or speaking. Each child or adolescent with a learning disability is unique, and may exhibit a diverse set of characteristics that will affect school performance. A LD is diagnosed when a student's achievement on an individually administered test in one or more academic areas is significantly below that expected for age, grade, and ability level. Simply stated, a student with a LD experiences unexpected difficulty and significant problems in learning to read, spell, write, or calculate math.

The prevalence of LDs ranges from 5% to 10% of the population, although higher rates have been reported (American Psychiatric Association, 1994). About 5% of school-age students are identified as having a LD. A higher percentage of students with LD are males, however, males may be more frequently referred by teachers because of the higher frequency of disruptive behaviors reported in males. There is a much higher likelihood of eventual school drop-out for students with a LD. There is no specific cause of LD, however risk factors include low birth weight, perinatal injury, genetic predisposition, and other neurological conditions or medical conditions.

Although as many as 20% of elementary students may have reading or academic problems, most of them will not receive or need special education services. The criteria established under IDEA for special education classification requires that the student must exhibit a severe discrepancy between achievement and intellectual ability in one or more of the basic areas. The disability is not caused by motor, hearing, or visual disabilities, or a result of environmental or cultural disadvantages.

Younger students with reading disabilities may exhibit mild speech delays, problems learning letter names, word-finding problems, and phonological-processing problems. Phonological processing involves the ability to distinguish the sounds in spoken words. In the upper grades a student's difficulty may be related to basic word identification and/or vocabulary knowledge and comprehension of text. Most students with severe reading disabilities continue to have difficulty throughout their school-age years and in adulthood.

Students with disabilities in math have either a primary math disability or have math problems associated with disabilities in reading and language. They often have difficulty memorizing math facts and understanding abstract concepts like place value and fractions. Students who have difficulty in reading, writing, or language will understandably have difficulty in understanding math word problems. Writing and spelling disabilities are similarly related to a student's phonological processing, reading comprehension, memory skills, and vocabulary knowledge. Children who experience difficulty with writing typically lack skills such as planning, organization, revising, and may lack knowledge about topics.

Although students with LD do not necessarily have behavior problems, many students with behavioral disorders, particularly ADHD, also have a LD. Between 19% to 25% of students with ADHD have a LD in at least one academic area (Barkley, 1990). Children who view school as difficult and frustrating over time may begin to act out or disrupt the classroom, therefore, several of the academic and behavior interventions found in Chapters 5–7 will be useful for these students.

SUMMARY

In summary, the prevalence of behavior problems in the school setting is significant and most classrooms will include at least 2–3 students with severe behaviors. About 7% of the school population will present a considerable challenge to educators and will require more intensive programs and interventions to be successful. There are several risk factors both inside and outside the child that contribute to the development of behavior problems in children, including temperament, genetics, neurological factors, parent-child interactions and characteristics, teacher and classroom variables, and school and community efforts. While the cause of behavior problems varies, and each child is unique, there are some important common characteristics shared by a majority of these students. These common traits that disrupt the classroom are the behavioral excesses of **noncompliance, rule breaking, arguing, disturbing others,** and **peer relationship problems**.

Teachers and school practitioners will quickly recognize those students who exhibit behavior and learning problems. Although a variety of educational and/or psychiatric labels are often used to describe these challenging students, a specific diagnosis or education classification is not required before implementing school-based interventions in the classroom. However, understanding the nature of a behavioral disorder and the essential features and associated deficits that often accompany such a disorder can be useful to educators when considering appropriate interventions. Most, if not all of the interventions listed in the following chapters have been specifically selected to address the varied behavioral, academic, and social deficits and excesses that students with behavior problems will present in the educational setting.

Whether or not a particular child meets the criteria for a specific disorder is less important than finding solutions that will help change a chaotic, unproductive classroom into a positive, productive one, and a student's negative school experience into a successful one. An important goal of this manual is to offer educators some solutions—solutions that are proven, practical, proactive, and positive in working with and helping these challenging students.

Chapter **4**

Classroom Basics—Preventing Problems Before They Begin

There are some important differences between classrooms characterized by productive learning environments and high levels of student engagement and classrooms with frequent disruptions and chaotic transitions, where teachers spend an excessive amount of time responding to unproductive student behavior. The difference is due to Classroom Basics—those teacher behaviors that lead directly to well-managed classrooms. Classroom Basics are methods of proactive classroom management that emphasize prevention of behavior problems by planning for and encouraging appropriate behavior, maintaining high levels of student participation, and reducing opportunities for student disruptions. Research evidence gathered over the past few decades suggests that successful teaching is not just responding to problems after they occur, but proactive planning for appropriate behavior—preventing problems before they begin (Gettinger, 1988). Using Classroom Basics will not prevent every problem from occurring, nor will it result in every child becoming a model student. Following Classroom Basics will, however, minimize occurrences of discipline problems, and help create a positive learning environment.

THE KEYS TO CLASSROOM BASICS

Managing and organizing an effective learning environment for children of any age—whether it is a class of thirty students, a small group, or a school-wide activity is not a simple task. There are a number of critical skills and procedures that are necessary to create and maintain a productive school environment. The emphasis of these skills is on prevention of—rather than reaction to behavioral problems. Although many of the interventions you may select from this manual can be used for specific problems, with an individual student, or if behavior problems increase, establishing Classroom Basics at the beginning of the year or at the onset of a new activity is perhaps the most important step of all. Classroom Basics consists of the following key components.

1. Establishing classroom rules and procedures
2. Teaching students appropriate behaviors and expectations
3. Maximizing student academic engagement
4. Structuring the classroom environment
5. Effective instructional skills
6. Establishing smooth transitions
7. Use of motivational techniques
8. Monitoring student behavior
9. Positive reinforcement for appropriate behavior
10. Clear and consistent consequences for misbehavior

Establishing Classroom Rules

Effective classroom management begins on the first day of school with instructing students in rules and procedures and monitoring student compliance with rules (Jenson, Andrews, & Reavis, 1996). The first few days of school are a critical period in which to begin classroom management. How effectively rules and procedures are established is a predictor of successful teaching in both elementary and secondary classrooms. Rules consist of directions regulating behavior in a particular setting (i.e., classroom rules, school rules, assembly rules, lunchroom rules, etc.). Procedures are routines or a particular course of action for a variety of activities (i.e., sharpening pencils, turning in assignments, putting toys away, etc.). Effective teachers, parents, and administrators are those who communicate rules, expectations, and consequences clearly and systematically to their students. Teaching rules with clarity involves teaching students to discriminate between appropriate and inappropriate behaviors. Do not assume that simply stating the rule is sufficient for understanding. It is important to devote time to demonstrating examples of rules and allowing students to practice examples of rules. (For specific examples of rule-setting interventions for different age groups refer to Chapter 5). Although teachers of secondary students may not need to spend as much time teaching and reviewing rules and procedures as elementary teachers, clear expectations for behavior and monitoring students for compliance is a critical proactive step. The following guidelines will help to establish classroom rules.

1. Rules should be positively and clearly stated in behavioral terms, emphasizing desirable behaviors rather than undesirable behaviors (e.g., Stay in your own space, Look at the teacher, etc., rather than, Don't talk, Don't bother others, etc.). Rules should represent what the teacher expects in the classroom.
2. Rules should be limited to five or less, particularly for younger children. Too many rules may actually make enforcing them more difficult.
3. Rules should be in a written form and posted in a prominent location where students can see them.
4. Students may be provided a copy of rules for inclusion in a notebook or placement on individual desks. A copy of the rules may also be sent home so that parents are aware of the rules their children are expected to follow.
5. Rules should be practiced and students should be taught to discriminate between examples and nonexamples.
6. Consequences for following rules need to be clearly explained.
7. Consequences for breaking rules need to be clearly explained.
8. Monitor students and consequate rule infractions consistently.

Establishing Class Procedures And Routines

Although establishing procedures and routines is similar to establishing rules in many ways, routines are provided to help students learn the steps necessary to accomplish tasks. Consistent routines help students move smoothly through activities and manage their own behavior. When students understand routines and procedures, they are less susceptible to distractions and interruptions and teachers can devote more time to providing instruction. Classroom routines should be taught to students in lessons, just as academic curriculum is taught. For example, each activity or task is analyzed by the teacher to determine what steps are necessary for students to perform the task. Daily routines should be broken into discrete steps that are demonstrated by the teacher and practiced by the students. Simple routines such as how to turn in assignments, how to come in from recess, or how to go to an assembly, may appear logical to adults, however, children need to be taught these skills, in a step-by-step manner, especially at the beginning of the year, or in a new situation.

Prior to the beginning of the school year, determine the procedures for various activities throughout the school day. Consider routines for student upkeep of desks, managing classroom equipment, entering and leaving the room, sharpening a pencil, going to the restroom or drinking fountain, collecting assignments, and transition periods. Students should also be taught procedures for handling problems or disruptions that might occasionally occur (e.g., illness, emergencies, injuries, explosive outbursts, etc.). Just as the classroom rules are taught and practiced by the

students, expectations for classroom procedures should be communicated clearly
and practiced by the students.

Teaching Students Appropriate Behaviors and Expectations

Many teachers complain that they must repeat instructions over and over,
however, children with behavior problems just don't seem to listen or follow the
instructions. For some students, simply giving an instruction, such as "get ready
for lunch" or "clean up the art supplies" is enough. Other students, especially
those with behavior problems, must be reminded several times and then continue
to ignore directions. For students to perform the appropriate behaviors they must
be taught what is expected of them. Teaching students the appropriate behaviors
and expectations by breaking the procedures into small steps, demonstrating each
step while describing it verbally, and allowing the students to practice the steps
several times prior to implementing consequences is an important proactive strategy. Students should be reinforced frequently with verbal praise for engaging in
the appropriate behaviors. Students should also be reminded of expectations prior
to beginning an activity.

For example, teachers of younger children may teach the students a ready position for sitting on the carpet while listening to instructions or sitting in a reading
group. To teach a ready position, the teacher describes the specific way to sit appropriately (e.g., straight, silent, legs crossed), the teacher demonstrates the ready
position and practices it with the students. One idea for teaching younger children
the ready position is to name it the "soldier sit" (Herschell, Greco, Filcheck, &
McNeil, 2002). The teacher explains that the students should sit just like a soldier, and models the appropriate way to sit. Several students may be selected to
demonstrate the "soldier sit" for the other students, or be called on to differentiate
correct from incorrect ready positions. Keep in mind that young children are learning an important behavior skill, just as they learn an academic skill. Learning and
mastering any new skill requires guidance, practice, and a positive atmosphere.

Maximizing Student Academic Engagement

Academic engagement is perhaps the most critical student behavior associated with effective classroom management. In fact, there is a significant relationship between levels of academic engagement and academic performance (Shapiro,
1988). When classrooms are running smoothly and efficiently, students spend a
larger proportion of the school day engaged in academic work and learning activities. Academic engagement is defined as the percentage of student involvement in
academic tasks rather than off-task, disruptive or passive behaviors. Academic engagement includes classroom behaviors such as writing, asking or answering questions, and reading aloud or silently. The more time students are actively engaged in

these tasks, the less idle time they will have to engage in inappropriate behaviors. Classrooms where teachers maximize instructional time and require participation by all students will convey the importance of academic engagement. One way of doing this is by giving students frequent opportunities to actively respond to academic requests. The literature suggests that increased rates of opportunity to respond at the appropriate instructional level results in increased academic productivity and decreased disruptive behaviors (Sutherland & Wehby, 2001). For example, faster presentation rate during practice or drill work has been shown to increase the attentiveness of students. In younger grades, frequent and active oral student participation may be more important, while in older grades students may spend more time involved in independent study, written responding, or group interactions.

The following factors contribute to increased instructional time and academic engagement:

1. Encourage and reinforce punctuality and attendance. Even a few minutes wasted while students straggle in late adds up to several hours of lost instructional time.
2. Plan and adhere to a consistent daily schedule. Posting a daily schedule listing assignments, academic information, homework, etc. is recommended.
3. Begin classroom activities immediately at the beginning of the school day or at the beginning of each class period.
4. Plan and reinforce smooth transitions between activities or settings.
5. Schedule important activities or instructional periods during students' optimal levels of attention and performance, with preferred activities following the completion of less preferred activities.
6. Use clear and brief verbal instructions and cues whenever possible.
7. Provide ready accessibility of materials and/or equipment needed for tasks.
8. Provide frequent opportunities for all students to respond correctly and provide frequent feedback or error correction.
9. During independent seatwork, monitor student behavior and work completion; however, give verbal reminders to individual students as unobtrusively as possible.
10. Minimize outside disruptions during the day. Schedule a regular time for announcements, business items, etc.
11. Develop a system to provide assistance for students who need individual help or have specific questions so they don't waste several minutes waiting.
12. Develop clear procedures and alternative activities for students who complete work early.

Structuring The Classroom Environment

In every classroom special attention should be given to the physical arrangement and structure of the environment to maximize efficiency and prevent potential problems. Classrooms that are well organized allow students to complete tasks and follow routines smoothly. Structural issues to consider include, designing spaces for specific classroom activities or functions that occur during the day, ensuring each student visual access to the teacher and/or the board, providing the teacher visual access to all students, minimizing distractions, and designing student movement to minimize congestion.

When designing spaces for classroom activities, consider the functions that will take place on a daily basis (Colvin & Lazar, 1997). Elementary and secondary classrooms will differ. Many elementary classrooms include an independent work area, small group area, whole group area, teacher's desk, penalty area, freetime area, and storage areas. Secondary classrooms usually include independent work areas, however, may include small group areas, teacher's desk, penalty areas, and storage areas. For optimal classroom structuring, independent work areas require minimum distractions and individual desks for students to complete assignments. Group areas may include a carpet area, group table, or circle of chairs, where students can watch the teacher. A penalty or think-time area is sometimes used for a student to spend time apart from the group. Such a space may include a desk in the back of the room, or a desk facing a wall.

It is also important to consider travel flow throughout the classroom. Frequently traveled areas should be wide enough for smooth travel and be free of obstacles. It may be helpful to rehearse traffic patterns that are likely to occur during the school day. Routines for students to move about the classroom for supplies, sharpening pencils, turning in assignments, getting a drink, etc. should be established. Specific rules for traffic areas such as "Only three students at the drinking fountain at a time" may also help with congestion.

To ensure that students are following daily classroom routines and to detect inappropriate behavior early, the teacher must be alert to what is happening at all times. To facilitate this, arrangement of classroom furniture to permit visual monitoring of the students is essential. The teacher must be able to quickly scan the classroom from either a sitting or standing position, and determine when students need help and what behaviors are occurring. The teacher may use low-profile techniques such as moving about the classroom to monitor student performance during a lesson or moving close to students who may be off-task during instructional periods. The placement of the teacher's desk should be in a low-traffic area. To effectively monitor the class, assist with problems, help students remain on-task, and reinforce student behavior, teachers should spend as little time as possible behind a desk.

Classroom seating arrangements also have a significant impact on levels of off-task behavior, particularly for students with behavioral disorders. Cluster or group seating arrangements where students face each other facilitate social and group interactions, however, interfere with on-task behavior during independent work periods. Students with behavior problems often need more personal space, therefore seating in rows or placing desks in a U-shape arrangement may reduce off-task behavior. Seating assignments, likewise, impact on-task behavior. When disruptive students are grouped together, they tend to encourage and increase disruptive behaviors. Disruptive students who are seated near well-behaved students tend to exhibit fewer disruptive behaviors. Disruptive students should also be seated so they are directly facing the teacher, rather than other students. Seating assignment can be varied periodically so that students are seated near different students. Choice of seating can also be used as a reward for students who demonstrate appropriate behavior, however, desks should be arranged so that students face the point in the room where they will need to focus attention during instructional time.

Effective Instructional Skills

There is a strong relationship between effective instructional delivery (teacher behavior) and appropriate student behavior. Effective teachers demonstrate those skills that maximize high rates of student academic involvement and student learning. Success in classroom management depends largely on the teacher's ability to maintain high levels of student engagement in academic tasks. Effective instructional strategies will reduce the need for special interventions.

There has been considerable research over the last several decades regarding effective instructional strategies. Models of instruction referred to as "direct instruction" are based on the principals of applied behavior analysis and were developed for classwide implementation in the 1960s and 1970s through the Follow-Through program (Engelmann & Carnine, 1982). Direct instruction refers to instructional methods that enhance academic engagement. The critical elements include, fast paced instruction, frequent opportunities to respond, frequent feedback, and reinforcement systems. These principles can be applied in designing any instructional program or with any age group. From this perspective, some recommended strategies for effective instruction are described below.

1. Select important foundational skills that students will need to learn. For students at-risk for failure because of academic or behavioral difficulties, instruction must be presented at the level of the student.
2. Prior to beginning a lesson, ensure that all students are attending. Effective teachers often use cues and signals to gain students' attention (e.g., hold up a hand, ring a small bell or chimes, use a key word, or key phrases such as, "Ready, set, look", "1—2—3", "Good listening ears", etc.). Acknowledge and reinforce students who are attentive.

3. Provide a meaningful rationale and instructional objective at the beginning of each lesson. Objectives and rationales help students understand what they are learning and the relevance of the lesson.
4. Give effectively stated task directions. Task directions (e.g., for assignment completion) should be clear and specific and tell students precisely what they are expected to do. Have a student or several students repeat or paraphrase directions to ensure understanding. For all children, keep explanations brief. For younger children you may need to limit directions to two or three steps or space directions for different activities apart rather than presenting them at the same time. (Steps for giving effective requests or commands are provided in the next section.)
5. Break tasks into smaller steps and demonstrate each step to students.
6. Use fast-paced, teacher led drill and practice. Students are usually more attentive during fast-paced presentations. Provide opportunities for frequent student responding (e.g., choral responding, use of response cards, call on individual students).
7. Provide immediate feedback and error correction when necessary. Error correction should be positive and systematic. A common procedure is to inform the student of the error, provide additional information or model correct response, and provide another opportunity for responding.
8. Use verbal praise and encouragement frequently to increase student participation.

Effective Requests

An additional factor in facilitating compliance is use of effectively stated requests or commands (Rhode, Jenson, & Reavis, 1993). Effective requests are often referred to as precision commands. If used correctly by teachers and parents, students will respond more quickly and accurately. Some suggestions for encouraging compliance and giving effective requests are listed below.

1. *Use a direct statement* rather than a question format. Stating, "I need you to pick up the toys" is more effective than asking, "Will you clean up the toys?" Tell the student to *start* a behavior rather than stop a behavior, for example: "Please start your spelling assignment", instead of "Don't play with your pencil." It is better to use *specific* and descriptive requests such as "Put your papers in your desk", than general statements such as "It's recess time."
2. *Use body basics.* Body basics are effective nonverbal communication skills. The most important skill is *eye contact*—look directly at the student as you give a request. Other body basics include, face the student and

move close to the student—give requests from a shorter distance (an arm's length), rather than from across the room, and use a soft but firm voice—don't shout.

3. *Build behavioral momentum.* With students who are often noncompliant, it is helpful to give them a few simple, easy to follow preferred tasks (high probability requests), prior to giving a less preferred, more difficult task (low probability requests). Students who are experiencing success will more likely continue the positive momentum and comply with the more difficult request.

4. *Give only one or two requests at a time.* Give requests that the student is capable of following.

5. *Allow enough time* for students to respond to a request (5–10 seconds), and do not interrupt this time period. Many adults immediately repeat instructions or give additional instructions without allowing students the time to comply. During this 5–10 second time period do not converse, argue, or respond to excuses. Waiting quietly and watching may prompt the student to respond without further reminders.

6. *Requests should be given only two times.* If teachers or parents need to repeat requests over and over, students are tuning out! Students who do not respond after two requests have learned that they can postpone following through for several minutes, and perhaps avoid the task altogether. If the student does not comply after the second request, the teacher should respond with a planned consequence (not an emotional outburst or ultimatum). Planned consequences might include moving near the student and guiding them through the first step, loss of two minutes of free time, working near the teacher's desk, loss of a privilege, etc.

7. *Recognize their effort with verbal praise,* smiles, or other positive reinforcement when students do follow requests appropriately.

Establishing Smooth Transitions

Transitions are periods of change or movement, from one activity to another or from one setting or classroom to the next. Most students spend several minutes of the school day—at least 15 minutes per day, involved in transitions. Establishing smooth transitions will increase academic engagement. Many times, students with behavior problems will exhibit more problems during transition periods, which are often less structured and less supervised. Changes in routine and moving from one area to another are difficult for students who are already distractible. To reduce behavior problems during these periods and to facilitate smooth transitions, it is necessary to plan ahead to determine what skills and procedures are necessary for each transition period. For younger students, transition periods might include entering the classroom, moving from desks to group or carpet areas, going out to recess, lining up to go to the gym, walking through the hallways, and getting ready to go home. For older students, transition periods might include moving within the classroom to different work areas (computers, labs, equipment, etc.), moving from classroom to classroom several times a day, going to the lunchroom, and going to assemblies. It is also important to establish times when students may move in and around the classroom to get drinks, sharpen pencils, turn in assignments, etc. This type of student movement should be designated and not typically allowed during instructional periods.

Just as classroom rules and expectations must be taught and monitored, transition rules and procedures must be explained and monitored. After identifying any problem behaviors of concern for each specific setting, the teacher should create a range of appropriate behaviors. These behaviors can be presented to the students through instructional lessons including positive examples and student practice. Skills such as waiting for a signal before leaving, walking quietly, watching where you are walking, keeping hands and feet to self, and entering classrooms quietly are important skills needed during transition periods.

To reduce problems during transition times, the following tips are also recommended.

Schedules. Provide students with a visual and/or written schedule of the day's activities to avoid confusion and to help establish consistent routines. For younger children, schedules incorporating pictures or symbols for each activity are useful. It is important to involve the students in reviewing the schedule, at the beginning of the day or period, as well as at transition times. Describe what students should expect, for example, "First we will review vocabulary flash cards, then we will work in our reading workbooks."

Cues. Utilize auditory or visual cues to signal changes in the routine. An example with younger students is singing a daily song during clean-up time or line-up time, or clapping to a rhythm to signal the transition. Give the students ample warning or remind students in advance that a transition period is approaching. The use of a clock or timer may also help students understand time periods. It may also be necessary to teach students a signal such as stating, "Freeze" to indicate immediate cessation of activity or that absolute attention is required.

Teach and practice. Discuss, teach, and practice skills that are important for transitions and activity changes. Review these skills occasionally throughout the year.

Calm down activities. It may be helpful to engage students in a calm down activity near the end of a class period, particularly when shifting from an unstructured to structured or informal to formal activity. Avoid rushed or abrupt transitions where students haven't had sufficient time to get ready (clear off desks, put materials away, etc.).

Supervise.   Adult supervision during transitions will greatly reduce problem behaviors. Stand at the door at the beginning of the period or during class breaks, and monitor hallways and group areas.

Be prepared.   Prepare materials for each activity ahead of time. It is sometimes helpful to present a transition activity immediately at the beginning of the period. For example, some teachers require ten minutes of silent reading immediately after the bell rings. Other transition activities might include timed 1–2 minute math tests, relaxation music or tapes, flash card review, answering a question of the day, or writing in a journal.

Reinforce.   Remember to reinforce smooth transitions, and praise students who demonstrate appropriate transition behaviors. Encourage smooth transitions by timing students during activity changes, and occasionally rewarding quick transitions with small reinforcers (extra recess minutes, a few minutes of free time).

Use of Motivational Techniques

Attending rates for students for students with behavior problems are influenced by classroom context, including teaching techniques used to motivate and stimulate student interest. Unfortunately, students today are bombarded with over-stimulation—from movies, television, computer games, advertising, and the media. How can educators expect to motivate and maintain student interest in daily tasks such as spelling, reading, algebra, or grammar? Teachers don't have to "put on a show" to teach effectively. The important key is to use effective strategies and teaching techniques that have been proven through educational research. In fact, many children with attention or behavior problems benefit more from greater task structure than over-stimulation, particularly on new or difficult tasks.

Incorporating motivational techniques in the classroom refers to increasing student interest through involving all students in the task or lesson, helping students connect learning with real-life, using a variety of presentation and questioning techniques, providing stimulation through the addition of color, texture, and hands-on activities, and letting students practice skills through a variety of performance tasks.

Effective teachers involve all students during recitation tasks by selecting students at random to recite, using group responses, asking listeners to comment, and alerting students they may be called on. During instruction, use of challenging comments such as, "You'll enjoy this one", or "Are you ready for a really hard problem?" will help to maintain focus and attention.

Students also maintain interest when lessons are meaningful and when they can relate the information to real-life situations. Connecting curriculum to real-life enhances understanding and insight. All students bring their prior knowledge and experiences to the classroom. Instruction that utilizes these experiences to capture student's attention will increase learning and success. It helps to get the students actively involved by letting them share experiences they have had with the subject.

The enthusiasm of the teacher in presenting instruction also plays an important role in maintaining interest and reducing behavior problems. To keep a smooth momentum during lessons, instruction should be fast-paced, with the teacher inserting the name of students into statements or questions, moderating voice tone, moving near inattentive students, looking directly at individual students, and directing questions to potentially inattentive students. Teachers who establish a positive climate by smiling, accepting student ideas, and showing genuine interest in the subject and the students will encourage positive behavior.

Although some topics and assignments require drill and repetition, and are not by their nature, particularly exciting, interest can be enhanced by using a variety of presentation techniques. Students with attention problems may attend poorly to tasks that they perceive as boring or repetitive. Presenting information in different ways or with a variety of applications will improve attention. For example, asking probing questions and providing opportunities for students to give input during teacher-led discussions will keep students engaged. Other instructional techniques that help to stimulate interest include use of visual aides (maps, pictures, cues, graphs, color, etc.), models or demonstrations, oral practice, games and contests, debates, special projects, films, use of computers, guest speakers, and field trips. Use of visual information to support verbal information is particularly effective for students with attention problems. Many students, especially inattentive ones are more successful at focusing their attention when teachers utilize an overhead projector to teach and explain new concepts (Jones, 1994). The use of an overhead projector also allows the teacher to look directly at the students and monitor the class while demonstrating a skill or providing examples.

Public posting (or visual advertising of student success) is another technique that can enhance motivation (Jenson & Reavis, 1996). The classroom bulletin board can and should be utilized to display student success. Public posting should be positive and can include student progress scores, highlight student accomplishments, or points earned toward individual, team, or class goals. Public posting provides visual feedback to students and it informs others (peers, parents, teachers) of student progress and achievement. It can be used in conjunction with many of the interventions presented in this book.

Monitoring Student Behavior

Adult supervision and attention to students is undoubtedly one of the most essential components of effective classroom management. Teachers who monitor their students communicate to the class that they are aware of what all students are doing, are likely to detect any inappropriate behaviors more quickly, and can immediately deal with misbehaviors. Monitoring student behavior refers to teacher awareness of the entire group behavior, rather than individual student behavior, through the use of low-profile techniques, such as simple comments or directives, eye contact with students, and moving close to a trouble spot. During large group instruction, the teacher should face the students, and the students' attentional focus should be on the teacher. Moving near students who are beginning to go off task, while continuing to give instruction is particularly effective. During independent work periods, the teacher may need to periodically move about the classroom to monitor student performance. The teacher should also be able to visually scan the classroom and continue to monitor events going on while working with small groups, or consulting with individual students. During transition periods—to and from the lunchroom or gym, while changing classes, or moving within the classroom, careful monitoring is particularly important. In secondary schools, the presence of hall monitors and adults in congested areas will deter behavior problems. Active adult supervision is critical, particularly in settings such as playgrounds, cafeterias, bus loading and unloading zones, or school entrances. To supervise such areas, adults must be visible and within a close proximity to students, continuously attend to students' movements and behaviors, and know the rules and procedures expected of the students.

Positive Reinforcement for Appropriate Behavior

Although providing positive reinforcement for appropriate behavior is not a new concept to educators, it is often easy to overlook this critical key when working with students who have behavior problems. Sometimes it is quite difficult to find any behaviors deserving of positive reinforcement when students are disruptive, aggressive, hyperactive, and noncompliant throughout the day. The desire for attention is universal, however, not all children gain attention through positive or desirable actions. Some students have developed a pattern of negative attention-seeking behaviors, such as interrupting, disturbing others, acting silly, teasing, or ignoring requests. These students may respond to a reprimand or reminder by stopping an inappropriate behavior temporarily, however, later they will most likely repeat the same behavior or another inappropriate behavior to seek attention. These students are actually reinforced by teacher and peer attention for their misbehaviors. Successful students are able to use desired academic and behavioral skills to access reinforcement in the school and home setting, whereas students with behavior problems rarely elicit positive comments for their appropriate behaviors from teachers. Positive reinforcement is so important it must be planned and used systematically. It is the teacher's role to create a classroom climate with high rates of positive reinforcement for desirable behaviors, and to design opportunities for all students, even those with challenging behaviors to experience success. In addition to providing positive reinforcement to individual students, proactive teachers emphasize group behavior, and communicate awareness of the group behavior by commenting frequently on the appropriate behavior occurring within the context of the group activity.

Adult praise is an extremely effective form of positive reinforcement that communicates recognition of appropriate behavior. There are important steps to making teacher praise more effective (Reavis, Jenson, Kukic, & Morgan, 1993).

- First, praise should be given more frequently than reprimands. We recommend at least a 4:1 ratio of positive to negative teacher comments.
- Second, praise should describe specific behaviors that warrant recognition, should be genuine, and be meaningful to the student. For example, a statement such as, "What a good job!" is less effective than, "It looks as if you really worked hard on that paper. Your writing is neat and you filled in every line!"
- Finally, praise that is delivered immediately and enthusiastically following a desirable behavior will be more reinforcing. Keep in mind that positive statements can become discouraging to students if qualifying comments such as, "it's about time" or "why can't you do this every day" are added at the end. Teachers may have to carefully attend to students with behavior problems to notice those infrequent appropriate behaviors and monitor themselves for praising those students.

For particularly difficult students, it may help to keep a record or tally of the number of times the student demonstrates desirable behaviors and also record how many times those behaviors were recognized and praised.

Middle and secondary level students may be embarrassed when teachers praise them in front of their peers. Communicating positive comments to these students can be more effective when given quietly or individually, either during or after class. With older students, praise may also be less explicit and more casual than with younger students.

There are several other forms of positive reinforcement that will encourage and increase appropriate behavior. Some easy examples are a smile, making eye contact, approving nod, a quick thumbs up, pat on the back, high five, a brief note on an assignment, or a positive note or phone call to parents.

Awarding special privileges for appropriate behavior is effective because they are easy to incorporate during the day, available in the natural environment, and can be adapted to match a specific student's interests and skills. Special jobs that elementary students enjoy are, being first in line, caring for a class pet, passing out or collecting papers, taking messages to the office, and tutoring peers. In a secondary classroom, special privileges might include, working as an office aide or teacher's assistant, giving building directions to parents or guests during conferences, helping at assemblies, or working as a peer tutor. Other suggestions include use of activity reinforcers such as playing a game, extra computer time, looking at magazines, listening to music, sitting by a friend, extra recess time, or going to lunch a few minutes early to reward appropriate behaviors. These reinforcers can be awarded to specific individual students or the entire class.

Small tangible or edible reinforcers can also be incorporated into a classwide reinforcement program. Such rewards can be given to the students contingent upon specific desirable academic or social behaviors. Classroom token economies involve awarding tokens or points that are later exchanged for activities, special privileges, treats, or objects. There are several variations of positive reinforcement programs and techniques that are included in Chapter 5—Interventions for Behavior Problems.

Clear and Consistent Consequences for Misbehavior

Although proactive classroom management techniques will certainly reduce the rate of student disruptions and the need to deal with discipline problems, an effective management plan must include clear and consistent consequences for misbehavior. When rules are explained to students, consequences for breaking the rules need to also be explained. Prompt response to misbehaviors will communicate to students an awareness of classroom events and interactions, and prevent minor behavior problems from turning into major problems. Some helpful guidelines in establishing and applying negative consequences include the following steps:

1. Consequences for misbehavior should be preplanned—identified and determined by the teacher in advance.
2. Consequences for misbehavior should be clearly explained to the students at the time rules are explained. A chart or list of positive and negative consequences should be posted with the rules (e.g., When I follow the rules I will . . . and When I don't follow the rules I will . . .).
3. Practice consistent use of positive and negative consequences for students' behaviors. Intervene promptly before classroom infractions develop into major behavior problems.
4. Apply consequences as unobtrusively as possible, avoiding reactive confrontations or ultimatums. Responding to inappropriate behaviors with corrective procedures and low-profile techniques is more effective that threats of punishment.
5. It is very important for adults to exhibit a professional demeanor with students and maintain a calm perspective when dealing with inappropriate behaviors.
6. Maintain a higher positive than negative ratio of reinforcement. A classroom environment that includes high rates of positive reinforcement for

students who exhibit appropriate behaviors will help promote a well-managed classroom.

7. Use mild negative consequences. Punitive consequences should be reserved for the most severe behaviors. In many situations, a variety of alternatives to suspension can be used, including administrative warnings, parent conferences, debriefing logs, other-class time-out, and/or indoor lunch or recess (refer to Chapter 5).

Examples of mild negative consequences include cues or prompts, verbal reprimands, loss of privileges (loss of 5 minutes of recess, or 1 minute of change time between classes), loss of positive reinforcers (points, stickers, treats, activities, free time, etc.), student conferences, and parent contact or conferences.

Verbal reprimands are the most common reductive technique used in the classroom. Reprimands can be effective in reducing problem behaviors, however, as with giving praise, the use of reprimands is more effective when specific rules are followed (Van Houten, 1980).

1. Reprimands should be *straightforward*—describing the inappropriate behavior, why it is unacceptable, and what replacement behavior should occur (e.g., "Jason, don't run in the hall. Someone could get hurt. You need to walk quietly.")
2. Reprimands should be stated in a *firm voice tone* (not overly emotional) and combined with a facial expression that conveys disapproval. Eye contact is important.
3. Reprimands should be delivered when *near the student*, not from a distance. It is unnecessary and unkind to publicly embarrass and humiliate students.
4. Reprimands should be delivered *immediately* and consistently, so students will know what to expect. When reprimands are delayed for even two minutes they are much less effective (Abramowitz & O'Leary, 1991).
5. If reprimands fail to reduce or stop the inappropriate behavior, other consequences or procedures may be necessary. Reprimands are ineffective, if after delivery the student is allowed to continue misbehaving.

SUMMARY

Designing a proactive management plan and structuring the classroom to prevent problems before they begin is an essential component of *School-Based Interventions for Students with Behavior Problems*. Classroom Basics include the critical skills and procedures that are necessary to establish an effective learning environment. The purpose of using Classroom Basics is to prevent and to minimize the occurrence of many behavior problems. There are several classroom and teacher variables that affect student behavior. These variables are based on educational research applications, and successful teaching practices. When a teacher establishes classroom rules and procedures, models and teaches expected behaviors, monitors student behavior, and provides reinforcement for appropriate behaviors, student behavior is positively affected. When a teacher structures the classroom to create an orderly environment, establishes smooth transitions, keeps students actively engaged, and uses effective, motivational and instructional skills, student behavior and learning are positively affected. A sound understanding and use of the Classroom Basics discussed in this chapter is the cornerstone of effective instruction. These skills are particularly important in initiating intervention to help students with behavior problems. The use of Classroom Basics will maximize success with all of the specific, individualized behavioral and academic interventions that are included in the following chapters.

Chapter 5

Interventions for Behavior Problems

Several effective techniques are presented in this chapter that educators can use with an individual student, with a small group of students, or with an entire classroom. While many students learn and flourish in a well-structured classroom and do not require specific or intensive intervention to behave appropriately, students with behavior problems and/or emotional disabilities will require more support and may require more extrinsic motivation to develop appropriate academic, social, and compliant behaviors. The goal of these interventions is not simply behavior management or using rewards to control behavior, rather it is to help students improve behavior and develop internal motivation to succeed. Based on the definition of the term *intervention* described in Chapter 2, the research-validated procedures presented in this chapter include methods of teaching new skills, and/or manipulation of antecedents and consequences. They include a range of effective or combination of effective positive interventions such as group contingencies, self-management, differential reinforcement, token economies, peer tutoring, as well as some mild reductive techniques such as response-cost and time-out from reinforcement. A complete list of behavioral intervention terms, definitions, examples, and cautions for each are provided in Appendix B. When selecting an intervention, it is always important to try the most direct or simple approach first. When classroom disruption is the result of only one or two student's misbehavior, the most appropriate intervention may be an individual intervention. When several students are misbehaving, class-wide interventions or group contingencies may be more effective. Most of the following interventions can be adapted for use with an individual student, a few students, or with the entire class.

Based on the Teacher Top Ten Problem Behaviors listed in Chapter 1, the interventions for behavior problems are organized to address the major concerns that continue to disrupt classrooms at all grade levels. Most, if not all of these problem behaviors are externalizing behavior excesses described in Chapter 3, and fall into one of the six categories listed below. Specific interventions for a variety of behaviors under each category are described. Although each intervention is listed in only one of the following six areas, many of these interventions can also be used to improve behaviors in some of the other areas as well. Additional behavior problems related to peer-relationships and social skills are addressed in Chapter 7. Refer to the subject index for additional information and page references.

1. Aggression—Aggression involves both verbal and nonverbal actions intended to hurt others ranging from name calling to physical assaults and threats. Behaviors addressed in this category are, anger management, arguing, bullying, fighting, and teasing.
2. Disruptive Behaviors—Disruptive behaviors are behaviors that annoy or bother others, including talking out, interrupting, making noises, out-of-seat, and self-control.
3. Following Directions—Following directions refers to compliance with teacher requests, obeying commands, and doing what the teacher asks and expects.
4. Following Rules—Specific strategies to teach and reinforce classroom, playground, bus, or transition rules are included in this category.
5. Noncompliance—Noncompliance includes active refusal to comply with requests, defiant behaviors, and deliberate rule-breaking behaviors.
6. Task Engagement—Task Engagement refers to behaviors such as initiating tasks, task maintenance, and work completion.

When selecting interventions for behavior change, the student's age and developmental level should be considered, as well as which behaviors are most likely interfering with a student's educational progress and will lead to repeated failure. Regardless of the intervention used, these basic considerations for implementing a behavioral intervention are recommended.

1. Determine specific target behaviors to focus on that are the most problematic—those behaviors that are the most salient and disruptive to the classroom and most detrimental to the student's success. It is best to limit targeted behaviors to only 1–3 specific behaviors. Although many times the primary complaint is actually quite complex and there are other underlying problems, this unacceptable behavior must change for success in other areas to follow.
2. Determine the possible functions (refer to ABC sheet in Appendix A) of the behavior and what antecedents or consequences may be contributing to the behavior before choosing an intervention.

3. Select and teach appropriate replacement behaviors if these behaviors are not already in the student's repertoire. The student must know what behavior is expected if he or she is to behave appropriately.
4. Not all positive reinforcement requires tangible rewards. Determine what is motivating to a student by asking the student(s), observing the student(s), and noticing the effect the reinforcement has on the student's behavior. Contingent verbal praise should be associated with the delivery of any tangible or token reinforcer. As a student gains internal motivation, the delivery of tokens or rewards can be faded out, but the praise is continued.
5. Implement intervention procedures consistently and uniformly over a sufficient period of time to obtain satisfactory results. Sometimes behaviors will seem worse before they improve—don't give up after one or a few days with no improvement.

AGGRESSION

Anger Logs   **E9 F9 E7 C10 T8 I6 V9 +9 T = 8.5**

Reference: Kellner, Bry, & Coletti, 2002.
Goal: This intervention is a class-wide program that provides an opportunity for students to evaluate and self-monitor their responses to anger-provoking situations.
Age Group: Secondary.
Materials: Anger Log recording sheets. A sample Anger Log is listed in Appendix A.
Steps:

1. The teacher explains to the students that they will use the Anger Log as a way to practice anger control either before or after anger-provoking situations occur at school.
2. The teacher reviews the need for practicing anger coping skills, stressing that anger is a normal emotion that everyone has when something is not right, however, anger should be expressed in a socially acceptable way that will help solve the problem.
3. The teacher introduces the Anger Log to the students. The Anger Log is a self-rating form on which students write their name and date and answer the following questions:
   (a) What was your trigger?
   (b) Where were you?
   (c) How angry were you? Students rate the degree of anger on a scale of 1 to 5, with 1 = not very angry, 2 = a little angry, 3 = angry, 4 = pretty angry, and 5 = furious.

       (d) What did you do? Inappropriate and appropriate responses should be listed (e.g., yelled at the person, hit or pushed the person, threw papers on the floor, cursed, or counted to 10 and calmed down, walked away, talked about it, ignored the person).

       (e) How did you do? Students self-rate their anger coping skills on a scale of 1 to 5, with 1 = poor, 2 = not good, 3 = OK, 4 = pretty good, and 5 = super.

4.   The teacher explains that the steps required for good anger management are; recognizing anger, interrupting anger before acting inappropriately (calming down), and using an appropriate anger coping skill. The appropriate skills should be reviewed so that students have a repertoire of positive coping skills.

5.   The teacher presents several anger-provoking situations to the students and demonstrates how to complete the Anger Log by reading and answering each question in a step-by-step progression, with student input and participation.

6.   Students are given several opportunities to practice anger-provoking situations and completing the steps on the Anger Log. The teacher may provide situational role-plays and ask students to act them out in the group setting (e.g., Another student is calling you names during P.E., or Another student grabs your shirt and tears it, etc.).

7.   The teacher places a stack of Anger Log forms in the classroom. When anger-provoking situations occur, the student involved completes an Anger Log form and returns it to a designated area or the students can keep their forms in an individual notebook.

8.   The Anger Log may be used as an in-class assignment or as homework for which students receive points or credit towards their grade.

9.   During weekly or bi-monthly group discussions, the teacher may ask students to review or reenact incidents that have taken place during the last week and report on the outcome.

Troubleshooting: Review of personal Anger Logs should occur in a supportive environment. Students should be encouraged to share their experiences with the class, but only if they are comfortable doing so.

Conflict Managers   **E8 F7 E6 C5 T9 I6 V9 +8 T = 7.3**

Reference: Johnson, Johnson, Mitchell, Cotten, Harris, & Louison, 1996.
Goal: The Conflict Manager program is a peer-mediation program in which students are trained to serve as conflict managers to mediate student conflicts such as verbal threats, bullying, name-calling and minor physical aggression (hitting, pushing, etc.).
Age Group: Elementary.

Materials: Mediation Report Forms and a poster listing possible solutions to arguments. A sample Mediation Report Form is listed in Appendix A.
Steps:

1. This program can be used in individual classes or on a school-wide basis.
2. The teacher or administrator explains that the class (or school) will be working on a new program to help reduce conflicts between students and help students to resolve problems with each other. Several students, including both boys and girls, are recruited or may volunteer to be trained as Conflict Managers. Students in 3rd through 6th grades may be included.
3. The teacher or other school staff member provides training for the students who will be the Conflict Managers. The training should include teaching communication skills (e.g., "I messages", listening skills, problem solving skills, etc.), as well as mediation skills (e.g., negotiation, compromise, making agreements). The students should be provided with a list of possible solutions commonly used by elementary students (e.g., stay away from each other, apologize, shake hands and be friends, compromise, take turns, tell yourself "It's OK", etc.). Students should have several opportunities to role-play conflict mediations prior to implementing the program with the rest of the class.
4. The Conflict Manager students are also trained in how to complete the Mediation Report Form. The information contained in the report form should include (a) the type of conflict reported, (b) the strategies used during the conflict, and (c) the agreed-upon solutions. The report form should also be signed by the students involved in the conflict and by the conflict managers assisting them.
5. The conflict managers are on duty during the lunch hour or during recess periods. The conflict managers are assigned to pairs and two students working as a team mediate each conflict. The teams can be rotated so that students have duty-free days. The teams are provided with a weekly schedule that lists which days they are on duty.
6. Students involved in a conflict can ask for help from the conflict managers or can be referred for mediation by another student, the teacher, a counselor, or an administrator.
7. When students are referred or seek mediation assistance, they sit down with the conflict manager team on duty, describe the problem, discuss possible solutions to the problem, and decide on the best solution. The mediation can take place in a designated location in the classroom or school building. When the students reach an agreement, they complete the Mediation Report Form, write the agreed-upon decision on the form, sign the form, and turn the form in to the teacher. The mediation procedure can usually be completed in a short period of time (5 to15 minutes). The

teacher reviews the forms daily and consults with the mediators if adult assistance is necessary.

Troubleshooting: The conflict manager program is a proactive approach, to diffuse and de-escalate aggressive behaviors and minor conflicts. For recurring conflicts or severe aggression, reductive techniques may be required.

Debriefing   **E10 F10 E7 C8 T8 I6 V9 +8 T = 8.3**

Reference: Sugai & Colvin, 1997.
Goal: The "debriefing" intervention is a brief, planned, teacher-student interaction used to provide feedback and reminders to students following a problem behavior. Teachers can also use debriefing following displays of appropriate behavior as a method of positive feedback.
Age Group: Elementary or Secondary.
Materials: Debriefing Form (optional). A sample Debriefing Form is listed in Appendix A.
Steps:

1. The debriefing strategy is a proactive procedure designed to follow pre-planned consequences. During debriefing, the student is reminded of, or taught more acceptable future behaviors, and prepared for return to the classroom.
2. Prior to implementing the debriefing strategy, the teacher or educator determines a hierarchy of reductive consequences for unacceptable or aggressive behaviors (e.g., throwing objects, profanity, yelling at teacher, etc.). Examples of typical consequences include, loss of privileges, referral to the office, removal from the classroom, noontime in-school detention, after-school detention, etc.
3. When the student displays the problem behavior, the teacher immediately assigns the predetermined consequence while telling the student calmly that the problem behavior is not acceptable.
4. The debriefing intervention is a transition between the administration of the reductive consequence and return to the classroom. Debriefing typically takes about three to five minutes. A written form can be used during debriefing to serve as a record of the behavior and to encourage student involvement in the process.
5. After the consequence has been administered or assigned, the educator introduces the debriefing strategy by stating something like, "You were assigned a consequence for _____. Let's discuss what we can do differently the next time you get upset and how you can go back to your class successfully."

6. During debriefing the student and educator discuss (a) what problem behavior occurred (e.g., "I pushed my desk over when the teacher told me to I had to I had to finish my math assignment."), (b) where, when, and why the behavior occurred (e.g., "It happened in my math class when the teacher told me I had to finish my math assignment before I could go outside. I was angry because I don't know how to do this part.") (c) what the student will do next time that is more appropriate (e.g., "I will ask the teacher to help me understand the math assignment."), and (d) what the student will do when they return to their classroom (e.g., "I will tell my teacher I will try to do the math assignment.").

7. If a debriefing form is used, both the student and educator can sign the form to acknowledge that the process was completed.

8. Students can be encouraged to give verbal responses prior to writing responses on the form. After completing the form they can be asked to review or elaborate on the written response. Following debriefing, students should transition back into the classroom setting and appropriately engage in the expected classroom activities.

Troubleshooting: Debriefing should not be used as a negative interaction or as a verbal reprimand or lecture for a rule infraction. It is important to focus on future, not previous behaviors. A simplified form that includes icons or pictures that students can circle may be used for younger students.

Inside-Outside   **E10 F9 E7 C8 T7 I7 V9 +9 T = 8.2**

Reference: Nelson, Thomas, & Pierce, 1995.
Goal: To reduce aggressive behaviors and help adolescent students resolve conflicts through a group discussion, problem-solving model.
Age Group: Secondary.
Materials: Notebook or agenda sheet located in the classroom.
Steps:

1. The Inside-Outside intervention is a structured session used to resolve conflict through discussion and use of problem solving steps. The Inside-Outside discussion uses a "fishbowl" arrangement, where a small group inside the class is involved in the discussion while the other students observe and listen.

2. The teacher and students establish basic ground rules to be followed during the Inside-Outside discussion. Cooperative behavior is required of all students.

3. The teacher explains to the students that the process is voluntary, and students do not have to participate. Alternative activities, such as a

study hall may be offered to students who do not participate or who
are disruptive.

4. The agenda notebook can be posted in the classroom and students allowed to write down problems they wish to discuss at the next scheduled
   time or the teacher can select a topic. The teacher should establish a regularly scheduled time for the Inside-Outside discussion.
5. The three components of the Inside-Outside format include a panel,
   a facilitator, and an audience. The class is arranged with chairs for
   the inside panel placed in a semicircle, concave toward the audience.
   Panelists are seated in chairs, with one empty chair left at each end of
   the semicircle. The audience may sit on the carpet or chairs around
   the panel. It is helpful for the facilitator to walk around the seated
   audience.
6. The teacher or counselor serves as the facilitator. The role of the facilitator is to introduce the topic, enforce the rules, keep the discussion
   moving, and close the discussion. The facilitator is a neutral member.
7. The panel is comprised of 5 to 7 students in the class, selected by the
   teacher. The role of panel members is to speak for the larger group
   and respond to issues, questions, or topics that are introduced by the
   facilitator.
8. The audience is composed of the remainder of the students in the class.
   The audience participates by listening to the comments made by the
   panel. If a member of the audience wishes to speak, they must go to one
   of the empty chairs at either end of the panel and wait until called on by
   the facilitator. After participating, they return to the audience.
9. A problem-solving format is used during the session. The facilitator
   describes the problem, and panel members discuss possible choices or
   solutions. The audience may provide additional solutions through the
   use of the empty chair. After several solutions are discussed the panel
   selects the best resolution to the problem.
10. The facilitator closes the discussion by summarizing what has been
    discussed and what has been decided.

Troubleshooting: It is important that all students follow the basic ground rules. It is
helpful to practice using Inside-Outside with non-emotional, less intensive topics
at first.

Recess Tickets   **E6 F9 E7 C7 T7 I9 V9 +9 T = 8.1**

Reference: Roderick, Pitchford, & Miller, 1997.
Goal: This intervention is a positive reinforcement program used to increase ap-
propriate recess behaviors and reduce aggression on the playground.
Age Group: Elementary.

Materials: Tickets, notebook with a page with each student's name on it, ticket container, and tangible prizes (one large prize or several smaller prizes can be used).
Steps:

1. The teacher explains to the students that they can earn tickets during recess and playground periods for behaviors incompatible with fighting and that a drawing will be held each week to select a student who will win the prize for the week.
2. Behaviors that are not allowed should be discussed, such as kicking, hitting, fighting, play-fighting, throwing objects or other aggressive behaviors.
3. The class should also discuss behaviors that are acceptable and incompatible with fighting, such as playing cooperatively, playing a game, taking turns, including all students, inviting others to play, etc.
4. During the recess period, the teacher or playground supervisor monitors students' behavior, watches for children playing cooperatively, and gives a ticket to students who are playing appropriately. Several tickets can be awarded during each recess period. For younger students, sticky tape can be used to attach the tickets to the child's clothing, like a sticker.
5. The teacher or playground supervisor also provides a positive comment to the student while giving them the ticket (e.g., "That's being a nice friend to invite Andy to join your game.").
6. At the end of the recess period, the students who received tickets put them into a booklet that has a page for each child's name in the class. This will allow the teacher to check the booklet to see which students are receiving tickets and also to praise the students for earning tickets.
7. It is important that all students have an opportunity to earn tickets throughout the week, and perceive them as attainable.
8. At the end of the week, the students place their tickets into a large container kept in the classroom (names should be written on each ticket). The teacher mixes up the tickets and draws one (or more) ticket out of the container. That student receives the prize for the week. If smaller prizes are awarded, several names can be drawn.
9. Each week, the container is emptied, and new tickets are awarded.

Troubleshooting: Tickets should not be removed once they are earned and students should not be given tickets for pleading or complaining that they didn't get a ticket. For students who continue to display playground aggression, this intervention can be combined with Sit and Watch also found in this chapter, or Structured Recess found in Chapter 8.

Sit and Watch   **E8 F9 E7 C8 T7 I5 V9 +5 T = 7.4**

Reference: White & Bailey, 1990.

Goal: This intervention is a modified time-out procedure involving contingent observation, used to reduce aggressive behaviors, noncompliance, or severe disruptive behaviors, particularly during recess periods, playground activities, or physical education classes.

Age Group: Elementary.

Materials: A timing device to monitor the time spent in "Sit and Watch." A timing device can be constructed from two plastic juice or soda bottles fastened together at the tops to resemble an hourglass. To create the hourglass, the lids can be fastened together with glue or electrical tape, and holes drilled in the lids that are large enough to allow sand to pass from one bottle to the other. One of the bottles should be filled with enough sand to make the time period about 3 minutes. Several timers may be needed, depending on the number of students on the playground.

Steps:

1. Specific rules regarding the playground, recess, or Physical Education periods are developed, explained, and reviewed with all students. The teacher explains the "Sit and Watch" program to the students. "Sit and Watch" is a consequence for aggressive or other severe behaviors that may occur on the playground. The teacher explains that during recess or P.E., rule-breaking behaviors such as aggression—hitting, slapping, pushing, or pulling others, or throwing objects such as sand, rocks, etc. will result in a 3-minute "Sit and Watch" period.

2. To ensure that the students understand the procedure, the teacher may wish to spend 15–20 minutes, modeling and role-playing specific examples of behaviors and how the "Sit and Watch" procedure will be implemented.

3. During the recess or playground activity, students are monitored for appropriate and inappropriate behaviors.

4. When a student is observed to be aggressive, the teacher or playground supervisor instructs the student to go to "Sit and Watch" and briefly explains the reason (e.g., "Sean, you need to stop throwing rocks. Go to Sit and Watch.").

5. The student picks up one of the timers, walks to a designated area at the side of the playground or away from the other students, and sits down on the ground with the timer.

6. The student begins the timer and remains in "Sit and Watch" until all of the sand has flowed through into the bottom bottle, approximately 3 minutes.

7. After the 3-minute "Sit and Watch", the student is allowed to rejoin the class or activity.

Troubleshooting: It is important to implement "Sit and Watch" immediately and consistently after aggressive behaviors occur. If more than one student is in "Sit and Watch" each should have his or her own timer and they should not be allowed to converse or sit near one another. Students in "Sit and Watch" should be monitored. Back-up procedures may be used if students engage in disruptive behaviors while in "Sit and Watch" or if they are sent more than once per period. Back-up procedures might include loss of free time later in the day, loss of computer time, or loss of points towards positive reinforcers.

Thinking Out Loud   **E9 F9 E7 C7 T8 I7 V9 +9 T = 8.1**

Reference: Meichenbaum & Goodman, 1971 and Camp, Blom, Herbert, & van Doorninck, 1977.
Goal: Thinking out loud is a procedure involving verbal mediation skills taught to students to improve self-control and reduce aggressive behaviors.
Age Group: Elementary.
Materials: Poster listing "Thinking Out Loud" steps.
Steps:

1. This procedure involves teaching students to use "self-talk" skills to increase self-control during interpersonal problem situations. This procedure was developed based on the work of Meichenbaum and Goodman (1971) and others. Refer to Camp and Bash (1985) for a complete "Think Aloud" program for use in elementary classrooms.
2. The teacher instructs the students that they will learn a game to help them "think out loud" to solve problems. The teacher provides a rationale by stating that thinking out loud can help students in solving many problems, including doing schoolwork or getting along with other students or adults.
3. First, the teacher introduces an easy problem (i.e., "I can't find my pencil" or "I want to play with a ball, but they are all gone."). The teacher models the procedure by talking out loud while the students observe. The teacher verbalizes four basic questions and the thinking process involved in answering them (questions can be listed on a poster).
   (a) The first question asks about the nature of the task such as, "What is my problem?" or "What is it I need to do?" The teacher might say out loud, "Let's see, I don't have a pencil, but I need to start my work. What is my problem? I guess I need to find a pencil so I can start my work."
   (b) Next, students ask a question about the plan needed to solve the problem such as, "What is my plan?" or "How can I solve this problem?"

The teacher might demonstrate by saying out loud, "How can I do it? I could ask the teacher to borrow one. Or I could ask a friend to loan me a pencil." It is important to model answers that include different solutions or possibilities.

(c) Third, students ask themselves the question, "Am I using my plan?" The teacher models by verbalizing the self-instruction involved, such as, "I will ask the girl next to me to loan me a pencil. I will ask her quietly." It is also helpful to model mistakes or revisions of the plan.

(d) Fourth, students evaluate their plan by asking themselves, "How did I do?" The teacher demonstrates by modeling self-reinforcement statements, such as, "Okay, I have a pencil. Now I can start my work."

4. After the teacher models the four steps, students are given the opportunity to practice the steps by role-playing examples, and verbalizing the steps out loud with the group or with a partner. A variety of problems can be used to teach students to use self-instructions, ranging from simple tasks to more complex problems.

5. After students demonstrate the ability to use self-instruction to control behavior, the overt self-statements are faded to a covert level (thinking through steps silently).

Troubleshooting: Some students may require individual assistance and repeated opportunities to practice self-verbalizations to develop adequate problem solving skills. Individual cue cards can be provided, if necessary to remind students of each basic question.

Wheel of Fortune   E6 F8 E8 C8 T7 I9 V9 +9 T = 8.2

Reference: Ninness, Ellis, Miller, Baker, & Rutherford, 1995.

Goal: The Wheel of Fortune intervention is a strategy in which students receive access to a reinforcement menu contingent on their self-assessment of appropriate responses to aggression-provoking situations during recess periods, transitions, or in-class periods. This intervention can be used with individual students, or with a group of students.

Age Group: Elementary or Secondary.

Materials: A Wheel of Fortune or spinner containing several (5 to 8) pie-shaped segments of different colors or numbers, daily point cards, back up reinforcers.

Steps:

1. The teacher explains the directions for the Wheel of Fortune. The students are informed that they can earn a chance at the Wheel of Fortune by demonstrating appropriate replacement behaviors in aggression-provoking situations.

2. The teacher selects a time period such as recess, lunch period, transition periods, or in-class periods, in which aggressive behaviors most frequently occur.
3. The teacher and students discuss ways to refrain from initiating aggressive behaviors, and refrain from responding to aggressive verbal or physical gestures by other students. For example, if a student initiates a conflict situation by making a rude comment, an appropriate replacement behavior might be to ignore the student and walk away. Other replacement behaviors include; control anger by counting to 10 and calming down, tell the student to stop in a calm manner, avoid eye contact with those who annoy them, make self-statements such as, "I won't get upset", joining a different activity, etc. The students are also told to remind themselves of the delayed beneficial outcome associated with appropriate replacement behaviors (e.g., the Wheel of Fortune).
4. The teacher models appropriate replacement behaviors and provides students an opportunity to practice behaviors in a variety of role-play situations.
5. Each student is provided a daily or weekly point card. Students are asked to self-assess their use of appropriate behaviors during the designated time period (e.g., recess), by rating themselves on a scale of 1 to 4 (1 = poor to 4 = excellent). Initially, students may be asked to assess their behavior several times per hour or day. The teacher reviews the students' ratings and students who rate themselves accurately (regardless of the point value) receive a bonus point from the teacher.
6. Students who meet the specified criteria (e.g., 4 points per period) are allowed access to the Wheel of Fortune. Each color on the Wheel of Fortune corresponds to a different tangible or activity-based reward to be given to the student at the end of the school day. These reinforcers can be changed frequently so that the reinforcement menu is unpredictable.
7. As student behavior improves, the number of self-assessments per hour or day can be gradually decreased, or the required criteria to receive the Wheel of Fortune can be increased.

Troubleshooting: Active physical abuse should not be tolerated. Reductive techniques (loss of privileges or points, time-out) or other disciplinary actions may be necessary with students who engage in harmful physical behaviors.

DISRUPTIVE BEHAVIORS

Behavior Badges   **E7 F9 E8 C7 T6 I8 V9 +9 T = 8.0**

Reference: Posavac, Sheridan, & Posavac, 1999.

Goal: The Behavior Badge is a visual cue combined with a positive reinforcement strategy used to reduce disruptive behaviors.

Age Group: Elementary.

Materials: Individual student badges (or cards) with the student's goal written on them, poster board with student's names, stickers.

Steps:

1. The teacher (and students) identifies specific individual student behaviors to target for this intervention. Targeted behaviors may be different for each student, depending on the disruptive behaviors a particular child may exhibit. The target behavior is written as an individual student goal. The goal should be recorded in positive terms (e.g., "Raise my hand before speaking" or "Sit in my chair and work quietly"). Other goals could include: keep my body facing my desk, keep my eyes on the teacher, keep my hands to myself, or stay in my seat, put my things away quietly, etc.

2. The students and teacher can also select a class goal to improve good classroom behaviors. The class goal can be written at the top of the class poster (e.g., "We are Great Kids").

3. The teacher creates personalized badges for each student. The badges can be made of plastic nametags, index cards, laminated cardstock, etc. Each student's target behavior goal is written on the badge. The students can also decorate their badges with markers, stickers, etc. if desired. The badges can be worn by the students during the monitoring period, or placed at the corner of the student's desks. The badges serve as visual reminders to cue appropriate behaviors.

4. A poster board listing the names of the students is posted in a visible location in the classroom.

5. During the designated period the teacher monitors student behaviors, prompting individual students if necessary to remember their goal. A timer is set for 5-minute intervals, or intermittent intervals. When the timer sounds, a goal check is initiated.

6. First, the teacher asks the students to self-evaluate (ask themselves if they think they have met their goal during the last interval). Students can be asked to report verbally if they believe they have met their goal. Second, students are asked to evaluate whether the class met their goal. Finally, the teacher evaluates each child's behavior and provides verbal praise for students who met their goal.

7. At the end of the period, if the student meets their goal at least 80% of the intervals (or other predetermined criteria), they earn a sticker to place by their name on the poster board. If desired, goal improvement can be rewarded with a smaller sticker.

Troubleshooting: It may be helpful to collect data on the frequency of disruptive behaviors prior to implementing this intervention. If there is a high frequency of behaviors, the initial criteria to earn the reward may be lower, then increased gradually as behaviors improve. To reduce teacher time, students may self-monitor after each short interval, and the teacher evaluates at the end of the period.

Behavior Contracts   **E7 F8 E9 C8 T8 I8 V10 +9 T = 8.5**

Reference: Downing, 2002.

Goal: A Behavior Contract is a formalized, written agreement between the student and the teacher used to improve classroom behavior. A behavior contract states that a student will receive a reward contingent on the performance of the specified behavior. Contracts can be used for a variety of classroom behaviors as well as academic and social behaviors.

Age Group: Elementary or Secondary.

Materials: Contract form and worksheet form (optional). A sample contract form is listed in Appendix A. The ABC Form listed in Appendix A can be used as a worksheet form.

Steps:

1. To develop a contract, the teacher collects data to determine the behavior concerns to target in the contract. On a worksheet form or ABC Form, the teacher collects the following:
   (a) A description of the problem behavior or behaviors.
   (b) Identify the situations in which the behavior occurs (where, when, with whom).
   (c) The antecedent events that trigger or maintain the behavior.
   (d) The antecedent events or consequences that decrease or inhibit the behavior.
   (e) A possible hypothesis about the function of the behavior or why behavior occurs.
   (f) The current levels of behavior (how often behavior currently occurs).
   (g) Desired or expected levels of behavior (behavioral goal).
   (h) Identify strategies that have already been attempted.
   (i) Develop a menu of effective reinforcers and how frequently needed.
   (j) Identify negative consequence for failure to fulfill the contract.
   (k) Determine who will be involved in signing and monitoring the contract.
   (l) Determine the time frame for implementation and evaluation.
2. After information is collected the teacher and student work together to determine a goal, negotiate the contract terms, and complete the written contract form. Discuss with the student why the contract is necessary.

The contract form should include the following:

(a) Statement of the behavior expected (e.g., "During the 45 minute instructional period I will raise my hand and wait to be called on before speaking for five days", or "I will work quietly at my desk during 10 work periods."). This statement should be specific, observable, and measurable and include the criteria for determining success within a specific time frame.

(b) Statement of reward if the agreed upon behavior is performed within the time frame (e.g., "If I am successful I will earn a hot dog and drink from the gas station.") It is helpful to have student input in selecting reinforcers or allow them to select from a list. Reinforcers should not be expensive or take too much time. A date when the contract will be evaluated and the reinforcer is received should be specified.

(c) Statement of penalty or consequence if the agreed upon behavior is not performed within the specified time frame. Not receiving the promised incentive is a natural consequence, however a negative consequence may also be required (e.g., "If I am not successful I will not attend the monthly class party.").

(d) Student and teacher signatures and the date.

3. The contract should be reviewed and evaluated periodically to determine the student's progress toward meeting their goal. At the specified date, it is important that the student receives the agreed-upon reinforcement if the contract terms have been met. If not, a new contract can be developed.

Troubleshooting: It may be necessary to begin with short-term contracts and criteria that are attainable. Long delays in receiving reinforcement are ineffective. Cumulative criteria work better than consecutive criteria (e.g., 10 cumulative "good work periods" rather than 10 consecutive "good work periods").

Chance Jars   E7 F9 E8 C7 T8 I9 V9 +8 T = 8.3

Reference: Theodore, Bray, Kehle, & Jenson, 2001.

Goal: The Chance Jars Game is a group game involving a group contingency program with random criteria and random reinforcers to decrease disruptive classroom behaviors.

Age Group: Elementary or Secondary.

Materials: A checklist with each student's name written on it, two opaque jars or containers, slips of paper listing different reinforcers, and slips of paper listing different criteria.

Steps:

1. The teacher explains the directions for the Chance Jars. The students are informed that they can earn reinforcers for compliance with class rules, and not engaging in disruptive behaviors.

2. The teacher explains the class rules, and a poster of the classroom rules is displayed in the classroom. Disruptive behaviors that are not allowed should be clearly defined and discussed with the students. Examples of disruptive behaviors might include, not touching or talking to other students who are working, no verbal putdowns, no swearing or obscene words, not playing with objects, not out of seat, etc.
3. The teacher explains that each time a student exhibits a disruptive behavior, they will receive a check mark by their name. The teacher determines the criteria level required for reinforcement (e.g., 5 or fewer checks).
4. The teacher labels the first jar "Criteria." In this jar are placed slips of paper with different criteria written on each. For example, the slips may state "Whole Class", "Highest", "Lowest", "Class Average", and slips with names of individual students.
5. The students are informed of possible reinforcers that can be earned. Ideas for reinforcers can also be generated by students. These reinforcers are listed individually on slips of paper and all slips are placed the opaque jars labeled "Reinforcers." The reinforcers can range from large to small, including edibles (soda, chips, candy) or activities (no homework pass, game, free-time).
6. During the designated class period, the teacher tracks student behaviors on a checklist that lists each student's name (kept on the teacher's desk or on a clipboard). Each time a student exhibits a disruptive behavior during the period, a check is placed next to that student's name.
7. At the end of the period, the teacher draws one slip of paper out of the jar labeled "Criteria." If an individual name is drawn, all the students are rewarded if that student met criteria (5 or fewer checks). If a slip labeled "Whole Class" is drawn, all students receive the reinforcer if the whole class met criteria. If the slip labeled "Lowest" is drawn, all students receive the reinforcer if the student with the lowest performance (most check marks) met criteria, etc.
8. Reinforcers are chosen contingent upon meeting the criteria drawn for the period. The teacher randomly selects from the second jar, labeled "Reinforcers" to determine what the reinforcer will be for the period or day. If the students did not meet the criterion selected, no reinforcement is given.

Troubleshooting: It may be beneficial to change the reinforcers frequently to maintain student interest. Some slips of paper labeled "no reinforcer" may also be added. The criteria levels may need to be higher or lower, depending on baseline levels of disruptive behaviors.

The Class Reading Jar   **E9 F9 E9 C9 T9 I8 V9 +8 T = 8.8**

Reference: Sprute, Williams, & McLaughlin, 1990.

Goal: The Class Reading Jar involves use of a group response cost contingency procedure to reduce classroom interruptions.

Age Group: Elementary or Secondary.

Materials: Class jar or container, 30 poker chips or tokens.

Steps:

1. The teacher determines a class period during which disruptive behaviors may be more likely to occur in which to implement the Class Reading Jar intervention (i.e., independent work periods). The teacher defines and explains the on-task behaviors that are expected in the classroom during this period, such as stay in seat, work quietly, raise hand, etc. Classroom rules stated to indicate appropriate behaviors should be posted in a visible location in the classroom.

2. The teacher introduces the procedure to the students and explains that the class will earn minutes each day towards a reading time at the end of class for demonstrating appropriate behaviors during the academic period(s) when they should be working quietly. The teacher explains that the class will begin each day with 30 poker chips or tokens (any other amount of chips ranging from 10 to 30 could also be used), placed in a class jar or container. Each chip represents one minute of reading time by the teacher (i.e., up to 30 minutes of possible reading time per day). By earning reading time, students are, therefore, not required to complete additional schoolwork during those minutes.

3. The teacher and students can select a favorite book or story from a collection of fiction for children or adolescents to be read aloud during the reading time. It is important that the teacher reading time is perceived by students as a positive reinforcement which is contingent on appropriate behavior, and not already available on a daily basis. Students can also be informed that minutes not available for the reading time are spent on additional schoolwork or assignment completion.

4. The teacher explains that each time a student exhibits a disruptive or interruptive behavior during the class period, one chip will be removed from the class jar. The teacher provides examples of disruptive behaviors that are incompatible with appropriate behaviors, such as out-of-seat without permission, talking out, moving around, playing with objects, disturbing other students, etc.

5. The teacher monitors student behavior during the period, and the teacher or a designee removes a chip for each disruptive behavior exhibited by any student during the class period. The teacher can remove the chip without comment or periodically state calmly why the chip was removed.

6. The amount of reading minutes is contingent upon reduced interruptions. The number of chips left at the end of the designated class period are

counted and exchanged for the number of minutes the teacher spends reading to the students at the end of the period or school day.

Troubleshooting: It is important to modify the program if students lose too many chips and become discouraged or if detrimental peer pressure occurs. Possible modifications include; allowing one warning before removing a chip, beginning with more chips, or rewarding bonus chips for improved behavior. The same format can be used for other positive reinforcements, such as Class Music Jar, for minutes of music, or Class Free-Time Jar, for minutes of free-time.

The Classroom Chart Game   **E7 F8 E8 C7 T8 I8 V9 +8 T = 8.0**

Reference: Brantley & Webster, 1993.
Goal: The Classroom Chart Game is an independent group contingency strategy with public posting used to decrease disruptive behaviors.
Age Group: Elementary.
Materials: Timer, chart with classroom rules, chart with students' names.
Steps:

1. The teacher explains the class rules and a poster listing the rules is posted in a visible place in the classroom. Classroom rules should be phrased to indicate appropriate, prosocial behaviors that are incompatible with disruptive, inappropriate behaviors (i.e., pay attention to the teacher, finish all your work, ask permission to leave your seat, raise hand to talk, etc.). The total number of rules for this activity should not exceed three or four.
2. The teacher introduces the procedure to the students and explains that they can earn a weekly reward by exhibiting appropriate, prosocial behaviors and complying with the posted class rules. This procedure involves an independent group contingency system. With an independent group contingency a criterion is determined for the class and only those students who meet criterion receive the reward.
3. Each student's name is listed on the board or on a chart posted in a highly visible area in the classroom. By each name is a space for the teacher to make several checkmarks. A new chart is used each week.
4. Weekly rewards are chosen at the beginning of the week from a list generated by the students and the teacher (i.e., popcorn party, class game, extra recess, etc.).
5. The class time or school day is divided into equal intervals or periods (i.e., 45–60 minutes each). A timer is used to indicate intervals to the students and to keep intervals consistent. The teacher may also choose to conduct this activity during only one or two periods per day, when disruptive behaviors most frequently occur. During or at the end of each interval, a checkmark is placed on the chart by the name of each student

who is compliant with the class rules and has exhibited at least two of the three appropriate behaviors during a given interval (i.e., raised hand, finished work, and stayed in seat). A student can earn only one checkmark per interval even if all three rules were followed. If used throughout the school day students could earn a maximum of six or seven checkmarks daily.

6. The teacher predetermines the initial criterion needed to earn the weekly reward and informs the students of the criterion needed. For example, the criterion might be to acquire 5 checkmarks daily on 4 out of 5 days. The criterion can be adjusted upward over time after student's behaviors are appropriate and stable.

7. Those students who do not reach criterion for the week do not earn the reward. For example they may have to complete an academic assignment in another room.

Troubleshooting: To provide structure, time intervals should be clear and manageable. Rules should be operationally defined and student behavior should be monitored consistently. The initial criterion should be set so that it is attainable for most students.

Dot-to-Dot Talk Outs   **E7 F9 E8 C8 T8 I8 V9 +7 T = 8.2**

Reference: Davies & Witte, 2000.

Goal: This intervention is a self and peer-management strategy combined with a group contingency to decrease disruptive behaviors during class time.

Age Group: Elementary.

Materials: Laminated dot charts and 5 dots for each group.

Steps:

1. The Dot-to-Dot procedure involves a group contingency system in which students work together towards a common goal. The same contingency is in effect for all members of the group, so that each student's outcome depends on the group's performance.

2. The Dot-to-Dot Talk Out strategy is conducted at the same time each day, during class periods when students are expected to work quietly and not disrupt others. In this procedure, students are assigned to a group. Groups can be determined according to seating arrangement and should include students who are seated near each other during work periods (i.e., tables or desks arranged together). Each group decides on a group name to allow for a sense of belongingness.

3. The teacher introduces the procedure to the class and explains that the students can earn reinforcers by participating in the game and how many dots the group has remaining in the green section of their chart at the end

of the period. One $9'' \times 12''$ group dot chart is located in the center of each groups' desks, within easy reach of the group members. The chart is constructed of laminated colored paper or poster board, divided into three colors (i.e., $1/2$ green, $1/4$ red, and $1/4$ blue). Each group also has five laminated black dots (about the size of a half-dollar). Each day, all five dots are stuck on the green portion of the chart (with sticky tape or Velcro tabs). The teacher explains that each time a student in the group displays a disruptive target behavior (e.g., a talk-out), he or she moves one dot from the group chart from the green section to the blue section. The teacher can verbally prompt a student to move a dot. If the student does not move the dot within 10 seconds, the teacher will move the dot into the red section of the chart.

4. The group receives the reinforcer according to how many dots the group has in the green section of their chart at the end of the period. The teacher determines the set criterion level required to earn the reinforcer (i.e., each group must have at least one dot left in the green section at the end of the period to receive the reinforcer). The students participate in selecting potential reinforcers they can receive for successfully meeting the set criterion (i.e., small tangible, social or activity reinforcers). Selected reinforcers may be delivered at the end of the class period or at the end of the day.

5. The teacher defines and discusses appropriate on-task behaviors that are expected during class time (i.e., in seat, working on assignment, not talking, etc.). The teacher explains which disruptive behaviors will result in a dot being moved out of the green section, such as inappropriate verbalizations (talk-outs or noises). Prior to implementing the procedure, students have an opportunity to role-play situations, differentiate inappropriate behavior from appropriate behavior, and determine which examples would lead to a dot being moved.

Troubleshooting: The teacher should emphasize appropriate reactions to the moving of dots, and students are not allowed to blame or make negative remarks to a student responsible for having a dot moved.

Earning Free-Time   **E10 F9 E8 C9 T9 I9 V8 +9 T = 8.8**

Reference: Higgins, Williams, & McLaughlin, 2001.
Goal: This intervention is a group contingency program in which students can earn minutes of structured free time as reinforcement for the absence of disruptive behaviors.
Age Group: Elementary or Secondary.
Materials: None.

Steps:

1. The teacher determines a class period in which disruptive behaviors oc-
    cur frequently to target for the structured free-time reward (e.g., math
    class, independent work periods, etc.) The teacher defines and explains
    the on-task behaviors that are expected during academic periods. These
    behaviors include in seat, working quietly, and not talking.
2. The teacher designates an area on the board on which to record check
    marks. The teacher informs the students that they will earn a check mark
    for the group on the board, at the end of each 5-minute period (or other
    specified time period) if they are demonstrating on-task behaviors and no
    disruptive behaviors are observed.
3. Disruptive behaviors are defined as out-of-seat behavior, talking-out,
    moving around, or playing with objects, etc. If disruptive behaviors occur
    during the 5-minute period, a check mark is not placed on the board.
4. The teacher monitors student behavior during the period and the teacher
    or another designated scorekeeper, records a check mark at the end of
    every 5-minute interval throughout the class period. The teacher can pro-
    vide verbal praise to the students as each check mark is recorded. At the
    end of the class period the check marks are counted. The resulting number
    indicates the number of minutes available to use for structured free time.
    Structured free time includes academic activities that involve practice of
    academic skills but are not typically available to students. For example
    the class may be allowed to play a group game (e.g., multiplication facts
    bingo), engage in individual or partner activities (leisure reading, com-
    puter games, practice flash cards with a partner or play a board game with
    a partner), or choose from a selection of worksheets rather than complete
    a math assignment from the book.
5. The total possible time available for free-time activities should be about
    10–15 minutes. If the length of the class period is such that more than 15
    check marks can be earned, the teacher may decide to add the number
    of check marks and divide by two to determine the number of minutes
    available for free time.
6. To use this intervention with an individual student, rather than the entire
    class, a small card or paper is taped to the corner of the student's desk.
    The teacher can monitor the student during the period and reward check
    marks at regular 5-minute intervals or at random intervals throughout
    the period. The teacher can also provide verbal praise for appropriate
    behaviors when the check marks are recorded. The teacher may allocate
    the last ten minutes of class or the first 10 minutes of class the following
    day to reward the free time.

Troubleshooting: To reduce the amount of teacher monitoring and recording required, the frequent continuous schedule of reinforcement (i.e., a check mark for each 5-minutes of appropriate behavior) can be changed to an intermittent less-frequent schedule once the behaviors have improved. Another option is to record check marks on designated days only and reward longer periods of free time (i.e., 20–30 minutes, once per week).

The Good Student Game   **E8 F8 E8 C7 T8 I8 V9 +9 T = 8.2**

Reference: Babyak, Luze, & Kamps, 2000.

Goal: The Good Student Game is a classroom management technique used to reduce disruptive behaviors and increase appropriate behaviors such as staying seated and working quietly. The game format provides an opportunity for students to self-monitor their behavior and to earn positive reinforcement for appropriate behaviors.

Age Group: Elementary.

Materials: Monitoring sheet for each group, and a timer.

Steps:

1. The teacher defines and selects target behaviors. The target behaviors should be appropriate behaviors that help students learn (i.e., stay in your seat and work quietly).

2. The teacher explains that they will learn how to play a game called the "Good Student Game." The teacher discusses the importance of good behaviors and describes the behaviors that are expected. Students should be given examples and nonexamples of good behaviors. The teacher can ask students to give a "thumbs up" if an example is a good student behavior, or a "thumbs down" if it is not a good student behavior.

3. The Good Student Game can be played during quiet, independent work periods, and can be played once or more times per day.

4. The teacher explains how students can monitor their behavior and demonstrates how to use the monitoring sheet. The monitoring sheet should include two columns labeled "yes" and "no", with rows numbered 1–10. There should also be a place to write the group name, and the name of the monitor.

5. To demonstrate how to monitor, the teacher sets a timer for a 1-minute interval. When the timer rings, the teacher checks the "yes" column if all of the students were in their seats and working quietly. If one or more students are disruptive when the timer goes off, the teacher checks the "no" column. Students practice using the monitoring sheet.

6. The teacher decides on group size. The Good Behavior Game can be used with small groups (3–6 students), with two or three larger

groups, or with individual students. A monitor is designated for each group. The group monitor is responsible to record the group's behavior. If small groups are used, students should be grouped according to seating arrangements so that members are able to see one another.

7. The teacher provides each group with a monitoring sheet and a cue card listing or depicting good student behaviors (optional). Good student behaviors can also be listed on the board or on a poster, visible for the entire class to see.

8. A specific criterion for success is set (e.g., 80% or better) and the students are told what the reinforcer will be if the criterion is met. Reinforcers can include tangibles or intangibles (e.g., stickers, treats, no-assignment coupons, extra recess, indoor games parties, etc.)

9. The teacher sets the timer to go off at 1 to 3 minute intervals throughout the work period (20–30 minutes). When the timer goes off, the teacher reminds the monitors to mark their sheets. At the end of the work period, the teacher collects the monitoring sheets.

10. The groups who meet criterion receive the reinforcer at the end of the period.

Troubleshooting: Intervals can be increased gradually, or shortened on difficult days. Provide feedback. Expectations should be clear and reasonable for success. Do not allow arguing among group members. Tell students arguing will result in a loss of 5 percentage points.

Home Notes   **E9 F9 E9 C7 T8 I8 V10 +8 T = 8.4**

Reference: Kelley & McCain, 1995.
Goal: The Home Note is a procedure used to improve classroom behavior by use of daily/weekly school-home report card to communicate with parents, combined with parent-managed reinforcement and/or contingencies.
Age Group: Elementary or Secondary.
Materials: Daily/Weekly Home Notes. A sample home-note is provided in Appendix A.
Steps:

1. A Home Note consists of a daily or weekly report completed by the teacher to communicate information (academic and/or behavioral) to the parent. The home note can function as a reinforcer for the student, provide feedback to parents, and provide on-going data collection for teachers. School-home notes require teachers to evaluate students' behavior on a regular basis and for parents to review this information and provide reinforcement or consequences at home based the student's performance.

Teachers can also use the home note to provide reinforcement or consequences at school.

2. The teacher can design a home note for a student of any age or grade level. Behaviors to be targeted should be identified and described in observable terms (i.e., on-time, completed 80% of assignment, stayed in seat, raised hand, etc.). The home note should contain sufficient detail about target behaviors and criteria, however, should be as simple as possible. The home note can include a place for the student's name, date, target behaviors, and a place for additional comments. Target behaviors can be rated (i.e., $0 =$ poor, $1 =$ OK, $2 =$ good, etc.), circled (i.e., yes, so-so, no), or icons (smiley-faces, sad-faces) can be used. The home note can also include a place for parents to sign indicating they have reviewed the note. Enough copies should be duplicated in advance to avoid running out.

3. The teacher explains to the parents the rationale for using the home note and enlists their support and cooperation in providing the reinforcement in the home setting. It is important to explain that the procedure is positive and parental participation is essential. Parents and students should select reinforcers ahead of time that are reasonable and motivating (i.e., money, activities with parent, special treats, videos, TV or video game time, late bedtime, etc.). Parents and students decide in advance on acceptable criteria (i.e., 80% satisfactory marks, 4 out of 5 days per week) and generate a contract outlining contingencies for reinforcement. Rewards can be delivered daily or weekly. A poor report results in not receiving the desired reinforcement or a mild consequence can be added (i.e., no TV, no computer games, no friends, etc.).

4. The teacher provides an example of the home-note to parents and students and explains the procedure. At the end of the day or class period, the teacher marks and initials the home note for the student to take home. It is best to avoid marking procedures that students can alter or counterfeit. Parents are instructed to review the notes daily with the student and reward according to the predesignated criteria. Teachers should also provide positive comments and encouragement to students for remembering to take their note home. The daily note can be faded to a weekly note once behavior is stabilized.

Troubleshooting: If students change or lose a note, the parent is instructed to not accept excuses and implement a consequence.

Mystery Motivators   E7 F9 E9 C8 T8 I10 V10 +9 T = 8.7

Reference: Musser, Bray, Kehle, & Jenson, 2001.
Goal: This intervention package combines a token economy, mystery motivators, and public posting to reduce disruptive classroom behaviors. It can also be used

to encourage compliance and rule following. It can be used with a few students or on a class-wide basis.

Age Group: Elementary or Secondary.

Materials: Rule poster, stickers, a poster listing each student's name with a place to put their stickers, envelopes, the names of various rewards written on 3×5 cards.

Steps:

1. The teacher develops and explains the class rules. The rules should include appropriate behaviors that are incompatible with disruptive behaviors, such as, "Sit in your seat" or "Raise your hand and wait for permission to speak." The rules should be posted in the classroom.

2. The teacher introduces the program to the students and explains that they can earn stickers by following the rules and by not disrupting the classroom (e.g., making noises, getting out of their seat, talking to others, etc.). The teacher explains that Mystery Motivators will be rewarded when students have earned a specific number of stickers (e.g., 10 stickers = 1 Mystery Motivator).

3. Mystery Motivators add an element of excitement, because the students never know in advance what the mystery motivator will be. Sometimes it could be a small reward (e.g., 5-minutes of free time or small piece of candy), and sometimes it could be a bigger reward (e.g., root beer floats, game party, listen to music, etc.) Be creative!

4. The stickers are awarded to students who observe the rules during each predetermined time period. For example, in an elementary classroom, the teacher may divide the intervals into 30-minute periods. At the end of each 30-minute period, every student who observed the rules and worked without exhibiting any disruptive behaviors is awarded one sticker. The stickers are publicly posted next to the students' names. The teacher can choose to reward stickers for each 30-minute period throughout the day, or only reward stickers during independent work periods, or during a specific time period when disruptive behaviors occur more frequently.

5. When a student has earned the required number of stickers to earn the Mystery Motivator, the student is given an envelope containing a card. On the card is written the name of a prize or reward. The student can redeem the card for the prize at the end of the day (or other designated time).

6. The teacher may wish to begin the program by requiring fewer stickers to earn the prize, so as to provide an opportunity to earn the first Mystery Motivator relatively easily. The number of stickers required can be increased gradually, as a way to train students to require less frequent reinforcement for appropriate behaviors.

7. To implement this intervention with the whole class, the teacher creates a class sticker poster, and only award 1 sticker for each 30-minute period when the entire class is working without any disruptions. The whole class would receive the Mystery Motivator when 10 stickers are earned.

Troubleshooting: If a few students continue to exhibit disruptive behaviors, a response cost can be used in which one sticker is taken from the student if he or she does not comply after the second request or warning.

Passing Notebooks　　　　　　　**E7 F9 E9 C8 T5 I7 V9 +8 T = 7.9**

Reference: Williams & Cartledge, 1997.
Goal: This intervention is a daily home-note strategy used to increase on-task behaviors in the classroom and to encourage parent-teacher communication.
Age Group: Elementary or Secondary.
Materials: Spiral notebooks personalized for each student.
Steps:

1. The notebook system is a procedure that provides written communication between teacher and parent regarding a student's behavior and performance at school.
2. Prior to implementing the notebook strategy, parents should be informed about the procedure, and encouraged to participate by reviewing teacher comments, and responding and signing the notebooks each day. Parents can be informed personally at parent-teacher conferences or by sending home a letter introducing the program. In the letter, expectations for classroom behavior should be emphasized as well as encouragement for parent participation in their child's educational program through regular communication. The notebook system is presented as a primarily positive strategy, with an emphasis on the positive behaviors exhibited by the students.
3. Each student is provided with an ordinary spiral notebook. Notebooks can be personalized for each student by decorating the cover with artwork, stickers, etc.
4. In each notebook, the teacher writes a brief comment on the student's behavior in class (e.g., comments about attentiveness, participation, work completion, etc.). On some days the teacher may make only minimal notations. It is important to begin this procedure as a means of conveying positive comments, and to convey information that will be useful to parents. Although negative comments are sometimes included, they should be written thoughtfully.
5. The students are instructed to take notebooks home daily. Notebooks can also be taken home on a weekly basis rather than daily. For example, the

notebooks can be taken home on Friday, with a brief comment on performance throughout the week. Another option is to establish alternating days for notebooks so that students are assigned a specific day each week to take their notebooks home.

6. Parents are instructed to review the teacher comments in the notebook and either respond with a written comment or simply sign the notebook, indicating they have read the notation. Parents are encouraged to write comments about their child, any questions about homework, or other information they may feel is useful to the teacher.

7. The students are instructed to place notebooks in a designated basket upon entering the classroom each morning.

8. A positive reinforcement system may be included to encourage students to return their signed notebooks each day. Students who return their notebooks signed by the parent can receive extra credit points, a small treat, or other small reinforcer.

Troubleshooting: It is important that the notebook system occur with sufficient frequency so that communication is regular. The notebook should not become an aversive form of communication. Stressing collaboration will help parents to feel valued.

Peer Attention Intervention   E9 F9 E8 C8 T7 I8 V9 +9 T = 8.4

Reference: Broussard & Northup, 1997.
Goal: The peer attention intervention is used as differential reinforcement to reduce disruptive behavior and to reinforce appropriate classroom behavior.
Age Group: Elementary.
Materials: Tokens (small paper coupons).
Steps:

1. The use of peer attention to reduce disruptive behavior and reinforce desirable behavior is based on results of classroom-based functional analyses for developmentally normal children that suggest peer attention is often associated with disruptive classroom behavior. This intervention involves the use of peer attention to ignore disruptive behavior (extinction) and reinforce desirable behavior (peer attention for other appropriate behavior).

2. This intervention can be used with an individual student or with a few students who frequently exhibit disruptive classroom behaviors that are maintained by peer and teacher attention. The teacher identifies disruptive target behaviors for each student (i.e., vocal noises or talk-outs, out of seat, playing with objects, etc.) and identifies desirable target behaviors to use in place of disruptive behaviors (i.e., raising hand to talk, body sitting in chair, writing on assignment with pencil, etc.).

3. Before implementing the peer intervention the teacher explains the procedure to the students. The teacher defines appropriate classroom behaviors, providing examples and defines the target desirable behaviors for which students can earn a coupon. The teacher informs the students that they will earn time with a peer contingent upon the occurrence of appropriate behaviors and nonoccurrence of disruptive behaviors.

4. The peer reinforcement is implemented by providing token coupons to the student that are equivalent to minutes of time with a peer. For example, each coupon may be equivalent to 1–2 minutes of time with a peer. During the class period, the teacher monitors student behavior. At regular or variable intervals (i.e., every 5 or 10 minutes), the teacher places a coupon on the corner of the student's desk, if during that interval none of the targeted disruptive behaviors have occurred. As the teacher places the coupons on the student's desk, no comment or interaction is made. If a student exhibits a disruptive behavior during the interval, the interval is started over. The schedule of reinforcement can be progressively increased in length as the level of disruptive behaviors improves.

5. The opportunity to exchange the coupons for minutes to participate in an appropriate interactive activity with a peer should be provided at the end of the period or another specified time. Peer activities could include, playing with games or toys, art activities, looking at magazines together, etc.

6. Prior to implementing this intervention, the teacher instructs the other students (when the target student is not present) not to interact with the disruptive student when disruptive behaviors occur. Other students may earn coupons for remaining quiet or following classroom rules. Coupons for the other students may represent a variety of common classroom rewards (e.g., extra recess minutes, a small treat).

Troubleshooting: The teacher may select peer "confederates" to interact with the target student during the activity time or the target student can be allowed to pick a peer of their choice.

Positive to Negative Ratios   **E8 F8 E8 C7 T6 I8 V9 +8 T = 8.0**

Reference: Friman, Jones, Smith, Daly & Larzelere, 1997.
Goal: This intervention involves increases in positive to negative interactional ratios to reduce daily problem behaviors and increase appropriate behaviors.
Age Group: Elementary or Secondary.
Materials: Individual point cards, back-up reinforcers.
Steps:

1. This procedure can be used with individual students who exhibit high rates of disruptive behaviors. Students with a history of behavior problems are much more likely to instigate negative than positive interactions

with teachers and parents, often leading to increasing rates of disruptive behaviors that are maintained by negative reinforcement. Students who experience years of misbehavior may feel like they are always in trouble, and the school atmosphere becomes very negative. The number of reprimands and criticisms is often high, and opportunities for positive interactions are few.

2. Positive reinforcement is much more effective when the number of positive interactions exceeds the number of negative interactions over the course of the class period or the school day. The goal of this intervention is to provide a minimum of 5:1 ratio of positive to negative teaching interactions.

3. Each target student is provided with a point card that they should carry at all times or place in a visible location on their desk. Each teaching interaction, positive or negative is recorded on the point card and initialed by the teacher.

4. A positive interaction should include the following components: (a) praise, (b) a description of the behavior being praised, and (c) a point award (a mark on the card indicating a + or a 1). A negative interaction should include: (a) description of the inappropriate behavior, (b) description of alternative appropriate behavior, and (c) a point fine (a mark on the card indicating a – or a –1). Negative interactions can also include asking the student to demonstrate the appropriate behavior and positive feedback for demonstrating the appropriate behavior. Effective praise should always include a point award and negative teaching interactions always include a point fine.

5. The students can add up the total number of points earned each day, minus the point fines and exchange them for privileges or other reinforcers, either on a daily or weekly basis.

6. To increase the number of positive interactions, the teacher may need to pay specific attention to the target students and make extra effort to notice behaviors that are appropriate for praise or reduce the number of negative interactions that target minor misbehaviors. Major misbehaviors, however, should not be ignored.

7. To determine the daily positive to negative interaction ratio, the number of positive interactions is divided by the number of negative interactions. An optimal ratio to aim for to increase appropriate behavior is 5:1.

Troubleshooting: It may be helpful to collect baseline data to obtain an idea of the positive to negative ratio prior to implementing the intervention. It is very important to significantly increase the number of positives even though it may seem artificial at first. This might mean that initially, teachers are making an effort to interact with target students more frequently than with the other students in the

class. Other adults (recess or lunchroom aides, etc.) can also be enlisted to watch
for appropriate behaviors and award points or fines.

Response Cost Raffle   **E7 F9 E9 C9 T8 I9 V9 +8 T = 8.5**

Reference: Proctor & Morgan, 1991.
Goal: The Response Cost Raffle is a procedure involving positive reinforcement
and withdrawal of reinforcers to reduce disruptive behaviors and increase appro-
priate classroom behaviors.
Age Group: Elementary or Secondary.
Materials: Colored slips of paper (raffle tickets), raffle jar, and reinforcers (prizes).
Steps:

1.   The Response Cost Raffle can be used with individual students, a small
     group, or with the entire class. Each student participating has an oppor-
     tunity to earn reinforcers by contributing tickets to a class raffle.
2.   Before implementing the Response Cost Raffle, the teacher explains the
     procedure to the students, through discussion and demonstration. The
     teacher defines appropriate classroom behaviors, providing examples and
     nonexamples and defines the target behaviors for which students can
     lose a ticket (i.e., out of seat, interrupting, talking to or bothering other
     students, etc.).
3.   Students are instructed that they will each receive five colored slips of
     paper at the beginning of each class period (or school day). If this pro-
     cedure is used with a small group of students, each student can be given
     a different color of slips. If used with the entire class, the students will
     need to put their name on their tickets. The five colored slips of paper
     remain on the student's desk during the period. At the end of the period
     students can enter their tickets into a prize drawing.
4.   The teacher and students can identify potential reinforcers (i.e., soda
     pop, candy bar, bag of chips, computer time, no homework coupon, etc.).
     Prizes can be posted on a reinforcer menu or list for students to select
     from. A second list can be posted listing group prizes (i.e., movie, game,
     extra free time, root beer floats, talking time, music, etc.).
5.   The teacher removes a ticket when a student engages in any of the targeted
     inappropriate or disruptive behaviors during the class period. Before re-
     moving the ticket the teacher states the specific inappropriate behavior
     that occurred. Students are instructed to respond appropriately when los-
     ing a ticket, without arguing or making negative comments, to avoid
     losing additional tickets.
6.   At the end of the class period, all slips remaining on students' desks are
     collected and placed in the group raffle jar. The teacher randomly marks
     two slips with the word "group."

7. The teacher conducts the raffle by drawing one ticket from the jar and stating the winner's name. The winner then chooses a prize from the posted list of potential reinforcers. If a ticket marked "group" is drawn the entire group wins a prize from the list of reinforcers designated as group prizes.

8. The remaining slips are discarded and the raffle procedure is started over at the beginning of each class period.

Troubleshooting: For this procedure to be effective, teachers must immediately and consistently consequate inappropriate behavior. It is also important that the teacher provide verbal reinforcement to students who exhibit appropriate behaviors. If some students continue to exhibit disruptive behaviors, and have no tickets remaining, other procedures may be required.

Self-Managed Response Cost   **E7 F9 E9 C8 T8 I8 V8 +8 T = 8.1**

Reference: Salend, Tintle, & Balber, 1988.
Goal: This intervention is used to reduce disruptive behaviors through student self-management and use of a response-cost system.
Age Group: Elementary or Secondary.
Materials: Token sheets or other tokens (chips, tickets, etc.).
Steps:

1. This intervention can be used with individual students, a group of students, or with the entire classroom. This behavioral technique includes use of free tokens. In this system, students are given a set amount of tokens at the beginning of the period or day. Students then monitor their own behavior by removing a token after each occurrence of an inappropriate behavior. If the student has any tokens remaining at the end of the class period, they will receive a reinforcer or can exchange the tokens remaining for available reinforcers.

2. The teacher selects inappropriate behaviors to target. Different behaviors may be targeted for individual students. Examples of disruptive, off-task behaviors to target include, leaving seat, talking to peers, blurting out or interrupting, playing with objects, looking around the room, and disruptive seeking of teacher attention.

3. The teacher defines on-task behaviors that are expected during the class period. For example, the teacher might explain that on-task behavior means looking at the teacher when instructions are given, eyes and/or pencil on the required book or assignment, sitting quietly in the chair, raising hand and waiting to be called on, desks clear of unnecessary items, etc. The teacher demonstrates specific observable examples of on and off-task behaviors, and students are given opportunities to identify whether or not the target behavior had occurred.

4. Each student is provided with a new token card at the beginning of each class period. The token card consists of a set of circles printed on a small index card. For example, each card may contain up to ten circles. Other tokens, visually related to the specific target can be used instead (e.g., small icons representing eyes, hands, pencil, etc.).
5. The teacher demonstrates the intervention and students have an opportunity to role play the system prior to implementing, using practice token cards.
6. The token cards are placed on top of the students' desks to be within easy access. Each time a student exhibits an off-task behavior, he or she crosses out a circle (token). The teacher may need to prompt students when an off-task behavior occurs and remind them to cross out a token. Teachers can also monitor students' accuracy in self-recording by circulating around the room and praising students who are completing their token cards correctly.
7. At the end of the class period, students who have any circles remaining on their cards receive the reinforcer. The teacher may select a surprise reinforcer each day, or allow students to select from a list of reinforcers (e.g., time with a friend, computer time, stickers, edibles, certificates of achievement, etc.). Teachers should also provide verbal praise for students who demonstrate or improve appropriate behavior.

Troubleshooting: To insure success, the number of free tokens given should not be below the mean of the baseline data. As student behavior improves, the number of tokens is decreased. This procedure is not appropriate for severe behaviors that must be decreased immediately.

The Reward Target Game   **E8 F9 E9 C8 T8 I8 V9 +8 T = 8.3**

Reference: Anhalt, McNeil, & Bahl, 1998.
Goal: The Reward Target Game (RTG) is a whole-classroom reinforcement program to encourage on-task behavior and following of class rules.
Age Group: Elementary.
Materials: Happy face tickets, sad face tickets, a target board containing the numbers 1 to 6 (or more), a ball (made of soft material), and back-up reinforcers.
Steps:

1. The teacher reviews the classroom rules and expectations and explains the Reward Target Game (RTG) to the students. The basis of the RTG is that groups of students try to follow the class rules and instructions in exchange for the opportunity to play the game.
2. The teacher explains that students can earn happy or sad face tickets. They can earn happy face tickets for on-task behaviors. If disruptive behaviors

occur the students will receive a verbal warning. The students are taught the warning signal, consisting of the teacher calling the student's name, holding up two fingers, and stating, "You have two choices. You can improve (behavior in question) or your group will receive a sad face."

3. The students are divided into groups or teams. The teacher decides on group size. The RTG can be used with small groups (3–6 students), or with two or three larger groups. If small groups are used, students should be grouped according to seat arrangements so that the teacher can monitor the group as a whole.

4. The teacher monitors student behavior during classroom periods in which students are expected to work quietly and follow instructions. Happy face tickets are given to groups of children for individual and group behaviors that are on-task and compliant. The happy face tickets are awarded frequently throughout the period. Verbal praise is also provided when children receive happy face tickets.

5. Individual or groups of children are given a verbal warning if they behave in a disruptive manner. The verbal "sad-face" signal is used to prompt students to change their behavior without delivering negative attention. If students continue to behave inappropriately following the warning, the group receives a sad face ticket. Tickets are given in a calm, matter-of-fact manner.

6. The teacher can designate one student from each group to manage the tickets or place a small container at each table in which to place the tickets.

7. At the end of the period, the groups that meet the criteria (more happy face tickets than sad face tickets, or other predetermined criteria) are allowed to play the RTG.

8. The RTG provides a short break from academic tasks. To play the game, a student from each team is allowed to throw a ball at the target. Each number on the target corresponds to a card that specifies a reward. Rewards can include activities or tangible reinforcers. The cards can be changed frequently so that the game remains novel and stimulating.

9. The RTG can be played several times per day. All children have an opportunity to participate each time the game is played. By starting over each time, students with behavior problems can regain interest because the opportunity to earn the reward is renewed.

Troubleshooting: The groups should contain a mix of students that misbehave and behave in order for groups to have equal opportunities to earn happy and sad faces.

Self-Recording   **E9 F9 E8 C8 T8 I8 V9 +9 T = 8.6**

Reference: Hutchinson, Murdock, Williamson, & Cronin, 2000.

Goal: This intervention is a self-management strategy, including self-recording with points, teacher praise, and back-up reinforcers to encourage on-task and non-disruptive behaviors.
Age Group: Elementary.
Materials: "I'm a Great Kid!" self-recording forms.
Steps:

1. This intervention can be used with individual children who exhibit off-task, disruptive behaviors in the classroom setting. It can be combined with a home-based reinforcement program to provide additional positive reinforcement.

2. The teacher develops a self-recording form individualized for specific problem behaviors. An example of the self-recording form, titled "I'm a Great Kid!" might include the following:

   Date   Name

   Today during Reading Period:

   Put an X in the boxes next to all the things you did during reading period.
   I read quietly. ☐
   I did not talk out without asking. ☐
   I did not bother anyone. ☐
   I stayed in my seat. ☐
   I did my work by myself. ☐
   The total number of things I did is _____.

3. The teacher instructs the student on how to complete the self-recording form and explains that the student can earn points for each box that is accurately checked on the form. For the first few days the teacher may need to help the student read and complete the form and check to see that it is completed accurately.

4. At the end of each recording period, the teacher reviews the recording form and provides teacher praise such as, "I am proud of the way you worked quietly during reading hour" when four out of five boxes are checked. If less than three boxes are checked, the teacher encourages future appropriate behavior

5. One point is given for each nondisruptive behavior (or box) exhibited. The points may later be redeemed for back-up reinforcers. The teacher can provide small reinforcers at school for a specified number of points (e.g., 5 points = 5 minutes free time, 10 points = small piece of candy, etc.).

6. The teacher may also combine the self-recording procedure with a home-based reward, by asking the student to sign the form and take it home each day. Parents can develop a reward menu and provide inexpensive prizes or activity reinforcers for a specified number of points (e.g.,

20 points = favorite candy bar, 30 points = extra half hour of Nintendo, or 40 points = an outing to buy ice cream, etc.).

Troubleshooting: If students have difficulty completing forms accurately, the teacher may complete the same form on randomly selected days and compare with the student's rating. If the student and teacher forms match exactly (regardless of the percentage of boxes checked), the student earns bonus points.

3-Steps   **E9 F10 E8 C9 T8 I8 V9 +9 T = 8.7**

Reference: Schmid, 1998.
Goal: The "3-Step" procedure is a simple whole-class intervention used to reduce classroom disruptions and instructional interruptions (tattletales) by teaching students to self-manage problems.
Age Group: Elementary.
Materials: Create a poster titled "3 Steps to Classroom Order" listing the following three steps: (1) Say, stop! I don't like that, (2) Try to ignore them or walk away, and (3) Report to your teacher what you have tried and ask for help.
Steps:

1. This procedure is helpful to use for many classroom disruptions that stem from children teasing one another or from annoying behaviors such as playing with objects, tapping pencil, making noises, etc., which then result in interruptions and complaints to the teacher.
2. At the beginning of the year, the teacher or other adult explains the 3-Step program to the students. The teacher provides a rationale for the program, by explaining that the class will be using a self-managed strategy to solve problems in the classroom and resolve conflicts without interrupting instructional activities. Students will learn to become active participants in resolving situations that bother them.
3. The teacher explains to the students that if another student bothers or annoys them, they must use the 3-Steps before interrupting the teacher and asking for help. 3-Steps has three parts that must be followed in sequential order. The purpose of the first two steps is for the students to attempt to solve the problem prior to going to the teacher to ask for help, thus reducing interruptions during instructional time. The third step is followed if disruptive behaviors persist and require teacher directed consequences.
4. The teacher shows the class the poster and explains the following three steps:
    a. Say (in a calm voice) to the person bothering you, "Stop! I don't like that."

    b. If you have said to the person "Stop, I don't like that" and they continue to bother you, the second step is to try to ignore them, or if you can, walk away.

    c. If you have said to the person, "Stop, I don't like that" and you have tried to ignore them and they continue to bother you, the third step is to go to the teacher or another adult and say, "First I said, stop. Second, I tried to ignore them, and they still didn't stop so I am asking you for help."

5. If students frequently go to the teacher with complaints, the teacher can provide a reminder by asking, "Did you do the 3-Steps?"

6. The teacher should provide verbal reinforcement to students who use the 3-Steps correctly. A positive reinforcement system may also be used to reward the class when they are using the 3-Steps. For example, the class may earn a smiley face (or point) during each instructional period that all students self-manage annoyances, or when all students follow the steps prior to asking the teacher for help. When the class has earned a specified number of smiley faces, they earn a privilege or activity reward.

Troubleshooting: If some students repeatedly bother or disrupt others, a mild consequence such as point loss, restriction from a privilege, or time away from the group may be required. Parents can use the 3-Step procedure in the home setting to teach self-control in resolving disputes between siblings.

The Timer Game   **E8 F9 E9 C9 T8 I8 V9 +9 T = 8.7**

Reference: Wolf, Hanley, King, Lachowicz, & Giles, 1970.
Goal: The Timer Game is a classroom procedure for managing students' out-of-seat and off-task-behavior.
Age Group: Elementary or Secondary.
Materials: Timer, backup reinforcers, individual point cards (small index or note cards).
Steps:

1. This procedure can be used with all students in the classroom or with individual students. Students who demonstrate on-task behaviors have the opportunity to earn points or token reinforcers each time a classroom timer rings or buzzes.

2. The teacher defines the appropriate behaviors expected during the class period, demonstrating examples and nonexamples to the students. On-task behaviors should include observable behaviors such as, sitting in their seat, materials (book and paper) on desk, working quietly, or the teacher can use work products (i.e., problems completed on worksheet) to measure on-task behavior. The teacher instructs the students that they

will earn points if they are exhibiting appropriate behaviors when the timer rings. If they are not exhibiting on-task behaviors when the timer rings they do not earn points. Specific off-task behaviors which will prevent students from earning points should be described, such as out-of-seat, wandering around room, prolonged pencil sharpening, playing with objects, talking to other students, etc.

3. The Timer Game can be used during any subject, however, works best when used consistently and during periods when students are more likely to be off-task, such as independent work periods. At the start of the class period, the teacher sets the timer or beeper to ring after intervals of varying duration. The timer should be set for random intervals, so that students will not know in advance when the timer will ring. Intervals should be varied so that the bell may be likely to ring after having just rung, as to ring after a long interval. The teacher can determine the number and duration of intervals, based on the baseline rates of off-task behavior. For example, the timer may be set to ring after varying intervals but on an average of every 10 minutes. Initially, shorter, more frequent intervals can be used, with interval duration increased gradually as behavior improves.

4. When the timer rings, every student who is in his or her seat and on-task receives a point on their point card. Students who are out-of-seat or off-task do not earn a point for that interval.

5. Students can self-monitor on-task behaviors by making a tally or + mark on their point cards, or the teacher can circulate around the room and reward points to students who are on-task when the timer rings (by making a tally or + mark with a colored pen on student point cards). The teacher may also circulate around the room to check for work completed by the students during the interval providing verbal reinforcement for students who are on-task.

6. Points can later be exchanged (at the end of the day or week) for backup reinforcers such as snacks, activities, small items, privileges, etc.

Troubleshooting: To reduce teacher time required to monitor and reward points, the teacher may choose to target only one behavior initially (i.e., out-of-seat).

Yes and No Bag   **E8 F9 E9 C10 T9 I9 V9 +9 T = 9.0**

Reference: Jenson, W. R., Andrews, D., & Reavis, K., 1994.
Goal: The Yes and No Bag is group contingency system used with a whole class to reduce inappropriate and disruptive behaviors.
Age Group: Elementary or Secondary.
Materials: An opaque container or bag, a set of at least 50 cards with either "Yes" or "No" written on each card, and a class reward (such as a Mystery Motivator—a sealed envelope with a reward written on a slip of paper). Happy-face or sad-face

cards or colored slips of paper can be used instead (i.e., red for "Yes" and green for "No").

Steps:

1. The Yes and No Bag is based on probability. The more Yes cards in the bag, the higher the likelihood that students will earn the reinforcer.

2. The teacher defines appropriate behaviors expected during the class period, demonstrating examples and nonexamples to the students. On-task behaviors should include observable behaviors such as; in seat, raise hands, speak in a quiet voice, etc. The teacher instructs the students that he or she will be watching students to catch them following directions and demonstrating appropriate behaviors. Each time the teacher observes appropriate behaviors a Yes card is placed in the bag. Similarly, if a student exhibits a disruptive behavior, a No card is placed in the bag. The card drawn at the end of the period or day determines whether or not the class will earn the reinforcer.

3. The teacher can vary the reinforcer or write a reward on a piece of paper placed in a sealed envelope to increase student interest and motivation. Reinforcers can include a small treat, 5–10 minutes of free time, listening to music or a story, visit with friends, etc. Larger reinforcers (e.g., movie or popcorn party) can be included occasionally to keep interest level high.

4. The Yes and No Bag can be used during any subject, however, works best when used during periods when students are more likely to be off-task, and when the teacher is able to monitor student behaviors. During the period, the teacher watches for appropriate behaviors to add Yes cards to the bag. When placing the card in the bag, the teacher describes the student's behavior (i.e., "Andrew, you raised your hand and waited quietly. I am putting a Yes card in the bag for the class", or "Andrew you were talking instead of listening. I will put a No card in the bag").

5. At the end of the day or class period the teacher or a student randomly picks a card from the bag. The cards should be thoroughly mixed and the student selects the card without looking. If the card selected is a Yes, the whole class receives the reinforcer—if the card selected is a No, the students continue with the regular academic activities. The bag is emptied each day after the card has been selected and the procedure is started again the next day.

Troubleshooting: To ensure a positive beginning, the teacher should make extra effort to add Yes cards to the bag, especially in the first few days of the program. If one or a few students try to sabotage the program and intentionally misbehave, they can be excluded from the group reward and placed on a separate team and allowed to rejoin the group when behaviors are appropriate.

FOLLOWING DIRECTIONS

"Clean Up—Hands Up"   **E8 F9 E8 C9 T8 I8 V9 +9 T = 8.5**

Reference: Connell, Carta, Lutz, Randall, & Wilson, 1993.
Goal: This procedure is a simple self-assessment strategy to teach young children
to follow directions during in-class transition times.
Age Group: Preschool or Early Elementary.
Materials: A poster containing pictures or photographs of students modeling targeted behaviors.
Steps:

1. The teacher determines specific tasks that the students are expected to follow during transition periods. For example, tasks might include stop playing, put things away, walk to the carpet, and sit quietly. A poster containing pictures of students demonstrating these target behaviors is created. Actual photographs of individual students performing the steps can be used, such as (a) a photograph of a child with his or her hand on the light switch to signal clean-up time, (b) a child putting a toy on a shelf, (c) a child standing in the group area, and (d) a child sitting with legs crossed on the carpet.
2. Other transition steps can be targeted such as (a) put away books, (b) clean up trash, (c) put on coats, and (d) line up to go outside.
3. During the class group time, the teacher explains the target behaviors by clearly defining appropriate and inappropriate performance of each behavior, giving examples, modeling the appropriate behaviors, and having students practice the behaviors.
4. After the students understand the steps required during the transition period and understand each target behavior, the teacher explains how students will self-assess their behavior. The behaviors they self-assess should be clearly observable, similar to the photographs. The students practice raising their hand above their head when a behavior has been performed correctly, and keeping both hands in their lap when the behavior has not been performed. The students practice assessing their performance of the specific target transition skills depicted on the poster by raising hands or keeping hands in lap.
5. Prior to beginning the transition, the teacher reviews the self-assessment procedure and reminds the students of the behaviors they are to self-assess.
6. A transition signal or prompt should be should be used to indicate the start of the transition (an assigned student flashes the light or rings a bell, or the teacher states, "It's time to clean-up.").

7. During the transition period, the teacher verbally praises students who are following directions.

8. After the transition, when all students are seated on the carpet, the teacher leads the students in the group response self-assessment procedure by (a) pointing to each picture on the poster of a student demonstrating a target behavior, while verbally describing the behavior, (b) asking the students to indicate by raising their hand above their heads if they had performed the behavior, and (c) providing verbal feedback about accurate self-assessment (e.g., "Dylan, you have your hand up. I agree you did a good job of putting toys away."). If students are inaccurate in their self-assessment, the teacher provides corrective feedback (e.g., Dylan, you have your hand up, but I don't agree. You didn't stop playing when the light blinked to stop playing. Let's work harder tomorrow.").

9. This procedure can be faded to once or twice per week, after behaviors are stable.

Troubleshooting: Teacher prompts and individual practice may be necessary with those students who have continued difficulty following directions.

High Probability Requests   **E10 F10 E9 C9 T9 I8 V10 +10 T = 9.4**

Reference: Davis, Brady, Williams, & Hamilton, 1992.
Goal: High Probability Requests are an antecedent strategy used to increase compliance to teacher directions and increase appropriate behaviors.
Age Group: Preschool or Elementary.
Materials: None.
Steps:

1. The use of High Probability Requests works on the principle of behavioral momentum. Behavioral momentum is similar to the momentum of objects in motion. A sequence of requests is used to establish a high rate of reinforcement for compliance that will increase the momentum and carry over to tasks that might typically have a lower probability of compliance. They can be used as an antecedent intervention by focusing on changing the context in which a request is delivered.

2. The high probability request intervention can be used with all ages. If children are extremely noncompliant and angry, giving requests initially that will have a high probability of compliance before making more demanding requests can prevent escalation of defiant behaviors and can prevent power struggles.

3. High probability requests are requests that a child will typically perform without argument. For younger children these requests might be

statements such as, "Give me five," "Thumbs up," or "Touch your nose." Children are likely to comply with these requests because of a history of being reinforced, and also because they are non-demanding. For older students, requests could be tasks students typically like to perform such as, "Turn out the lights", "Pass out the papers", or "Take this note to the office."

4. Low probability requests are requests that a child does not typically perform, and has not received regular reinforcement for performing. Examples include, "Pick up the toys," "Go to the table," or "Get out your crayon." Children who don't comply with these requests are sometimes inadvertently reinforced for their nonperformance if the noncompliance is ignored, or they get out of performing or escape the required task.

5. To increase compliance to requests, teachers can (a) give three high probability requests, (b) deliver verbal or gestural praise for performance (e.g., "way to go", "give me five", smile, pat on back, thumbs up, etc.), then (c) give a low probability request, and (d) deliver verbal or gestural praise for performance of the low probability request. When a child performs several high probability requests and is subsequently reinforced, the momentum of the behavior will likely continue when a low probability request is delivered.

6. The high probability request sequence should be delivered immediately prior to presenting each low probability request. The behavioral momentum is more effective when the low probability request is delivered within 5 seconds of reinforcement of the performance of the high probability request.

7. If a student does not comply with a high probability request, the teacher continues to deliver high probability requests until two consecutive compliant responses are made before giving a low probability request.

Troubleshooting: To assist with generalization of compliance, requests should be delivered in various settings and with more than one adult.

Picture Prompts   **E7 H9 E9 C7 T7 I9 V10 +10 T = 8.5**

Reference: Lazarus, 1998.
Goal: Student photographs are used as visual prompts to follow routine requests and teacher directions.
Age Group: Preschool or Elementary.
Materials: Photographs of individual students demonstrating appropriate classroom behaviors.
Steps:

1. The teacher takes photographs of individual students (or groups of students) demonstrating desired classroom behaviors. To create the

photograph for an individual student, the student is instructed to perform different tasks. For example, the teacher might say, "Show me what
you look like when you raise your hand" or "Show me what you do when I
tell you to get out your paper and a crayon." Other examples of behaviors
include, lining up, putting toys away, sit on the carpet, look at a book,
sit at the table for snack time, etc. The teacher may wish to target only
one or two specific behaviors that are the most problematic for individual
students.

2. It may be helpful to take a few pictures of each task and let the student
   choose which one to use. Pictures can also be taken of a small group of
   students and posted in a visible location in the classroom.

3. At the bottom of each picture, the teacher writes the classroom rule it
   represents (e.g., Raise your hand or Stay in your own space, etc.). The
   teacher explains to the students that they will use the pictures as prompts
   to help them follow directions.

4. The teacher demonstrates how to use the pictures by showing the picture,
   stating the rule, and modeling the appropriate behavior. The teacher may
   also demonstrate a gesture such as pointing to the picture that can be used
   to remind students of the expected behaviors. Use of the visual prompt
   and gesture will help to reduce repeated verbal directives.

5. During group time, the students are given several opportunities to practice
   using the picture prompts. The teacher shows a picture and states, "show
   me what it tells you to do."

6. The selected pictures are then laminated and posted at the student's desk
   or work area.

7. Students can use the picture prompts to self-monitor behaviors during
   transition periods, instructional periods, or independent work periods.
   Each student is given a separate card on which to record points. The card
   is attached or placed below the pictures on their desks. At the end of the
   period (or at different intervals during the period) the teacher instructs
   the students to give themselves a point or tally mark on their card if they
   were doing what the picture shows them to do.

8. Students can earn a reinforcer when they accumulate a specified number
   of points on their card.

9. Personal Picture prompts can also be used to cue and self-monitor other
   skills or situations, including social skills (smiling, sharing, helping,
   playing together, etc.), playground behaviors, or lunchroom behaviors.
   Parents may also use personal picture prompts at home to encourage
   following directions and reduce verbal reminders.

Troubleshooting: If students have difficulty self-recording on their point cards, the
teacher can circulate around the room providing verbal praise, and placing a sticker
or smiley face on the cards of students demonstrating their target behavior.

Student Checkbooks **E7 F9 E8 C6 T6 I8 V9 +9 T = 7.8**

Reference: Metzler, Biglan, Rusby, & Sprague, 2001.

Goal: This intervention is a positive reinforcement program (point system) used to motivate students to follow directions, comply with classroom rules, and engage in other appropriate behaviors (good attendance, punctuality, organized binders, prepared for class, etc.). The use of student checkbooks can also be incorporated into the math curriculum to provide opportunity for students to practice calculation skills, keep a checkbook balance, and budget their money.

Age Group: Secondary.

Materials: A notebook or checkbook register and checks for each student, tickets or paper "dollars" to be used for points, and a classroom store which contains edible and/or tangible reinforcers and activity coupons.

Steps:

1. The teacher selects target behaviors to reinforce and determines how many points (dollars) will be awarded for each behavior. For example, each completed assignment may be worth $1.00. Coming to class prepared and on time may be worth $1.00 per day. A range of points or dollars may be assigned to different behaviors, homework assignments, or larger projects, depending on the effort and difficulty of the task. The more difficult or challenging the task, the more dollars it is worth.

2. The teacher also determines the cost of each material or activity reinforcer available in the classroom store. For example, a small candy is priced at $1.00, a soda pop is priced at $5.00, and a class party is priced at $20.00. Prior to determining the value assigned to behaviors and reinforcers, it is helpful to estimate how many points students will earn in a typical day, and how many points students should have to pay for each item.

3. Students are taught how to use the checkbook procedure. Students must be able to record deposits and withdrawals into their checkbook register. In the notebook or checkbook register, students will enter the date, amount earned (deposited), amount spent (withdrawals), and a keep a running balance. Students are also taught how to write a check and how to deduct the check amount from the register balance.

4. At the end of each period, the teacher pays the students with tickets or play dollars for the targeted appropriate behaviors. Students add up the dollars or tickets and enter the amount into their checkbook register as a deposit.

5. At the end of the week, the funds available in the checkbook can be spent or exchanged for purchases at a classroom store. Store items might include small prizes, pencils, sodas, snacks, etc. Funds might also be

spent on activity reinforcers, such as free time or no-homework coupons. When students make purchases, they write a check to the teacher, and subtract the amount from their checkbook balance.

6. The teacher may wish to award a group reinforcer for the entire class such as a class party or activity once per month. To participate in the activity, each student must pay a predetermined amount and subtract it from their checkbook balance. Students can be encouraged to accumulate dollars from week to week to spend on larger purchases.

Troubleshooting: It is important to provide sufficient opportunities for all students to earn "dollars." Be careful not to take away points for noncompliance, particularly in the first few weeks. Students will give up easily if they have not earned any dollars by the end of the week. Bonus points can be awarded occasionally, to increase motivation.

Time Out Ribbons   **E8 F8 E9 C8 T8 I8 V10 +7 T = 8.3**

Reference: Yeager & McLaughlin, 1995.
Goal: The time-out ribbon procedure is used to increase compliance to teacher directions. The time-out ribbon is most effective when combined with precision requests (refer to the "Sure I Will" intervention in this chapter).
Age Group: Preschool or Early Elementary.
Materials: A poster or chart located in a visible spot. On the poster is each child's name with a place for a happy face card underneath. Also needed are happy face cards (one per student). The cards can be attached to the poster with sticky tape or Velcro, but should be removable.
Steps:

1. The time-out ribbon is a form of in-class time out as a consequence for noncompliance. For example, the student remains in the classroom, and is given a ribbon to wear for compliance with requests. While wearing the ribbon, the student has access to reinforcers. When the student does not comply with requests, the ribbon is removed, and the student does not have access to reinforcers. In the procedure described below, students are given happy faces cards, rather than wearing ribbons.
2. The teacher explains that students can earn reinforcers when they comply with a teacher request. Small reinforcers such as pretzels, Teddy Grahams, Cheerios, marshmallows, and M & M's can be used. Other reinforcers include a small sticker, or tokens towards a later reinforcer. It is important to also provide verbal reinforcement frequently to those students who are following directions. The students are told, however, they can only earn the reinforcers when they have a happy face card by their name on the poster.

3. The teacher places a happy face card underneath each student's name on the poster.
4. The teacher informs the students that they can earn a "treat" (or sticker) because they have a happy face card for doing what the teacher asks. The teacher explains that as long as the happy face card is by their name, students can continue to earn a treat (or other reinforcement) for doing what is asked. If the students do not do what the teacher asks them to, they will lose their happy face card.
5. Teacher requests should be delivered in the format of precision requests. In precision requests, the teacher asks the student to do something by stating, "Please ... (requested behavior)" and given five seconds to respond. If the request is followed, the student continues to earn the happy face and receive positive reinforcement. If the request is not complied with, a second request is given. The student is told, "You need to ... (requested behavior)." If the request is not followed within five seconds, the happy face card is removed from the chart (or turned over), and no reinforcement is given.
6. Students can earn back their happy face by following the next request given by the teacher. All students should start over each day with a happy face by their name.
7. The happy face cards could also be kept on a corner of each student's desk, and removed or turned over during the time-out period.

Troubleshooting: Students who do not comply after the second request may be told to sit in a time-out chair for four minutes, while losing their happy face card. After the time-out period, the request procedure should be followed again, allowing five seconds to comply before reinforcing compliance.

FOLLOWING RULES

Following Classroom Rules

"High Five Rules"   **E8 F9 E9 C8 T7 I9 V10 +9 T = 8.6**

Reference: Taylor-Greene, Brown, Nelson, Longton, Gassman, Cohen, Swartz, Horner, Sugai, & Hall, 1997.
Goal: To increase positive student behaviors by developing age-appropriate classroom rules, defining and teaching specific student behaviors for each rule, monitoring student behavior, and providing positive reinforcement for appropriate behaviors.
Age Group: Elementary or Secondary.
Materials: Large "High Five" poster, "High Five" tickets, and small reinforcers.

Steps:

1. During the first few days of school, all students participate in "High Five" training. The teacher presents the "High Five" poster (listing five important rules) to the students. Rules should be posted in a prominent location in the classroom. The rules listed below are examples of classroom rules appropriate for an elementary classroom, however, each teacher may choose to develop classroom rules based on age level and class needs:
   High Five Rules
   a. Be respectful.
   b. Sit in your seat.
   c. Keep hands and feet to self.
   d. Follow directions—do what your teacher asks.
   e. Be there—be ready.
2. The teacher reads and explains each rule, describing both positive and negative examples. The teacher demonstrates positive examples, asks individual students to demonstrate examples, and provides all students an opportunity to practice each rule. For example, the teacher may demonstrate how to be respectful by modeling a respectful tone of voice while asking to borrow something from a student (e.g., "May I borrow your eraser, please?"), saying kind words to others, taking care of school property, or using good manners (e.g., saying "excuse me" when bumping into someone). The students should role-play these skills with other students. Several examples should be provided to ensure that students have a clear understanding of expectations.
3. The teacher explains that students will receive "High Five" tickets for demonstrating the "High Five" rules. Tickets will be exchanged for a small reinforcer at the end of the day. The teacher prompts students to follow rules throughout the day by holding up a hand and stating, "Give me five."
4. During the day students are monitored for rule following behaviors. As students demonstrate appropriate rule following behaviors, the teacher, recess aide or other adult rewards the students by giving them a "High Five" ticket, along with verbal praise for their behavior. Verbal praise should be specific and describe the behavior and rule observed (e.g., "Joey, nice job being respectful, and putting the toys away carefully.")
5. At the end of the day, students with "High Five" tickets exchange the tickets for a small reinforcer (small candy, etc.). Tickets could be accumulated during the week instead of daily, and then exchanged for a reinforcer (5 tickets = piece of candy).

Troubleshooting: The "High Five" ticket reinforcement should be used in the first few weeks during the training period and then faded, however, intermittent reinforcement and periodic review of the rules may be needed throughout the year. This intervention can also be used as part of a school-wide intervention (refer to Chapter 8).

Magic Five   **E8 F9 E8 C7 T7 I9 V9 +9 T = 8.2**

Reference: Carpenter & McKee-Higgins 1996.
Goal: This intervention is a proactive behavior management program that combines classroom rules and a group contingency based on students working together on a common goal of demonstrating appropriate behaviors.
Age Group: Elementary.
Materials: Poster with class rules, laminated class goal poster, and a large cartoon character, laminated and cut into several puzzle pieces.
Steps:

1. The teacher presents and reviews a set of classroom rules termed the "Magic Five" with the students. The "Magic Five" rules are based on five class behaviors (e.g., legs crossed, hands in lap, eyes on teacher, mouth closed, ears listening).

2. The teacher explains to the students that they will be working on a class goal each day to follow the "Magic Five" during carpet time, or instructional periods. The teacher explains that during each activity, if the class meets their goal, a piece of the cartoon character puzzle will be attached to a goal poster. When the entire cartoon is completed, the whole class will receive a reinforcer.

3. The teacher and students decide what the reinforcer will be. Activity reinforcers, such as a class game or extra recess time, or a small edible reinforcer are suggested.

4. The teacher presents a large laminated poster, titled "Our Class Goal." On the poster, two or three activities are listed (e.g., story, math, calendar, etc.) and next to them, a line to write in the class goal. The class goal is a pre-determined number of rule violations allowed during each activity. For example, the teacher and class may decide the goal is no more than 4 rule violations during math instruction, 4 during story, and 3 during calendar. These numbers are written next to the name of the activity. During each activity, the teacher marks a tally mark next to the activity, whenever a student breaks a "Magic Five" rule.

5. At the end of the activity, the tally marks are added. If the number of rule violations tallied during the activity is less than the pre-determined goal, the class has met their goal and the teacher puts up a puzzle piece of the cartoon character on the poster.

6. If the number of rule violations tallied exceeds the pre-determined goal, the class did not meet their goal and the teacher does not put up a piece of the cartoon character.

7. When the entire cartoon character is completed on the poster, the whole class receives the pre-selected reinforcer.

Troubleshooting: Prior to implementing this intervention it is important to determine when problem behaviors occur, which behaviors are most problematic, and count how frequently these behaviors occur. The class goal should be determined in relation to baseline levels of off-task behaviors, and gradually decreased as behaviors improve.

Stoplight Rules   E9 F8 E9 C8 T8 I6 V9 +6 T = 7.9

Reference: White, Algozzine, Audette, Marr, & Ellis, 2001.
Goal: This intervention is designed to reduce the incidence of problem behaviors and improve classroom discipline by developing and explaining classroom rules, monitoring student behavior, and delivering consequences in a sequential hierarchy for instances of rule violation.
Age Group: Elementary or Secondary.
Materials: For younger students—a posterboard or bulletin board with a paper stoplight for each student in the classroom, and colored paper circles (green, yellow, and red) can be used. For either younger or older students—a posterboard with a pocket for each student and colored paper cards or tickets (green, yellow, and red) can be used.
Steps:

1. At the beginning of the school year, the teacher develops and explains the classroom rules. Examples of rules appropriate for 3–6 grade classrooms are:
    a. Follow all teacher directions promptly.
    b. Stay on task.
    c. Be prepared for class.
    d. Raise your hand.
    e. Respect the rights and property of others.
2. The teacher reads and explains each rule, discussing both positive and negative examples.
3. The teacher explains that the students will receive consequences for rule-breaking behaviors. The consequence hierarchy is 1) verbal reminder, 2) loss of privilege, 3) 3–5 minute in-class penalty, and 4) 15–20 minute penalty in another class. Each student has a pocket on the poster that contains a green, yellow, and red card (or stoplights containing a green, yellow, and red circle). The first time a student breaks a classroom rule, the teacher will verbally remind the student to follow the specific rule, e.g., "Brian, remember to keep hands to yourself." If the student repeats the rule violation a second time, the green card is removed from that student's pocket (or green circle removed from the stoplight), and the

student is required to lose a privilege (e.g., loss of recess minutes). If a rule is violated a third time, the yellow card is removed from the student's pocket (or yellow ticket is removed from the stoplight) leaving only the red card remaining in the pocket. Following the third violation the student is escorted to a "thinking spot" (a penalty area in the classroom) for 3–5 minutes, for a chance to regain control. If a student continues to misbehave the student receives a "classroom pass." A "classroom pass" means that the student is sent to another classroom for 15–20 minutes to complete work (see Other Class Time-Out intervention for details on an inter class time-out program).

4. After the completion of the 20-minute "classroom pass" time, the student returns to his or her own classroom and the ticket sequence is started over.
5. Students should be verbally reinforced if, after receiving a ticket and/or a consequence, they are able to follow rules correctly.
6. Students that demonstrate appropriate behaviors and do not receive tickets, can earn positive reinforcers at the end of the day or week.

Troubleshooting: Reminders and consequences should be stated quickly and calmly. Do not give the student attention while in the classroom penalty area. Once the consequence is over students should rejoin their classmates, and be given an opportunity to demonstrate correct behaviors. At the secondary level, teachers may carry a clipboard with a list of students, and record or tally rule infractions.

Following Recess Rules

Recess Wristbands   **E8 F9 E9 C8 T7 I9 V10 +10 T = 8.7**

Reference: Lewis, Sugai, & Colvin, 1998 and Eddy et al., 2000.
Goal: This intervention is a classroom group contingency used to increase compliance to recess rules, and to encourage positive peer relations on the playground.
Age Group: Elementary.
Materials: 100 or more small plastic or elastic wristbands, large container to hold wristbands.
Steps:

1. At the beginning of the school year, the teacher develops and explains the playground/recess rules, demonstrating both positive and negative examples. Examples of playground rules include, invite others to join, let everyone play, follow game rules, use equipment appropriately, line up on time, etc.
2. The teacher explains that the class will be working on a class goal to fill up the container with wristbands. Students who demonstrate rule following

and positive playground behaviors will receive small plastic wristbands to place on their wrist during the recess period. The teacher explains that many wristbands will be given each day, and when the container is full, the class will receive a group reinforcer. The teacher and students can select or vote on the desired reinforcer prior to beginning the activity.

3. During the recess period, the teacher or playground monitors give wristbands to students who demonstrate positive behaviors. When students are given the wristbands, the teacher provides verbal praise and feedback (e.g., "nice job inviting Alex to play the game with you."). Students keep the wristband on their wrist until they return to the classroom.

4. After the recess period, students who received a wristband report to the class why they earned it, and then place it in the class container.

5. When the container is filled, the entire class receives a group reinforcer, and the process is started over.

Troubleshooting: Teachers should initially distribute as many wristbands as possible to all students who demonstrate positive behaviors at recess, gradually decreasing distribution as behaviors improve. Teachers may need to target specific students who have a history of problem behaviors during recess and try to catch them behaving appropriately.

NONCOMPLIANCE

Other Class Time-Out   **E9 H8 E9 C7 T7 I5 V9 +7 T = 7.7**

Reference: Nelson & Carr, 1996.
Goal: This intervention combines precision requests, other class time-out, problem solving, and teacher feedback to reduce noncompliant and disruptive behaviors.
Age Group: Elementary or Secondary.
Materials: Debriefing Form. A sample Debriefing Form is listed in Appendix A.
Steps:

1. This procedure includes a combination of behavioral strategies described elsewhere in this chapter (Debriefing, Sure I Will, Stoplight Rules). Refer to the "Think Time" manual developed by Nelson and Carr (1996) for a complete description of a school-wide strategy involving an interclass time-out procedure.

2. A time-out procedure involves removing a student from a reinforcing environment to a less reinforcing environment. Other Class Time-out (OCT) involves removing a student from his or her own classroom to a different classroom for a limited period of time. Although time-out is a reductive procedure, it can be effective in reducing negative verbal

interactions and increasing compliance, particularly when combined with precision requests, an opportunity to think about the behavior, and teacher feedback and encouragement for future behavior.

3. Use of other class time-out requires cooperation between two or more teachers. Each teacher participating will designate a specific area for a student to spend while in time-out (i.e., a desk or corner in back of the room).

4. The teacher provides instruction to the class through discussion and modeling, on classroom rules and consequences for misbehavior. Other class time-out is introduced as a consequence used to help create a calm, orderly classroom and to help students regain self-control. The teacher demonstrates the signal when a student needs to go to other class time-out. The signal can include a precision command, or a warning in the form of pulling a colored card (see Stoplight Rules), followed by a verbal directive after the second warning (i.e., "You need to go to OCT."). The teacher demonstrates and discusses how students are to leave the classroom and how to proceed to the designated class. A nearby classroom is preferable to reduce student travel time and distance.

5. When students arrive at the other class time-out location, they are instructed to wait at the door until the teacher signals them to enter and sit at the designated spot. Students are expected to enter the classroom quietly and proceed directly to the designated area.

6. An other class time-out period is limited (usually 20–30 minutes maximum). During the time-out, students are expected to work quietly on their schoolwork or complete a Debriefing Form (see appendix). The time-out teacher can ask the student to describe the problem behavior prior to giving them the form to complete.

7. After the designated time period, or when the student has completed the Debriefing Form, the student waits for direction from the teacher to return to his or her class. When directed, the student returns to class, rejoining the ongoing class activity. The classroom teacher can check the Debriefing Form when convenient. It is important that the student have an opportunity for positive reinforcement when he or she returns to class.

8. Additional intervention (i.e., loss of privileges, lunch detention, etc.) may be needed for students who are chronically referred to other class time-out. A positive reinforcement incentive (such as a monthly class party) may also be added to reward those students who are not referred or referred less than two times per month to OCT, or students who have reduced the number of referrals over a period of time. To add an element of chance, and to encourage those students with several referrals to behave appropriately, a mystery motivator envelope can be placed in front of the classroom. In the envelope a mystery number is written on a slip of paper

(i.e., any number from 1–5). This number indicates the number of times a student can be referred to OCT and still attend the class party at the end of the month, however, the envelope is not opened until the day of the party.

Troubleshooting: Students unwilling to go to the time-out class quietly or quickly can be escorted by an adult or receive additional consequences (e.g., call to parent, minutes of recess, administrative intervention, etc.).

Read-My-Fingertips E10 F9 E8 C9 T9 I4 V9 +7 T = 8.1

Reference: Reitman & Drabman, 1996.
Goal: This is a simple intervention involving time-out and use of a non-verbal cue (counting fingertips) to reduce arguing and encourage compliance during the implementation of time-out.
Age Group: Preschool or Early Elementary.
Materials: Timer and a designated time-out location.
Steps:

1. After the class rules have been established and explained to the students, the teacher discusses consequences for noncompliance to the rules. One consequence for noncompliance is that students may be asked to sit for a short period in a "think spot." A "think spot" is a designated place, such as a chair placed in the back of the room or away from the other students that is used for a short time-out period.
2. The teacher explains that a student may be given only one warning before they are asked to go to the "think spot."
3. The teacher explains that if children argue, whine, or ignore directions after they are asked to go to the "think spot", the teacher will add additional minutes to the original time period by using the "Read-My-Fingertips" technique.
4. The "Read-My-Fingertips" technique is a non-verbal cue that additional minutes will be added to the original "think spot" time period. For example, if after directions are given to go to the "think spot", the child begins to argue or complain, the teacher calmly holds one hand up in the air, with fingers extended. With the other hand, the teacher touches a finger on the hand that is held up. Each time a fingertip is touched, the student must spend one additional minute in the "think spot." The teacher can begin with the thumb and count additional minutes (on each finger) as needed.
5. Prior to implementing this procedure, the teacher should demonstrate to the class by holding up a hand with fingers extended, and point to each finger on the hand while explaining that each time a fingertip is touched,

an additional minute will be added to the "think spot" time period. The teacher explains, however, that during the actual implementation of the procedure, no verbal explanation will be provided.

6. A timer can be used to monitor the time period and to signal the end of the "think spot" time. About one minute per year of age is an appropriate length of time for younger children (e.g., preschool). Children nine years and up can spend longer periods (10–15 minutes). After the time period has ended, if students have behaved appropriately, they are allowed to rejoin the group activity without further comment or consequence.

7. During this procedure and while students are in the "think spot", it is important that the teacher does not engage in any verbal interaction with the student, and does not give verbal reminders about the extra minutes.

Troubleshooting: This procedure should be combined with a positive reinforcement program for appropriate behaviors. This procedure should be implemented immediately and consistently each time the student misbehaves. The student's behavior should be calm and under control before returning to the group.

"Sure I Will"   **E9 F9 E9 C9 T9 I7 V10 +9 T = 9.0**

Reference: Neville & Jenson, 1984.
Goal: The "Sure I Will" program is a simple procedure that teachers or parents can use to effectively deliver requests and commands and reinforce compliance.
Age Group: Preschool or Elementary.
Materials: None.
Steps:

1. This procedure includes the steps teachers can use to encourage students to comply with requests, by giving clear instructions, allowing the student a chance to comply without interrupting, reinforcing students who follow the initial request promptly, or implementing a brief consequence when students don't comply. This procedure is used to prevent coercive patterns that often occur between an adult and child when teachers or parents ask repeatedly or make threats. A positive "Sure I Will" incentive is used simultaneously with the precision command to reinforce behaviors that are incompatible with noncompliance.

2. A precision request is a standard approach to giving clear, effective instructions or commands. The "Sure I Will" precision request includes specific compliance cues used to encourage a positive response from students.

3. The teacher explains to the students that they can earn a reinforcer when they respond promptly to teacher requests. To earn the reinforcer, students must verbally respond with "Sure I will" and begin immediately to

comply after the first request. The teacher can demonstrate and practice the procedure with the students by giving them simple requests that they are likely to follow. The teacher identifies small reinforcers that students can earn (i.e. chips, M & Ms, animal cookies) or the reinforcer can be combined with a variable ratio reinforcement system such as a dot-to-dot with a surprise bag or spinner (see Spinners and Chartmoves).

4. The request sequence includes the following steps:
   (a) The teacher makes a calm request in a quiet voice beginning with the word "*Please*" (i.e. "Please pick up the toys"). The teacher allows 5 seconds before repeating the request. The student earns the reinforcer (or earns points toward the reinforcer) for responding to the initial "Please" instruction by saying, "*Sure I will*" and beginning to comply (i.e., begins to pick up toys).
   (b) If the student does not verbally respond or initiate a compliance behavior within 5 seconds of the "please" request, the teacher gives the second compliance cue, "*You need to*" (i.e., "You need to pick up the toys"). The teacher allows 5 seconds for the student to comply with the second request. The teacher provides verbal praise if the student complies, however, the student has missed the opportunity to earn the "Sure I will" reinforcer. If the student does not initiate the requested behavior within 5 seconds, the teacher implements a preplanned consequence such as a brief time-out (i.e., head down 1 minute, 3 minutes to a chair, move away from group for 3 minutes, etc.). For example, the teacher might say, "No, Joey, that's not picking up the toys. You need to sit in the chair."
   (c) After the consequence, the teacher repeats the request stating "*I need you to ...*" (i.e., I need you to pick up the toys) and the procedure is repeated.

Troubleshooting: It is important to have preplanned consequences and apply them consistently when a student continues to be noncompliant or the behavior problems escalate.

Therapeutic Storytelling **E9 F10 E8 C8 T8 I9 V9 +10 T = 8.8**
"Grizz the Bear"

Reference: Painter, Cook, & Silverman, 1999.
Goal: Therapeutic storytelling is a proactive technique that involves use of a teacher or counselor-told story that corresponds to the behavior problems that students are experiencing (e.g., noncompliance). In the story, the main character meets a wise person who teaches problem-solving steps and helps to identify alternative behaviors and increase student compliance.
Age Group: Preschool or Early Elementary.

Materials: Pictures of animals (e.g., a young bear and an older bear) or animal puppets.
Steps:

1. Therapeutic storytelling involves creating a story that corresponds to a particular behavior, feeling, or problem occurring in the classroom, with one or several different students. There are five steps to the story, which follow a problem-solving sequence.
    a. Introduce the main character (usually an animal or a child) that shares many characteristics with the students in the class. This character is presented as positive and likeable, however, has one small problem that needs to be resolved.
    b. Identify the problem. For example, the character may be a bear that sometimes doesn't listen to his teacher, and doesn't do what he is supposed to do.
    c. Talking to a wise person. For example, the character meets a wise old bear that helps him resolve his problem.
    d. Thinking of alternative approaches. The wise bear talks to him about why he should listen to his teacher and helps him think of different ways he can follow directions without getting upset.
    e. Summarizing the lesson.
2. The teacher identifies target problem behaviors (i.e., noncompliance) to address in the story. A variety of problems could be targeted in subsequent stories.
3. The teacher should clearly describe the positive behavior expected (compliance), and provide both positive and negative examples. Students can practice complying with teacher requests to do a variety of tasks such as, "Touch your nose," "Stand up," "Clap your hands," "Hold up a blue crayon," etc.
4. The teacher tells the students that they will hear a story about "Grizz the Bear", a young bear who would not listen or mind his Teacher Bear. The teacher can use animal pictures or puppets to represent the characters in the story. Since Grizz did not listen, he had many negative experiences. In the story, the teacher can describe Grizz's many adventures and problems because he didn't follow directions (e.g., getting stung by a bee, almost falling in a hole, getting muddy, losing his book, missing play-time, etc.). Then Grizz talks to a wise old Grandpa Bear (or any wise, older character) who helps him to understand that it just doesn't work for a young bear to try and be the boss of the class. Grizz the Bear is a very smart bear who learns this lesson quickly. The students are challenged to try and learn as quickly as Grizz does. After the story, the students can be questioned about the story and asked to retell parts.

5. The teacher may use prompts during the day to remind the students how to comply, such as stating, "I wonder what Grizz the Bear would do?"

Troubleshooting: To improve compliance, teachers should give clear, specific directions, avoid arguments, and allow enough time for students to comply (refer to the "Sure I Will" intervention in this chapter).

TASK ENGAGEMENT

"Beat the Buzzer"   E9 F9 E9 C9 T9 I9 V9 +9 T = 9.0

Reference: Adams & Drabman, 1995.

Goal: This intervention is a positive reinforcement contingency strategy to increase student on-task behavior and to decrease teacher attention to negative behaviors. "Beat the Buzzer" involves setting time limits for children to begin and then continue to work on assigned tasks until tasks are completed. Positive reinforcement is given to students who complete the tasks within the time limit.

Age Group: Elementary.

Materials: A timer or "buzzer", and student self-monitoring cards for each student. Each card is numbered (e.g., 1–10) with a smiley face or star next to each number.

Steps:

1. The teacher explains the student's responsibilities for the class period (e.g., reading, math, or spelling assignments, etc.). A list of tasks to be completed should also be written on the board. For young children, a picture depicting each activity can be posted on the board. The teacher should designate how many of the tasks need to be completed to "beat the buzzer." This number may vary depending on individual skill levels or length of time allowed.
2. This intervention can be used with all the students in the class or implemented on an individual basis for students who tend to dawdle or delay beginning tasks.
3. The teacher explains how many minutes the students have to complete the required tasks. For example, for younger children who are required to complete three or four worksheets or tasks during the work period, the teacher may choose to set the timer for 30 minutes.
4. After directions for completing the tasks are given, the teacher sets the timer for the desired number of minutes.
5. The students are instructed to begin working and keep working until the assignments are completed or until the timer goes off.

6. During the time period, the teacher may remind or prompt a student or class one time to "keep working" on their assignments.

7. When the timer "buzzes" or rings, the teacher checks to see which students have completed the required tasks. Those students who "beat the buzzer" by completing the assigned tasks may color in a smiley face or star on their self-monitoring cards. Another option is for the teacher to monitor the work completion by quickly walking around the classroom and placing a small sticker or drawing a colored star on the cards of those students who have the completed papers on their desks.

8. Failure to complete the tasks on time and "Beat the Buzzer" results in not coloring in a smiley face or not receiving a small sticker for that period.

9. The "Beat the Buzzer" strategy may be used for one specific activity or repeated several time periods per day.

10. Students who accumulate a designated number of smiley faces or stickers receive a reward at the end of the day (or week), such as extra playtime, small treat, 5 minutes to talk or read with a friend, a fun art activity, etc. The teacher may also decide to reward a student immediately after the buzzer goes off or on a daily basis.

Troubleshooting: If students consistently fail to "beat the buzzer", the time limit may be too short or the tasks may need to be broken into smaller chunks or steps (e.g., only require one task for each buzzer period).

Choice Cards   E9 F9 E8 C8 T7 I8 V9 +9 T = 8.5

Reference: Cosden, Gannon, & Haring, 1995.
Goal: Choice Cards are used as an antecedent-based intervention to increase task engagement by allowing students the opportunity to choose from a selection of academic activities.
Age Group: Elementary or Secondary.
Materials: Choice cards, Reward Cards.
Steps:

1. This procedure provides students with choice-making opportunities to choose from multiple academic tasks as well as choice of reinforcers. Choice-making is a proactive, self-management strategy that improves academic performance and productivity by allowing students to choose preferred activities.

2. The teacher instructs students that they can participate in the Choice Card activity contingent on following rules. Some days can be designated as "Choice" or some, "No-Choice" days. The teacher provides specific

instructions for completing various tasks prior to the independent work periods.

3. The teacher prepares several cards displaying pictures or photographs of preferred reinforcers (i.e., music—picture of a Walkman, game—picture of a checkers game, magazines—picture of various magazines, etc.). The reward card pictures can be placed on a poster and displayed in the room.

4. The teacher prepares several different task cards. Each card describes 1–4 assignments to be completed during regularly scheduled periods of independent seatwork. The assignments should reflect academic activities appropriate for the age and grade level and commensurate with normal class assignments in the content area. For example, a card might include the following four reading tasks: journal entry, workbook page, read a story, illustrate story. Task cards containing only one assignment might include the following different tasks: write spelling word 5 times each, make a sentence for each spelling word, decorate your spelling words, cut out letters from magazines and spell each word, put spelling words in alphabetical order, etc. An empty token circle is drawn next to each written task assignment.

5. Each task assignment card includes the instructions, "return to seat and begin assignments." Cards with more than one task should include some high preference tasks and some lower preference tasks. Task assignment cards can also be used as a visual reminder of the tasks to complete. As students complete each assignment, they mark a checkmark in the empty token circle.

6. During the Choice Cards activity, the teacher allows students to choose a task card from the selection of three or more cards spread out on a table, or placed in pockets at the front of the room. Students also choose from one of the picture reward cards posted in the room.

7. Once students have selected a Choice Card, they are to return to their seat and begin working on the assignments listed on that card. Each time they complete an assignment, students mark the empty token circle next to it.

8. When students have earned a predetermined number of checkmarks, they earn the reinforcer pictured on the Reward Card they selected.

Troubleshooting: Students should not take excess time to choose from the provided options. "No-Choice" days can be used as a consequence for students with inappropriate behaviors.

Computerized Self-Graphing   E9 F9 E9 C7 T7 I8 V9 +9 T = 8.7

Reference: Gunter, Miller, Venn, Thomas, & House, 2002.

Goal: Computerized self-graphing is a self-monitoring technique used to increase on-task behavior and work completion by use of a procedure for students to record and graph data regarding their academic progress and/or social behavior.
Age Group: Elementary or Secondary.
Materials: Classroom computer and software program (e.g., Windows). If a computer is not available, students can be taught to graph data on regular graph paper.
Steps:

1. The teacher identifies the student behavior to target for the self-graphing procedure. Target behaviors can include rates of work completion (i.e., number of math problems completed, number of pages read), academic progress (i.e., number of words spelled correctly each week, number of math problems completed correctly), on-task behaviors (i.e., number of on-task tally marks recorded during a class period), or social behaviors (i.e., number of positive statements made to peers).
2. To use the computerized graphing procedure, the teacher creates a folder for each student on the desktop of a classroom computer. If using "Windows", this is done by "right clicking" the computer mouse on the desktop window that opens a menu with a "New" option. When opened, "left click" on "Folder." A new folder will appear on the desktop. The words "New Folder" that appear under the folder icon, should be highlighted and the student's name should be typed to appear there instead.
3. Once student folders have been created, Excel files for different academic subjects can be opened, such as math, spelling, or reading. Each file should contain a teacher-generated Excel spreadsheet with an embedded graph for each academic or behavior target. The teacher determines the data entry dates and selects the cells when designing the graph.
4. A folder should be created on the designated computer's desktop for each student in the class who will be graphing their own behavior. To train students to self-graph, the teacher demonstrates the procedure of entering the data. The student should double-click first on the folder, then on the appropriate file. When the spreadsheet appears, the student enters the day's data value in the cell corresponding to the day's date. After entering the data, the student presses "Enter" and the data point should automatically be graphed. The graphic display can be presented as a line graph, or students may have the option to choose a bar graph. Students should have several opportunities to enter data with assistance, if needed, before doing so independently.
5. The teacher can provide the data for entry to the student (i.e., number of words read correctly), or a student can self-grade his or her own math sheets, or self-count the number of problems completed.

6. The computerized self-graphing can also be used as a method for teachers to analyze student performance at regular intervals. The teacher can insert a predesigned celebration line into the graph to determine if a student is meeting expected learning rates.

Troubleshooting: If a computer or software is not available, the students can self-graph behavior or performance by plotting the data on a piece of graph paper at regular intervals. Even younger children (first and second grade) can be taught to self-graph with simple bar or line graphs.

Dots for Motivation   **E9 F9 E10 C9 T9 I9 V9 +10 T = 9.3**

Reference: Doyle, Jenson, Clark, & Gates, 1999.
Goal: The Dot program is an effective motivation system used to increase work completion by use of a reinforcer that can later be exchanged to avoid or skip some assigned work.
Age Group: Elementary or Secondary.
Materials: Small colored stick-on dots used to mark folder files (can be purchased in office-supply stores).
Steps:

1. The dot program can be used as a reinforcement program to increase work completion in any subject. The dots can be used to skip math problems, written assignments, spelling drills, or homework assignments. It can be used with individual students or a small group of students who are nonmotivated, unproductive, and who do not usually attempt or complete daily assignments.
2. The sticky dots are available in different sizes and colors, usually in sheets of 20 or so dots per sheet. The teacher cuts the sheets, so that each dot is separate, but still attached to the backing paper.
3. The teacher explains the procedure to the students, telling them that they can earn dots when they are on-task and working. Each student is given an envelope that is taped on the side of their desk in which to store the dots. During the class period, when students are asked to work independently on daily assignments, the teacher circulates around the room monitoring student behavior and task completion. The teacher rewards students with a dot when they are on-task and working on the assignment. The teacher may also choose to reward a dot each time a student completes a set number of problems (e.g., one dot for each five problems completed) or when the student completes the entire worksheet. The students place the dots in their envelope. When they encounter a problem, sentence, or question they cannot or do not want to complete, they can use one of their

dots to skip the problem by sticking it next to the problem or question. This would mean they get a free problem they do not have to do. In other words, students work to get out of work!

4. The teacher can choose from several variations on the dot program. Larger dots can be used and cut in half, and students must use both halves to skip a problem. Different colored dots can also be used for different subjects. Two or more dots can be required to skip longer problems or test questions. Students can save up dots to use on a later assignment or dots can be saved to use for a choice of activity or tangible reinforcers. Or, on a larger scale, dots can be given after completing several assignments and a dot can be used to skip a future assignment (similar to a no homework coupon).

5. The teacher will need to evaluate current rates of work completion to determine the desired ratio of dots to work completed. At first, it is important that students don't wait too long for a dot. As students increase their rate of work completion, teachers can increase the ratio or reward half or quarter dots instead of whole dots.

Troubleshooting: The teacher may need to initial each dot, to prevent older students from buying their own. The teacher may also need to establish rules about students not giving or taking dots from other students.

Homework Teams   **E8 F9 E9 C8 T8 I9 V10 +9 T = 8.7**

Reference: Olympia, Sheridan, Jenson, & Andrews, 1994.
Goal: The Homework Team strategy is a group contingency procedure used to improve work completion and accuracy rates of daily assignments.
Age Group: Secondary.
Materials: Team scorecards, a class scoreboard with the name of each team and a space next to the name to place stickers, stickers, raffle tickets, and raffle prizes.
Steps:

1. The Homework Teams consist of small groups of students of mixed abilities who work cooperatively to encourage work completion to receive a group contingency. Optimal group size is 3–5 students per group. The teacher may group students according to seating arrangements so that members are seated near one another.

2. The Homework Team strategy can be used when students are given an assignment that they are required to complete in class or take home and complete as homework, such as a daily math assignment. Each team establishes a goal or criteria that they will work individually to meet (e.g., Team Goal = 90% or more assignments completed with 90% accuracy).

3. Each team member is assigned a team role, including coach, scorekeeper, manager, and pinch hitter. Team assignments may be rotated on a weekly basis so that each student has an opportunity to participate in each assignment. Prior to beginning the Homework Teams, the teacher instructs the class through direct instruction, modeling, and practice in filling out the scorecards and the role and function of each team assignment.

4. Each team meets together briefly (5-minutes) at the beginning of class. During the team meeting, the coach verbally prompts the group and reviews the daily team goal.

5. The scorekeeper counts the number of assignments completed from the previous day and completes a team scorecard. On the scorecard should be written the team name, the date of each assignment, and the percentage of assignments completed by each date. For example, if all team members completed the assignment, the score would equal 100%. If 4 of 5 team members completed the assignment and one team member only finished 50%, the group average would equal 90% (450/500). The scorekeeper collects the completed assignments and turns them in to the teacher.

6. The manager totals the daily team score and declares a win or loss depending on whether the team matches or exceeds its daily goal. The manager also posts a win sticker publicly on the class scoreboard if the team has matched or exceeded its daily goal and distributes raffle tickets to team members who completed the assignment.

7. The pinch hitter fills in if another member of the team is absent or unavailable.

8. Raffle tickets are placed in a container for a once-a-week drawing, held by the teacher.

9. Teams can earn group reinforcement (small treat, soda, free time, no homework coupons, etc.) when they reach a specified number of stickers on the class scoreboard.

Troubleshooting: The teacher may wish to award bonus points for accuracy of completed work. Team goals may be teacher selected or team selected, however, students may tend to select lower performance goals. The teacher may choose to require a minimum performance goal of 80% for all groups.

Probability Chips   E9 F9 E8 C8 T8 I8 V9 +9 T = 8.5

Reference: Martens, Ardoin, Hilt, Lannie, Panahon, & Wolfe, 2002.
Goal: Probability Chips is a game-like activity based on a lottery system in which chips are placed in a bag and students who complete work earn the opportunity to receive reinforcers.
Age Group: Elementary or Secondary.

Materials: Red and white chips, worksheets (i.e., math sheets), small slips of paper with easy problems, and back-up reinforcers.

Steps:

1. This activity involves an intermittent schedule of reinforcement to increase academic responding and work completion. It can be conducted during a specific class period or subject in which students are required to work independently on worksheets or assignments (i.e., math, spelling, phonics, etc.).

2. The teacher explains that the students will be participating in a class game in which they will have the opportunity to earn reinforcers. The teacher can select the reinforcers or have students choose from a list of reinforcers. Reinforcers can include small items, snacks, "good work" certificates, or activity reinforcers.

3. The teacher explains the concept of probability by demonstrating with small colored plastic chips (i.e., red and white) placed in a bag. For example, if three red chips and one white chip are placed in the bag, the probability of choosing a red chip out of the bag is three of four, or 75%. If four red chips and no white chips are placed in a bag, the probability of choosing a red chip out of the bag is four of four, or 100%.

4. Each day, before students begin to work on assignments independently, the teacher informs the students what the exchange rate is for the day and places the required number of red and white chips in the bag. The teacher restates the chances of drawing a red chip that day. The teacher can select various probabilities each day, so that the schedule of reinforcement is intermittent, beginning with a higher ratio of red to white, and systematically lowering the ratio over a period of time.

5. During the instructional and independent work periods, students are given work to complete (i.e., math worksheets based on appropriate instructional level). Students are instructed that when they complete the entire worksheet, they can exchange the completed paper for a slip of easy problems (i.e., a small slip of paper with 4–5 easy problems). Students who complete more than one worksheet per class period can earn an easy problem slip for each paper completed.

6. At the end of the period the teacher or a student draws a colored chip from the bag. If the chip drawn is red, students who have completed easy problem slips can exchange the easy problem slip for the back-up reinforcer. If a white chip is drawn, students cannot earn the back-up reinforcer, however, they can save the easy problem slips for another day.

Troubleshooting: The teacher can modify the activity several ways, to have some no-lottery days, to require that students have a specified number of correct problems to earn an easy problem slip (i.e., 85% accuracy), or require that students earn two or more easy problem slips before they can receive the reinforcer.

Response Cards   **E7 F9 E9 C9 T8 I8 V9 +9 T = 8.8**

Reference: Gardner, Heward, & Grossi, 1994.

Goal: This intervention is a method used to increase active student participation and on-task behavior (writing responses to questions) during whole-class instruction periods. Use of response cards allows all students to participate and increases the frequency of active student responding. It also provides immediate reinforcement and feedback to students.

Age Group: Elementary or Secondary.

Materials: Response cards (a white laminated card) for each student in the class, dry-erase markers, and small cloth or old sock used to clean the response card. Response cards can be made by cutting 23 cm by 30 cm (or any size desired) cardstock or poster board and laminating them. White laminated particleboard may also be used, if available.

Steps:

1. Each student is provided with an individual response card and dry-erase marker. Students will also need something to use for cleaning the card, such as a wet paper towel, or an old sock or piece of cloth.

2. The teacher instructs the students on how to respond to questions by using the response cards. Practice sessions can be conducted so that students are familiar with the response card procedure.

3. During the lesson, when the teacher asks a question, all students are instructed to write their response on the response card, rather than the teacher calling on individual students to raise their hand and answer the question. Response cards can be used for any subject or grade level, examples are: answers to math problems, math symbols, letters or numbers, spelling or vocabulary words, test review, and social studies and science questions (e.g., facts and definitions). The procedure is (a) the teacher asks a question (e.g., "what is 2 plus 5?" or "what is paper made from?"), (b) students write the answer on the card and, (c) students hold the card up for the teacher to see.

4. After each question, the teacher visually scans all of the response cards held up by the students and provides praise or corrective feedback. If every student has the correct answer, the teacher might say, "Good class, 2 plus 5 equals 7." If some of the responses are incorrect, the teacher provides corrective feedback by stating, "I see that many of you have 7 as the answer. That is correct, 2 plus 5 equals 7." If none of the answers are correct, the teacher states, "I don't see any correct answers. The correct answer is 7, 2 plus 5 equals 7."

5. Low-achieving students who are reluctant to participate by answering
    questions orally may be more likely to respond by using response cards,
    because making a mistake may not be as embarrassing. When giving
    corrective feedback, the teacher responds to the entire class, without
    correcting individual students.

Troubleshooting: Pacing is important, so that most students have enough time to
write responses, but not spend too much time waiting for other students to write
their response. Response cards are best used with questions that can be answered
that require minimal writing (e.g., one-word or short responses).

Spinners and Chartmoves   **E9 F9 E9 C9 T8 I10 V9 +10 T = 9.1**

Reference: Jenson, Neville, Sloane, & Morgan, 1982 and Peine, Darvish, Blakelock, Osborne, & Jenson, 1998.
Goal: This intervention involves the use of two components, chartmoves and spinners to provide a practical contingency management system to increase on-task
behavior and work completion.
Age Group: Elementary or Secondary.
Materials: A chart containing a picture with 30 to 100 dots for each student, a
spinner consisting of an unevenly divided circle with each section referring to a
different reinforcer, and invisible marker pens (if available).
Steps:

1. The Spinners and Chartmoves intervention combines a self-recording
    system with a variable schedule of reinforcement. Students have the op-
    portunity to earn reinforcers for exhibiting on-task behavior and/or for
    completing schoolwork. The teacher first determines the target behaviors
    for which students will earn a chart move and explains to the students
    that they will be able to connect a dot on their chart when they exhibit
    the target behaviors. Generally, only one target behavior is designated at
    a time. For example, the student is allowed to connect one dot for each
    completed math paper or the student is allowed to connect one dot for
    remaining in seat during each 15-minute period. Students can also be
    given the opportunity to earn more than one dot per period or several dots
    throughout the day.
2. The teacher prepares a chart for each student. Charts can be made from
    a student's favorite picture (i.e., rocket, racecar, animal, etc.) by placing
    30–100 dots around the outline (or a dot-to-dot page can be used). Charts
    can also be designed like a series of connected squares going up and
    down the page and students color in one square each time they earn a
    chartmove. Reinforcers are determined by larger dots randomly placed
    among the smaller dots. To create an element of suspense, invisible ink

can be used to randomly mark the reinforcer dots or squares with hidden stars, so that the student does not know when he or she will connect with a reinforcer dot or square.

3. The teacher also creates a spinner that can be used by all students. The spinner consists of a circle divided into unequal sections (about 5 sections). On each section can be written a specific reinforcer or numbers can be used which correspond to five different reinforcers. The spinner is used to indicate which reinforcer will be given randomly. Typically, the spinner contains four low value reinforcers and one high value reinforcer. The low value reinforcers correspond to the larger sections on the spinner.

4. At the end of each period students who meet the predetermined criteria are allowed to "take a chart move." The student connects one dot to the next dot and marks the dot with a special marker used to reveal invisible ink. If the revealed dot has a hidden star, the student is allowed to spin the spinner for a reinforcer. The student receives the reinforcer corresponding to the number or prize on which the spinner lands. If the revealed dot has no star, no spinner reinforcement is given.

5. When the chart is completed, the student can receive a bonus prize and charts can be publicly posted or sent home with a positive note of accomplishment.

Troubleshooting: Chartmoves should be dated and initialed by the teacher to keep track of progress and to prevent students from inaccurate recording. Students who attempt to manipulate the spinner to a more desirable reinforcer can be told to close their eyes while spinning.

Chapter 6

Interventions for Academic Problems

The interventions in this chapter are designed to enhance academic skills in the areas of reading, written language, spelling, math, and organization skills. Many students with behavior problems also exhibit low academic skills and poor academic performance—either because their behavior has interfered with the learning of new skills, because they have learning disabilities, or both. Without basic academic skills, these students are destined for failure. Early identification of students who are at-risk for academic difficulties and behavioral problems and providing strategic intervention to address these problems is particularly important in helping them to achieve a successful school outcome.

Effective instruction is essential to children's success in learning academic skills and most teachers are well prepared with the academic curriculum and teaching skills to provide this instruction. While most children (about 80–85%) respond favorably to basic academic instruction, a significant number of children including nondisabled learners have not mastered the important academic skills needed to function successfully as adults by high school graduation. In practice, teachers need to incorporate a large repertoire of strategies and techniques to meet the needs of these students. Effective teachers utilize varied instructional activities, a range of grouping arrangements, quick instructional pacing, and active student involvement to increase the academic growth of both high and low achieving students.

The interventions described below are designed to supplement the repertoire of instructional strategies and techniques, not to supplant the existing classroom curriculum. Tailoring academic instruction to meet the individual needs of students with learning and behavior problems may require extra teacher support and individual guided assistance, as well as personalized adaptations to curriculum and assignments. However, most of the interventions presented in this chapter are practical and low maintenance. They may be incorporated within a general education classroom to benefit students with learning difficulties while helping other low achievers and without detriment to average or high achieving students. They can be incorporated into a typical instructional period (20–50 minutes), as part of a daily or weekly schedule.

Effective academic interventions incorporate the principles of (1) quick pacing and including a variety of instructional activities, (2) high levels of student engagement, (3) challenging standards of achievement at individualized levels, (4) self-verbalization methods, and (5) physical or visual representations of difficult concepts. They are designed to increase student active participation and time on-task, increase student motivation and interest, and provide immediate feedback and reinforcement. They utilize well-established strategies such as peer-tutoring, self-monitoring, and positive reinforcement contingencies.

A critical step in prevention and reduction of behavior problems is helping students with behavior disorders develop academic competence. Unless academic deficits are remediated and these students are successful in their efforts, they will continue to become frustrated, will develop a negative perception of school, and will most likely act-out or dropout. It is our hope that the academic interventions listed below will provide some practical instructional strategies for educators faced with this difficult challenge.

READING—SIGHT WORDS

Keywords   **E9 F9 E8 C9 T7 I8 V8 +9 T = 8.3**

Reference: Uberti, Scruggs, & Mastropieri, 2003.
Goal: Keywords is a method of instruction in which students are taught sight words by use of a similar sounding keyword as a verbal and visual cue.
Age Group: Elementary or Secondary.
Materials: List of vocabulary words to be learned, vocabulary cards with pictures of keywords.
Steps:

1. The keyword method is an application of mnemonic instruction in which a concrete, acoustically similar word is selected for students to use to help learn and remember the meaning of an unfamiliar vocabulary word.
2. The teacher and/or students can create keywords to use with any vocabulary list or sight word list they are learning. The teacher previews the reading material (stories, chapter in textbook, chapter books, etc.) and determines a list of important and challenging vocabulary words for

students to learn. Students can be given a pretest before the vocabulary words are selected to determine which words they already know.

3. The teacher creates a list of the unknown words and their definitions (i.e., abandon—to leave behind, inquisitive—asking many questions, curious, etc.). The teacher then examines each vocabulary word and recodes the word to an acoustically similar, but familiar, concrete word. This becomes the keyword. For example, "abandon" sounds like "band" and "inquisitive" sounds like "quiz." Band and quiz are the keywords.

4. The keyword is then related to the vocabulary word in an interactive picture using the definition. For example, "inquisitive" can be illustrated as a teacher giving a "quiz" with many questions, and "abandon" is illustrated as a band with people leaving their instruments behind. The teacher can use clip art to create pictures to go with the vocabulary word and its' definition or ask students to illustrate.

5. The teacher instructs the students how to use keywords by explaining it is a new way to help them remember the definitions of some new vocabulary words. The teacher shows the students the vocabulary cards by reading the words one at a time, then reads and points to the keyword and the picture, telling the students it is a "cue word" to help them remember the definition. The teacher should practice each vocabulary word, keyword, and definition several times with the students. Word cards with pictures can be posted on the board or placed in a folder for students to practice individually.

6. Students are taught three steps when using the keyword method. First, students learn the keyword—students are instructed to think of the keyword when they hear the new word (i.e., "Think of a quiz when you hear the word "inquisitive." "Quiz sounds like inquisitive and it is easily pictured."). Second, students are to remember the picture of the keyword and the definition of the vocabulary word interacting together—students visualize the picture (i.e., "Visualize a teacher giving a quiz with many questions."). Third, when asked the definition, students are to think of the keyword and what is happening in the picture to retrieve the information from their memory—they think about what was happening in the picture and it reminds them of the definition.

Troubleshooting: It may be difficult to identify a keyword for every vocabulary word, however, the keyword does not need to have a similar meaning—just sound acoustically similar. It is important to incorporate the definition of the vocabulary word into the visual picture.

Pupil-Made Picture Prompts   **E9 F9 E9 C8 T9 I7 V9 +9 T = 8.3**

Reference: Rivera, Koorland, & Fueyo, 2002.

Goal: Pupil-Made Picture Prompts are an effective and direct method to assist students in learning basic sight words by creating their own picture prompts materials through illustration of word meanings.

Age Group: Elementary.

Materials: Index cards, colored markers, crayons, or colored pencils.

Steps:

1. The Pupil-Made Picture Prompts are a technique used to increase reading fluency and discrimination of basic sight words. Sight words generally include a lot of words recognized without phonetic analysis. Once learned, basic sight words can facilitate fluency of other reading in context.

2. The teacher determines the sight word list to use based on grade and reading level of each student. Teachers may choose to select words from previously identified basic vocabulary lists essential for reading (e.g., The Dolch Basic Sight Word List, Fry List, etc.). The teacher also determines the number of words to target in each set of words (e.g., 7–15 unknown words).

3. The teacher or teacher aide writes a word from the first set on a large index card using a black marker. Words can also be computer generated and printed. The teacher reads each word aloud to the student and discusses its' meaning. The teacher asks the student to draw and color a picture that best illustrates each word next to the printed word. The student-drawn pictures represent stimulus prompts to set the occasion for a correct response. The student creates an illustration for each word in the set.

4. A duplicate of each index card, displaying the word alone should also be available. The word-only cards represent a fading procedure that removes the addition of the prompting stimulus (picture cards).

5. The picture word cards are shuffled before every session. The flashcards are shown to the student by the teacher, a teacher-aide, or another student, and the student is given 5 seconds to say the word correctly. Words said incorrectly or not said within 5 seconds are read to the student and placed back in the deck. At the end of each session the student practices reading the word-only cards as a prompt fading step and to probe sight word accuracy.

6. When students have mastered most of the words in the first set (85–90%), they can create illustrations for the next set of words, and so on until they have completed the entire list. Words not mastered can be included with the next set. A review of all words should be conducted over time.

Troubleshooting: An illustrated model may be provided to the student in the initial steps, to show the student what general steps are expected, however, illustrations should be chosen by the student. Some basic words may be more difficult to illustrate (i.e., is, were, when, etc.) and illustrations may need to embed the word in context (e.g., The dog *is* black).

Reading Racetracks   **E9 F9 E8 C8 T7 I9 V9 +9 T = 8.6**

Reference: Rinaldi, Sells, & McLaughlin, 1997.
Goal: Reading Racetracks is an intervention used to practice sight word acquisition and fluency that employs error correction, timing, and drill and practice.
Age Group: Elementary.
Materials: Sight word reading lists, stopwatch, reading racetrack sheets, data collection sheets.
Steps:

1. Reading Racetracks is a procedure that allows students to actively practice reading skills through drill and practice, through timed readings, and student self-charting. It is a strategy that can be used with individual students or as part of a class-wide peer tutoring strategy.
2. The teacher determines the sight word list to use based on grade and reading level of each student. Teachers may select words from previously identified basic vocabulary lists essential for reading (e.g., The Dolch Basic Sight Word List, Fry Word List, etc.) or from a prepared reading curriculum.
3. The teacher creates reading racetrack drill sheets designed to resemble an automotive racetrack (oval-shaped). Each racetrack sheet contains about 28–30 cells. In the cells are written from 7–10 different vocabulary words repeated in random order to fill each cell. A new racetrack is designed for each set of 7–10 words. A review racetrack containing all 28–30 different words should also be created.
4. The teacher introduces the reading racetrack and instructs the student to read the words around the track as quickly as possible when they hear the cue, "On your mark, get set, go!" The teacher allows one minute before saying, "Stop!" The teacher keeps track of the number of words read by placing a tally mark on the sheet each time the student completes a full circle around the track. When the teacher says stop, the teacher or student marks the word just read.
5. Upon completion of each 1-minute timing period, the student counts up the total number of words read and self-records the data on a data collection sheet that includes the date, a space for the number of words read, and a space to record the number of errors.
6. At this point, the teacher may use a direct instruction procedure to teach or review any words missed by the student. This procedure includes first modeling the correct pronunciation of the word, saying the word with the

student, allowing the student to read the word independently, and asking the student to reread the word correctly.

7. Students should remain on a given racetrack until they reach a specified criterion (e.g., 90% of words read correctly per minute with zero errors, or until they have completed five sessions on the racetrack).

8. To use reading racetracks on a class wide basis, students can practice with partners taking turns timing each other. This intervention requires less than 10 minutes of daily classroom time if conducted with class wide peer tutoring.

Troubleshooting: The review racetrack can be used as an efficient initial assessment tool as well as a cumulative assessment review. If students are able to read the words on the review racetrack at a target rate, they can move to the next review racetrack until reaching a point at which they are unable to read at an acceptable rate.

Self-monitoring Sight Words   **E9 F9 E9 C9 T6 I9 V9 +9 T = 8.3**

Reference: Lalli & Shapiro, 1990.
Goal: This intervention includes the use of audiotaped words and self-monitoring to increase the acquisition of sight word vocabulary in students with reading skills deficits.
Age Group: Elementary or Secondary.
Materials: Sight word lists, audiotapes of word lists, tape recorder.
Steps:

1. This strategy provides students with the opportunity to self-correct reading of sight word vocabulary lists. Students listen to the correct pronunciation of each word on an audiotape after they read the word, and self-monitor whether or not they read the word correctly. This procedure is used to increase sight word vocabulary through practice, modeling, and increased academic engagement. Although teacher time is required initially to create the tape-recorded word lists, student time required is minimal.

2. The teacher creates several word lists containing 15–20 sight words selected from the basal series or other vocabulary list appropriate for individual student reading levels. Students should be pre-assessed to determine known and unknown words and to select a starting point that will vary for each student.

3. The teacher creates an audiotape of each word list containing the correct pronunciation of each word as it is written on a corresponding worksheet. A 5-second pause is recorded before each word is pronounced. Each word list can be repeated several times so that the total length of time on each audiotape is about 5 minutes. Each word list should be recorded on a

separate tape and labeled and numbered so that students can easily select
the correct tape from a box or container placed near the tape recorder.

4. The teacher instructs students on use of the tape recorder before they begin
   the self-monitoring procedure. The teacher explains that each student will
   have an opportunity to practice reading his or her word list for 5-minutes.
   After students complete their 5-minute session, they are instructed to
   rewind the tape and place it back in the container.

5. This activity can be conducted in a separate location in the classroom
   while the other students are working independently. Students can take
   turns reading with the tape recorder. Headphones can be used to reduce
   distractions.

6. Students are instructed to take their assigned word list, sit at the tape
   recorder, and push the play button. The student is given 5-seconds to read
   the word before the taped voice is heard giving the correct pronunciation.
   After reading each word, the student waits and listens to the correct
   pronunciation of the word. If the word is read correctly, students are to
   put a plus sign after the word on their list. If the word is read incorrectly,
   students are to put a minus sign after the word on their list. At the end
   of each session, students tally the number of words read correctly. This
   provides students with an accurate measure of how many words were
   read correctly.

7. Prior to beginning this intervention, the teacher demonstrates how to
   self-monitor, allowing students to practice the procedure, and providing
   corrective feedback if needed.

8. When students have reached a criterion of 80% accuracy (i.e., 12 of 15
   words) on two consecutive sessions, they may select the next word list
   and tape to use.

Troubleshooting: Self-graphing of daily progress may increase the effectiveness.
The addition of external contingent rewards can also be used (i.e., 11 or more
pluses = a piece of candy).

Taped-Words   **E9 F9 E8 C7 T6 I8 V9 +9 T = 8.2**

Reference: Sterling, Robinson, & Skinner, 1997.
Goal: This intervention is a self-management strategy used to increase sight word
reading in students with reading skills deficits.
Age Group: Elementary or Secondary.
Materials: Sight word lists, audiotape of word lists, tape recorder.
Steps:

1. The Taped-Words strategy provides students with opportunities to model
   a tape-recorded reading of word lists. The tape-recorded list of words is

played and students are instructed to read the list aloud with the tape. Modeling is an effective way to increase sight word vocabulary and with Taped-Words, the rapid pacing also increases on-task and learning rates. Although teacher time is required to create the tape-recorded word lists, the Taped-Word intervention requires only a few minutes of academic learning time for each student.

2. The teacher selects a list of sight words appropriate for a student or group of students. Words selected can be unknown but within the students' reading ability. From a larger pool of words, a list of 10–20 words is assigned to each taped set. Words can be grouped by phonetic or other categories. Words can be grouped by phonetic or other categories. Worksheets containing each 10–20-word set are constructed for students to read as they listen along with the taped words.

3. For each worksheet, the teacher prepares a corresponding audiotape by reading the words in sequence into a tape recorder. Words can be read at both rapid rates (1-word each second) and slow rates (1-word each 5 seconds).

4. When students practice reading with Taped-Words they are instructed to listen to the audiotape and to read the worksheet aloud with the corresponding tape. Students should practice reading the word lists at the slow rate, and then the rapid rate for each session. Sessions can be repeated several times.

5. During assessment sessions, students are asked to read from the word lists without the audiotape. When students are able to read 80–90% of the words accurately within three seconds, a new list is presented.

Troubleshooting: For each set of words, additional worksheets can be prepared with the words listed in a different sequence to prevent students from responding to a memorized sequence of words.

READING—PHONICS

Word Boxes   **E6 F7 E8 C7 T6 I8 V8 +9 T = 7.8**

Reference: Joseph, 2002.
Goal: Word Boxes involve a phonic approach to help readers make connections between sound and print.
Age Group: Elementary.
Materials: Magnetic Board or individual dry erase boards for each student, with a drawn rectangle divided into boxes according to the number of sounds in a presented word, small magnets (used for counters) for each student, magnetic

letters, pictures representing each word (optional), dry erase markers, and tissue paper (to clean dry erase boards).
Steps:

1. Word boxes consist of connected boxes created by drawing a rectangle on a magnetic board or a small dry erase board. The rectangle is divided into sections that correspond to the number of sounds heard in a word. For example, words that include three distinct phonemes (e.g., sit, hit, fit, etc.) would be represented by a rectangle with two vertical lines to create three connected boxes. If desired, a picture representing the word can be placed above the rectangle. Magnetic word boxes are engaging because students manipulate the materials and make frequent responses rather than completing pencil and paper worksheets.
2. Word Boxes can be used on a class wide basis, with the teacher providing direct instruction, in small groups, or on an individual basis in a peer tutoring procedure.
3. Each student is given a magnetic board and counters (small magnets can be used as counters). The number of counters corresponds to the number of boxes in the rectangle. In the first phase, the teacher instructs the student in how to segment each sound in the word. The teacher models the task by saying the word slowly and placing a counter in each divided section as the sound is articulated.
4. Next, students place their counters in each divided section as the teacher says the word slowly. Students may also respond chorally as they place counters in each section.
5. The next step involves letter-to-sound matching. The students as a class, a small group, or individually, simultaneously say the sounds of the word slowly and place magnetic letters in each divided section of the rectangle.
6. The final phase involves students writing the letters of the word in the connected boxes as they slowly repeat each sound. Tissue paper is used to wipe the letters off of the board when each word is completed.
7. Once students understand the one-to-one correspondence between letters and sounds, the sections of the rectangle can be represented as drawn dotted lines and then removed altogether to fade out the word boxes.

Troubleshooting: Students should have several opportunities to practice each step on every presented word. Students should complete all three steps—segment sounds, letter-to-sound matching, and writing letters before moving on to a new word.

Word Sorts   E9 F9 E8 C7 T7 I8 V9 +9 T = 8.5

Reference: Joseph, 2002.

Goal: Word Sorts are a procedure to help students increase reading skills by categorizing words that share common phonological and orthographic components.
Age Group: Elementary.
Materials: Index cards with sets of words printed on them that share common spelling or sound patterns, colored chips for each student, list of words the teacher will read out loud, prepared work sheets with selected category words printed horizontally across the top of the paper.
Steps:

1. The teacher identifies reading words to use for the Word Sorts. Groups of words are selected that share common spelling or sound patterns. Two or more sets of words (categories) are needed. For example, the sets might include these three category words; sit, sat, and set.

2. Each student has one word from each set to serve as a category word. The printed category words (on index cards) are placed horizontally on the students' desks. For example, these three words would be placed across the top of the desk:

Sit   Sat   Set

3. Each student also has a deck of note cards containing words that share the sound patterns of the category words (e.g., fit, bit, hit, cat, bat, hat, bet, pet, met, etc.). The rest of the cards are shuffled and sorted below the appropriate category words. Students pick up each printed note card and place it below the matching category word according to the shared spelling pattern. After completing the task, students can practice reading each list and referring to the category word to self-check. Teachers can also check for accuracy by scanning the card layout on students' desks, and provide corrective feedback, if needed.

4. Another word sort procedure can be used on a classwide basis. Each student is provided with the category words printed on note cards and a small colored chip.

5. The printed category note cards are placed horizontally on the students' desks as described above. The teacher says a word aloud, and each student places a chip below the category word that sounds similar to the word read aloud. The teacher can quickly scan the students' responses to check for accuracy and provide corrective feedback, if needed. Then, another word is introduced. The student moves the chip to place it below the correct category word. The process should be repeated until several words for each category are presented.

6. Students can also practice writing spelling words read aloud by the teacher by writing each word below the appropriate category word that is printed across the top of a sheet of paper.

Troubleshooting: This procedure can also be used for students to categorize words by different features (e.g., beginning consonants, blends, or conceptual (meaning) sorts. The number of categories can vary but if the task or concept is new or too difficult, the procedure should initially include only two categories and the number of words presented increased gradually.

READING—FLUENCY AND COMPREHENSION

Cooperative Story Mapping   **E9 F9 E8 C8 T9 I7 V9 + 9 T = 8.7**

Reference: Mathes, Fuchs, & Fuchs, 1997.
Goal: Story Mapping is a technique used to increase students' reading comprehension by participating in a cooperative activity to analyze and discuss stories using a graphic organizer.
Age Group: Elementary.
Materials: Story Maps, reading books. A sample Story Map is listed in Appendix A.
Steps:

1. This activity can be conducted with small groups or with an entire classroom. During Cooperative Story Mapping all students read the same story. The teacher may select stories from the reading basal text, or from selected children's literature. The chosen stories should be at the appropriate reading level for most students in the class or group.
2. Cooperative Story Mapping consists of partner or individual reading of the selected story, skimming it for essential story elements, mapping the essential elements on a Story Map sheet in a cooperative group, followed by teacher directed discussion with the class.
3. The teacher can create a Story Map similar to the example in the appendix or adapted as desired. The Story Map is a graphic representation or visual schema of the story elements, including main character(s), setting, problem or conflict, main events, and story outcome or ending. Creating boxes or graphic organizers around each element provides students with a visual representation.
4. The teacher discusses and demonstrates how to use the Story Map by selecting a story in which the elements are easy to identify, modeling the procedure for the students and asking students to practice analyzing a story together.
5. The story elements are defined as:
    (a) Main character—Who or What the story is about (animal or person(s).
    (b) Setting—Where the story happens (place and time).
    (c) Problem—What the main character must solve or do.

     (d) Main events—What are the important things that happen in the story?

     (e) Story outcome—How the problem is resolved (or not).

6. The teacher assigns students to cooperative groups of 4–5 students. Students can be assigned randomly, or each group can be composed of students with varying skill levels.

7. The students first read the story independently or with a partner. When the story has been read by all of the students, they map the stories in their assigned cooperative learning group. During the first two minutes of the activity, the students skim the story silently, then for the next 15–20 minutes they complete the map in their group. Groups must decide collectively on the best answers and write them on the Story Map. Every student in the group is assigned as a "leader" for one story element (i.e., main character, setting, etc.).

8. The leader for each element follows a set routine consisting of telling the answer and evidence, asking other students for input, discussing with the group, recording the answer, and reporting to the class during the class discussion.

9. After the groups have completed the Story Maps, the teacher leads a class wide discussion of the elements, asking groups to share their answers with the class.

Troubleshooting: Students may need to be taught specific rules on how to "get along" in a cooperative group by taking turns, disagreeing politely, allowing each member to speak, paying attention to each other, and offering encouragement. The teacher may need to monitor group participation to provide assistance if needed.

Partner Reading   **E9 F9 E8 C8 T9 I7 V9 +9 T = 8.6**

Reference: Mastropieri, Scruggs, Mohler, Beranek, Spencer, Boon, & Talbott, 2001.

Goal: Partner Reading is a class wide peer tutoring strategy in which students work in pairs to listen to each other read and ask questions to promote reading comprehension.

Age Group: Secondary (see Story Sharing intervention for elementary students).

Materials: Reading materials, folders, and Partner Reading Checklist.

Steps:

1. Partner Reading is a class wide peer tutoring model used with middle school students, in which all students within a single class are paired to tutor one another to provide increased opportunity to practice. Partner Reading can be implemented for 15–30 minutes daily during the regularly assigned English or Reading periods. Reading materials can include stories or text within the reading range of most students.

2. To pair students, the teacher ranks students from highest to lowest performance in reading levels, splitting the list in the middle to form two lists (highest half and lowest half). The teacher then pairs the top-ranked highest reader with the top-ranked lowest reader, the second-ranked highest reader with the second-ranked lowest reader, and so on until each student in the class is paired with another student of adjacent ability. The teacher can also make adjustments in pairing based on students' social behavior and ability to work together. The stronger reader can be assigned as "coach" and the weaker reader assigned as the "reader."

3. The teacher introduces tutoring roles, rules, and materials to the students. Students are told that when they enter the room they should pick up their tutoring folders and sit by their reading partner. Folders contain reading materials (stories and checklists). Students are instructed to talk in quiet voices, and to cooperate with their partners.

4. During partner reading students will complete three tasks, (a) partner reading and error correction, (b) story retell, and (c) paragraph summarization. The Partner Reading Checklist provides a checklist for students to follow and check off as each task is completed. The teacher provides an opportunity for students to practice each step. During the first 5 minutes, the first reader reads orally until a timer goes off. The first reader is the stronger reader in the pair. During the oral reading activity, tutors provide corrective feedback when necessary. To provide feedback, the tutor identifies an incorrectly read word, prompts the correct response, states the correct word, and prompts re-reading. While learning the steps, students are asked to make errors for their partners in order to practice the correction procedure. After the first reader has read, the timer is reset and the second student reads the same passage for the next 5 minutes.

5. After students understand the partner reading and error correction procedure, they are taught to ask questions to help them understand and remember what they read. The teacher demonstrates that after reading for 5 minutes, partners ask the reader to retell what they have read by asking, "What was the first thing you learned?" and "What happened next?" Students then ask the reader to summarize the most important facts in the passage in 10 words or less. As with partner reading and correction, the first reader reads for 5 minutes and answers questions, then the second reader reads for 5 minutes and answers questions. This procedure can be repeated one or several times.

Troubleshooting: Ongoing monitoring of student interactions and awarding points for good behavior may be required to ensure that procedures are conducted appropriately. If a partner is absent, groups of 3 can be created or students can work independently that day.

Story Sharing   E9 F9 E8 C9 T9 I8 V9 +9 T = 8.7

Reference: Mathes & Babyak, 2001.
Goal: Story Sharing is a peer-tutoring strategy in which students are paired with a partner to practice reading and comprehension skills.
Age Group: Elementary.
Materials: Reading materials (stories from children's literature), pair scorecards.
Steps:

1. This procedure can be conducted with the entire class in 15–20 minute sessions about 2–4 times per week. During Story Sharing, all students in the class are paired with other students in the same class to participate in the activity.
2. To pair the students, the teacher can rank order the students from the strongest to the weakest reader and split the list in the middle forming two lists (stronger and weaker readers). The teacher then pairs the top-ranked stronger reader with the top-ranked weaker reader, the second-ranked stronger reader with the second-ranked weaker reader, and so on until each student in the class is paired with another student of adjacent ability. The stronger reader can be assigned as the "coach" and the weaker reader as the "reader."
3. The teacher designates the story each pair is to read during Story Sharing. Stories can be selected from the reading text or from children's literature appropriate for the reading ability of the stronger reader and the reader's ability to restate information. Text should also be selected that pairs could read two times in the time allowed. The teacher could create a Book Bag containing an assortment of children's books and decodable books with enough books for each pair in the class.
4. The teacher instructs the students on how to conduct Story Sharing by explaining and modeling the procedure. During the Story Sharing activity, students are to practice three activities (a) Pretend-Read, (b) Read-Aloud, and (c) Retell.
5. During the first 2 minutes of Story Sharing, the pairs "Pretend Read" by looking through the book together and predicting what is happening on each page based on the pictures. This activity is intended to teach previewing skills and enhance oral language skills.
6. The next 12–15 minutes students engage in a "Read-Aloud" activity. The coach and reader take turns reading each sentence (or paragraph) of the story aloud while sliding his or her finger under each word, with the coach providing a fluent model of oral reading. When the pair finishes reading the story, the reader and coach can switch positions and re-read the story with the "reader" reading each sentence first.

7. The pairs conduct the "Retell" activity in the last few minutes of the Story Sharing. During "Retell" they sequence the events of the story, by asking each other "What happened first?" and then, "What happened next?", and so on.

8. If desired, the teacher can assign each pair to a class team (A and B) for which they can earn points. The pairs will work together to earn points for Story Sharing. The pairs can earn a point for each Story Sharing activity completed during the session (i.e., 3 points per session). Points are marked on a shared scorecard. Scorecards can be a simple note card containing the students' names, date, and a space for the number of points earned. At the end of the week, the total points for all pairs on each team are added and the winning team announced.

Troubleshooting: The teacher should supervise and provide assistance to students if needed, during Story Sharing. The teacher can award bonus points to individual pairs for cooperating with each other and remaining on-task.

LANGUAGE ARTS—SPELLING

Add-a-Word   **E9 F9 E9 C8 T8 I7 V9 +9 T = 8.6**

Reference: Schermerhorn, 1997.
Goal: This intervention is an individualized spelling program used to improve spelling skills by providing students with a word flow rather than a fixed list and planning spelling instruction on the basis of assessment information.
Age Group: Elementary.
Materials: Basal spelling text appropriate for age and grade level, spelling study sheets.
Steps:

1. The Add-a-Word program provides students with an individualized spelling list in which words spelled correctly are dropped from the list and a new word added. Words are retested at a later date and words spelled correctly over time are removed from the list.

2. The teacher can create the spelling word lists from words taken from a basal spelling series used by the school. To begin, each student receives a list of 10 words. Words should be presented in list form and should be learned whole rather than broken down into smaller parts.

3. Students should spend at least 60 minutes practicing spelling words each week. Students can be given exercises from their spelling book, asked to copy the words three times, fill in missing letters, or students can use the

Cover, Copy, & Compare procedure described in this chapter to practice their word lists. The Cover, Copy, & Compare procedure works well when combined with the Add-a-Word intervention. Students first copy a word from their list on to a spelling study sheet. Then they cover the word and write it from memory. Finally, they compare the word to the original copy to see if it is correct. Students should practice each word until they have written it correctly from memory twice.

4. An important component of this procedure involves frequent exams with high mastery. At the end of their daily practice, the students take a quiz of their 10 words. The daily quiz can be given by another student, the teacher, or an adult volunteer but should be checked weekly by the teacher. Words that are spelled correctly are noted on the student's master list. When a word is spelled correctly two days in a row it is removed from the list and replaced with a new word. After one week, the words that are removed from the list are tested again on the daily quiz as a review word. If spelled correctly, the word or words are retested again 30 days later. If the word or words are spelled correctly after the second review they are removed from the list. If the word is spelled incorrectly at any point in time, it is added to the list again as one of the 10 spelling words.

5. To provide reinforcement, students may choose a goal (e.g., 100 words) and when they reach their goal, student names are publicly posted and they receive a reward (e.g., certificate of achievement, etc.).

Troubleshooting: To reduce teacher time required each day to give and correct each spelling test, the teacher might test 4–5 different students per day and allow the remaining students to sit with a partner and quiz each other. Students can be allowed to self-correct their spelling study sheets or exchange papers with each other.

Cover, Copy, & Compare   **E9 F10 E9 C9 T9 I7 V9 +9 T = 9.0**

Reference: Mclaughlin & Skinner, 1996.
Goal: This intervention is a self-management procedure to help students increase spelling skills through modeling, drill and practice, and self-correction.
Age Group: Elementary or Secondary.
Materials: Spelling words, Cover, Copy, & Compare sheets.
Steps:

1. The Cover, Copy, & Compare procedure can be used to increase academic performance across various curriculum. Subject areas in which the Cover, Copy, & Compare procedure can be used include weekly spelling words, individual lists of words commonly misspelled in creative writing, math facts, geography facts, etc. It is typically used to learn material that involves recognition, memorization, or automatic responding.

2. The Cover, Copy, & Compare intervention includes the following sequence of steps:
   (a) The student looks at an academic stimulus (e.g., spelling word or math problem).
   (b) The student covers the academic stimulus either with their nonwriting hand or by placing an index card over the stimulus.
   (c) The student makes an academic response (e.g., writes the word),
   (d) The student uncovers the original stimulus, and
   (e) The student then compares his or her response to the original stimulus and evaluates it for accuracy.
   (f) If the student response is accurate, the student moves to the next item on the list (e.g., spelling word or math problem) and repeats the procedure.
   (g) If the last response is incorrect, the student does an error correction procedure before moving on to the next item (e.g., repeats the Cover, Copy, & Compare procedure), or writes the word three times.
3. To use the Cover, Copy, & Compare procedure with spelling words, the student needs a list of words printed down the left side of a page, with space to copy these words.
4. The teacher instructs the students to use the Cover, Copy, & Compare procedure by modeling the steps and verbalizing each step. The students then practice the procedure independently.
5. To use the Cover, Copy, & Compare procedure with math facts, the student needs a list of math problems and the answers printed down the left side of the page. After covering the problem and answer, students write the entire problem with the answer, then self-evaluates for accuracy.

Troubleshooting: To increase motivation, intervals should be brief. For example, students can be encouraged to complete as many trials as possible in three minutes. Students can also set a goal and track their personal completion rate. Because the Cover, Copy, & Compare procedure is a self-management procedure, the error correction component should not be too aversive. Students may cheat if they are required to rewrite words too many times.

SPELLER   **E8 F9 E8 C8 T8 I8 V9 +9 T = 8.3**

Reference: Keller, 2002.
Goal: SPELLER is an intervention that combines class wide peer tutoring and a spelling strategy to help students acquire and maintain spelling skills.
Age Group: Elementary.
Materials: Poster board, pencils, spelling lists, SPELLER practice sheets, cue cards, and a timer.

Steps:

1. The SPELLER strategy involves a mnemonic designed to help students follow seven steps including visual imagery, systematic testing, and auditory reinforcement.
2. To use the SPELLER strategy with an entire class, the students are paired into teams of two. Students may be paired randomly, by ability level, or by matching students who work well together. The teacher determines which type of pairing works best for a particular classroom. New dyads can be reassigned weekly or as needed throughout the program.
3. During the SPELLER strategy, one student is the tutor and one the tutee for 10 minutes; the students then change roles for another 10 minutes. Each student has the opportunity to serve as tutor and tutee. Tutoring sessions take place 20 minutes per day, about three times per week.
4. The teacher prepares a poster board with the SPELLER strategy and rules written on the poster. A smaller version of the SPELLER strategy can be printed on a cue card for each student to use during the SPELLER sessions. The SPELLER Steps to be written on the poster board and the cue cards should include the following steps and rules (1) **S**pot word; say it (in the first step, the students look at the spelling word and pronounce it out loud). (2) **P**icture it (next, they visualize the image the word represents with their eyes open). (3) **E**yes closed (students then close their eyes and visualize the word). (4) **L**ook to see if right (students open their eyes and check the word). (5) **L**ook away, write it (students recall the word from memory and write it on the practice sheet). (6) **E**xamine it (students check the spelling of the words with their flashcards). (7) **R**epeat or Reward (the students repeat steps 1 through 6 with the same word if they spelled the word incorrectly, or reward themselves if they spelled it right). The reward is a verbal praise statement given by the tutor (e.g., "Great spelling").
5. On the first day, students are given their list of spelling words for the week as a class assignment. Students write each spelling word on a flash card, so they will have their own set.
6. The teacher instructs the students on how to use the SPELLER strategy by explaining and modeling each step. Students can role-play examples.
7. During the class wide peer tutoring sessions, the students sit with their partners. Students will need their spelling flashcards, a practice sheet (on which to write each word from memory), and a SPELLER cue card. The teacher sets the timer for 10 minutes and instructs the students to begin. During the tutoring session, the teacher can circulate around the room, monitoring and providing assistance if necessary. At the end of 10 minutes, students change roles and the timer is reset.

Troubleshooting: Establish tutoring rules prior to implementing. Tutors should be instructed to remember to use positive words, particularly during error correction. Teachers may need to monitor students' practice sheets to ensure students are completing the procedure accurately.

The Spelling Game   **E9 F9 E8 C8 T8 I8 V9 +9 T = 8.6**

Reference: Delquadri, Greenwood, Stretton, & Hall, 1983.
Goal: The Spelling Game is a peer-tutoring strategy that includes team competition, distributed practice, and an error correction procedure to improve spelling accuracy of weekly spelling words.
Age Group: Elementary.
Materials: Weekly spelling lists, point cards, colored tickets (red and blue).
Steps:

1. The Spelling Game can be implemented in a regular spelling classroom, or with a small group of students. The Spelling Game provides increased opportunity for students to respond and practice spelling words in a short period of time by using a peer-tutoring procedure. It provides social and token reinforcement for students, and includes an error correction procedure. This intervention is conducted during the spelling period and takes about 15 minutes of class time per session. The Spelling Game will help to increase spelling skills for students with and without spelling deficits.
2. The teacher selects the spelling word list to be learned by the class or group of students based on grade and ability levels. This list should include 10–20 spelling words on which the students will be tested at the end of the week.
3. Every Monday, students are randomly assigned to one of two teams (Red and Blue) by drawing a red or blue ticket from a box. The teams, once selected, remain the same for the entire week. The two teams compete for the highest team point total. Each week new teams are randomly selected, to ensure that students have the opportunity to participate on a winning team.
4. The teacher pairs each student in the team with a partner. Students can be paired randomly, by ability level, or by matching students who work well together.
5. The teacher instructs all of the students in the tutoring procedure and explains how they play the Spelling Game by demonstrating and modeling the steps. The teacher outlines the rules and method for earning and scoring points by comparing it to basketball. The teacher tells the students that they will make "baskets" (two points) or "foul shots" (one point). During tutoring the first student tutors the other student for 5 minutes. After 5 minutes the teacher signals for the pairs to reverse roles for another 5 minutes.

6. Tutoring consists of the tutor presenting the spelling words to the tutee. The tutor says the word and the tutor writes it on a spelling paper. The tutee then orally spells out the word as it is written. If correct, the tutor states, "Correct, give yourself 2 points." A 2 is scored next to the word. If incorrect, the tutor says, "Take a foul shot" and spells the missed word correctly. The tutee is required to write it correctly 3 times before the next word is presented. A 1 is scored next to the word. The students can go through the list as many times as possible during the 5 minute period (thereby earning more points).

7. At the end of the each session, the students add their points, and report the score to the teacher, who sums the points for each team. The team points can be posted each day on a class chart. Students may also earn points for their team for each word spelled correctly on the Friday spelling test. At the end of the week, the teacher announces the winning team and the class cheers for the "team of the week."

Troubleshooting: To provide additional reinforcement for "good tutoring", the teacher can monitor the game and randomly reward bonus points. The teacher may wish to randomly spot check students' scoring each day.

Word Wizards   **E10 F9 E8 C8 T9 I8 V8 +9 T = 8.6**

Reference: McDonnell, Thorson, Allen, & Mathot-Buckner, 2000.
Goal: Word Wizards is an intervention used to improve spelling performance through a partner learning, peer-tutoring strategy.
Age Group: Elementary.
Materials: Spelling word lists.
Steps:

1. The Word Wizard procedure can be implemented with a small group of students or with an entire classroom. This procedure involves a peer-tutoring strategy in which each student has a turn as the tutor, tutee, and a tutor-helper. Partner learning is a method used to enhance rates of academic responding, provides students with direct instruction and error correction, and provides opportunity for repeated practice in a short period of time.

2. The teacher pairs students into groups of three. Students may be grouped randomly, by ability level, or by matching students who work well together. The teacher determines which type of grouping works best for a particular classroom. New triads can be assigned weekly or as needed throughout the program.

3. Before each partner learning program, the teacher develops spelling word lists for each student. The lists can be taken from the grade level basal

spelling text or individualized lists can be developed for students with spelling or reading disabilities.

4. Prior to implementing, the teacher provides instruction to all students in the class on the partner learning procedure, through demonstration and modeling. The students can role-play examples.

5. During the partner learning, each student in the triad serves in one of three learning roles. The first role is the "Word Wizard." The Word Wizard (tutee) writes the spelling word and verbally spells each word presented by the tutor. The second role is the "Word Conjurer." The Word Conjurer (tutor) selects a word from the appropriate word list, presents the word to the speller (Word Wizard), and provides feedback to the speller. The third role is the "Word Keeper." The Word Keeper is a tutor-helper. The Word Keeper holds the word lists, checks the written and verbal spelling of the word with the Word Conjurer, and shows the written word from the list to the speller as part of the standard error correction procedure if the speller makes an error.

6. For example, the Word Conjurer selects a word from the spelling list, presents it (i.e., "Spell ___") and gives the Word Wizard 5 seconds to write and spell it verbally to the other members of the group. After the Word Wizard spells the word, the Word Conjurer and Word Keeper check for accuracy together. The Word Conjurer then states, "I agree" or "I disagree." If the word is incorrect, the Word Keeper shows the correct spelling from the list, and repeats the steps.

7. Each partner learning session lasts about 20 minutes. During the session, the roles are rotated so that each student has a turn as the Word Wizard, Word Conjurer, and Word Keeper. If, during the role as the Word Conjurer, a student is unable to read a word on the spelling list to the Word Wizard, the Word Keeper can be consulted for assistance.

8. During the partner learning sessions, the teacher monitors the activities, provides assistance when necessary, and provides feedback to triads about their performance.

Troubleshooting: The teacher should establish tutoring rules prior to implementing. Tutors should be instructed to remember to use positive words, particularly during error correction.

Write-Say   **E10 E9 E9 C9 T8 I5 V9 +8 T = 8.3**

Reference: Kearney & Drabman, 1995.
Goal: The Write-Say spelling method is a strategy used to improve students' spelling accuracy by providing immediate feedback to dual sensory modalities following the presentation of a daily spelling test.
Age Group: Elementary or Secondary.

Materials: Weekly spelling word lists.
Steps:

1. The Write-Say strategy is a cost-effective strategy to help students retain new information. In includes the use of immediate feedback targeting both visual and auditory modalities.
2. The Write-Say strategy can be conducted during a regular classroom spelling period, typically 20–30 minutes per day. The teacher selects appropriate spelling word lists for each student based on the student's age or grade level and words not previously taught. Students should be able to read the words they are to spell. Word lists should contain from 6–12 new words per week. New spelling word lists are given each week.
3. Students are given a word list on Monday and instructed to study the list on their own. The following day, the teacher assesses the students for spelling accuracy by asking them to write each word from the list after it is verbally presented. The teacher or adult can present the word list to students or students can be assigned to a spelling partner and take turns presenting the word lists to each other. Spelling accuracy is defined as the number of words spelled without any errors (e.g., reversals or omission of letters), divided by the number of words on the list.
4. Following the initial test, the teacher or spelling partner gives verbal feedback on incorrect and correct spellings. Students are then instructed to practice the misspelled words by simultaneously spelling the word orally (letter-by-letter) as they write the correct spelling of each misspelled word. Students are instructed to write-say each misspelled word five consecutive times.
5. During the next and subsequent days, students repeat the procedure, by writing each word from the list as it is presented by the teacher or spelling partner. Students are instructed to write-say each misspelled word 10 consecutive times.
6. On the last day of the week, students are re-assessed for spelling accuracy by writing words from the list after each word is verbally presented by the classroom teacher.
7. The write-say procedure can also be used to teach math facts, such as multiplication tables to children with math difficulties. The teacher verbally states the math problem as the flash card is visually presented (i.e., multiplication facts, addition facts, etc.). Students are instructed to rewrite each incorrect problem and answer five times on their paper. Students are also asked to say the answers to the problems aloud.

Troubleshooting: The rewriting of incorrectly spelled words may serve as a negative reinforcer to increase a student's motivation to improve accuracy. The teacher can also provide positive reinforcement in the form of verbal praise, points earned towards a reward, or public posting of test scores to increase motivation.

LANGUAGE ARTS—WRITING

Advance Planning Strategies   **E9 F9 E9 C8 T8 I6 V9 +9 T = 8.5**

Reference: Troia & Graham, 2002.
Goal: Advance Planning Strategies include explicit, teacher-directed instructions used to teach three planning strategies for writing—goal setting, brainstorming, and organizing.
Age Group: Elementary or Secondary.
Materials: The acronyms STOP & LIST printed on a classroom chart.
Steps:

1. Students should have pre-instruction to become familiar with the basic structure and key elements of stories and/or persuasive essays. To teach the five primary elements of a well-developed story the acronym SPACE (Setting, Problems, Actions, Consequences, Emotions) can be printed on a small chart. The teacher presents an example of each element from a sample story. The teacher and students then read a story and identify the key elements together. Finally, students are asked to independently identify the elements in one or more stories until students achieve mastery. For additional practice, students can be asked to tell a story about a picture that includes each of the key elements.

2. The Advance Planning Strategies include three planning strategies: identifying the purpose of the activity and setting appropriate goals, brainstorming ideas, and organizing ideas. The acronym STOP & LIST (Stop, Think Of Purpose, and List Ideas, Sequence Them) is printed on a chart and used to teach these components. The teacher introduces the planning strategies by introducing the STOP & LIST acronym and modeling how to use the strategies in various contexts, such as reading a passage, planning a trip, going shopping, and writing a story.

3. The teacher first explains and models how to use the strategies to perform several different types of tasks (including story writing), and how planning strategies may be adapted for different tasks. The teacher models the use of planning strategies for story writing, emphasizing the importance of generating as many ideas as possible for each of the five elements of a story (SPACE), adding, and deleting ideas as necessary. After modeling use of the strategies for other tasks, (i.e., reading a passage, planning a party, planning a trip) and writing a story, the teacher compares how the strategy is similar or different for each of the tasks.

4. Students are asked to practice the STOP & LIST mnemonic during subsequent lessons until they can recite it accurately. The teacher explains how using the STOP & LIST mnemonic can help them write stories. After the teacher has modeled use of the strategies to compose a story, the teacher and students write a story collaboratively using the advance planning strategies. When the story is completed, the teacher and students discuss how the STOP & LIST strategies helped them complete the story.

5. The students are given several opportunities (including homework assignments) to practice using advance planning strategies in a variety of situations (i.e., planning a birthday party for a friend, going on a vacation, etc.) with teacher review and feedback. Students then practice using STOP & LIST to compose a story with teacher assistance. The teacher and students discuss how they used the strategies. Finally, students use the STOP & LIST strategies to write stories by themselves.

Troubleshooting: Students can be taught how to use a checklist or a scoring rubric (refer to Writing Assessment Rubrics) as they are planning stories to remind them to complete each step of the strategy. Students can also work in pairs to evaluate each other's use of the strategies.

Check-off System   **E9 F9 E8 C8 T8 I7 V8 +8 T = 8.5**

Reference: Martin & Manno, 1995.
Goal: The Check-off System is a self-management procedure designed to improve writing skills by teaching students to plan stories using identified story elements and monitor the use of these elements with a check-off system.
Age Group: Upper Elementary or Secondary.
Materials: Writing stimuli (e.g., pictures or story starters), and a Story Planner Form. A sample Story Planner Form is listed in Appendix A.
Steps:

1. The check-off system is a procedure that is used to help students improve their planning and story writing ability by providing story schema training, and by providing a simple checklist of story elements students can use as an aid to self-regulate writing performance. Story schema is the ability to understand the general structure of a story that includes a sequential ordering of story elements.

2. The teacher can select writing prompts such as story starters; story enders, and/or pictures to use as writing stimuli. Pictures that would be interesting for the appropriate age and grade level may be obtained from issues of various popular magazines and mounted on cardstock or poster board.

3. The teacher provides direct instruction in how to include essential elements in a story by demonstrating and modeling each step. At this point,

the emphasis is on content and ideas rather than mechanics of writing. The teacher explains the Story Planner Form and teaches the students to plan and monitor their story writing. The Story Planner Form consists of three columns; (a) the first column lists six (or more) essential story elements, (b) the second column provides spaces for students to fill in brief notes as they plan their stories, and (c) the third column provides spaces for students to check-off each element as it is included in the written story.

4. The teacher may select story elements that would be appropriate for the age and grade level. Six story elements that are suggested to include are:
   (a) Main character—A person, animal, or fantasy character.
   (b) Supporting Characters—People, animals, etc. that interact with the main character.
   (c) Setting—Place(s) where the story occurs, or a place and time for the story.
   (d) Problem—Story premise, or a situation or dilemma involving the main character.
   (e) Plan (action)—Activities of the main character to resolve the problem.
   (f) Ending—Problem resolution.

5. The teacher should provide several examples of simple stories containing the six elements and model how to complete the Story Planner Form. Each student can keep a two-pocket folder containing notebook paper and a supply of Story Planner Forms. Students are instructed to write brief notes on the Story Planner Form while planning their story, then check off each element as they include it in their written story.

6. This procedure works best if students have regular opportunities (e.g., 20 min. at least three times per week) to practice their story writing skills.

Troubleshooting: The teacher can encourage students to participate in the check-off system by allowing them to earn free time points for each story completed.

Self-Regulated Story Writing   **E9 F9 E8 C8 T9 I8 V9 +9 T = 8.8**

Reference: Mason, Harris, & Graham, 2002.
Goal: This strategy is an integrated instructional approach for writing that combines academic strategies with self-regulation to increase story writing skills.
Age Group: Elementary or Secondary.
Materials: Classroom poster listing the strategy steps.
Steps:

1. The teacher introduces and describes two strategies for story writing. The two strategies are referred to as "POW", and "W-W-W, What 2, How 2."

The first strategy, POW, is an acronym used to remind students to: Pick an idea, Organize notes, and Write and say more. The teacher tells the students that stories have more "power" when they use POW. The second strategy, "W-W-W, What 2, How 2." is used to remind students to ask seven questions as they plan their stories. The five "W" questions and two "How" questions include: Who is the main character? When does the story happen? Where does the story take place? What do the characters do? What happens then? How does the story end? and, How does the main character feel?

2. The steps to these two strategies can be presented on classroom posters and placed in a visible location in the room to remind students of the steps. Students should orally rehearse and memorize the acronyms for the two strategies after the teacher discusses them with the class. The teacher can read age-appropriate stories to the class and have them practice identifying the seven story parts. Picture cues for the seven parts may be helpful for younger students. Students should demonstrate knowledge and understanding of the strategy parts through class discussion. The teacher can present a simple story on the overhead projector and have students practice identifying the seven parts or can give students a copy of a student story to read and identify the parts. A graphic organizer (refer to Graphic Organizers described in this chapter) can be used to chart each story part.

3. Next the teacher models the complete writing and planning process, using each part of the two strategies, and modeling "things I ask myself" out loud (i.e., "What do I need to do next?" and "Do I have all seven steps?"). Students can assist the teacher and suggest ideas throughout the process. Modeling should begin with the "P"—Pick an idea, by developing an idea from a picture prompt or story starter. While modeling the next step, "O"—Organize my notes, the teacher uses the seven steps from the "W-W-W, W 2, H 2" strategy. While explaining the last step in POW—Write and say more, the teacher discusses the importance of detail and word choice in a story.

4. Next, students should begin to plan and write their own stories, with teacher assistance as needed. Students can continue to use graphic organizers to plan their story, writing notes for each story part. Assistance and the use of graphic organizers can be gradually faded as students demonstrate independence.

5. Students can self-evaluate their use of the story-writing strategies by counting and recording the number of story parts included in their stories. The teacher prompts students that the goal is to write stories with all seven parts. Reinforcement can be provided to students who meet the goal.

Troubleshooting: The teacher should monitor students' use of strategy steps prior to having students self-evaluate. Several sessions may be needed for students to learn the steps.

Sign Up Sheets   **E8 F9 E10 C8 T7 I9 V9 +10 T = 9.0**

Reference: Godt, Hutinger, Robinson, & Schneider, 1999.
Goal: Sign Up Sheets are a self-managed turn-taking procedure used to encourage pre-academic writing and reading skills in preschool children in a naturally occurring situation.
Age Group: Preschool or Early Elementary.
Materials: Sign-up poster board, sign-up sheet pages, laminated photographs of each student (optional), photograph of sign-up activity, markers or pencils.
Steps:

1. The sign-up sheet is kept next to the sign-up activity area so that students can use it to schedule a turn. The sign-up sheet can be used with a variety of activities in a preschool, Kindergarten, or elementary classroom. For example, it may be used to sign up for a turn at the computer, a turn at the reading corner, a turn to check out playground equipment, a turn to read with a tutor, or any other special activities. It may be used as a classroom attendance sheet, where each child signs in when they arrive at school and signs out when they leave. When children who are learning emergent writing and reading skills repeat this activity daily, they can make visible gains in their skills over the course of the year.

2. To create the sign-up sheet, the teacher designs a poster board titled with the name of the activity (e.g., "Computer Center" or "Reading Time"). A photograph of the activity is attached to the poster board under the title. The poster board is divided into three columns, with the headings Number, Photo, and Signature. Under the Number heading, the first column is numbered (e.g., 1–10, depending on the class size). The poster board can be laminated.

3. Each day, the teacher provides a new sign-up sheet page with the current date, and attaches it with a paper clip to the poster board, under the Photo and Signature column. The poster board should be placed near the activity, within easy reach of the students. Pencils or markers should be available for students to use.

4. The teacher demonstrates how students use the sign-up sheet by writing their name on the signature line next to the first available number, to denote their turn at the activity. The teacher provides sufficient opportunities for students to practice signing their name and assistance if needed, prior to signing independently. The first student to sign up writes his or her name by the number one, and so on.

5. Preschool students or young children may not be able to write their name initially, however, they should be encouraged to practice pre-writing skills by writing the first letter in their name, or attempting to make a mark or scribble on the paper.

6. To assist children who have difficulty writing or recognizing their own or others marks, children can attach a picture of themselves next to the number denoting their turn. Laminated photos of each child (school or digital pictures work well) are provided. The pictures can also have the child's name written below, to provide a visual model for the student to copy. The pictures can be attached to the poster board with tape, a paper clip, or Velcro fasteners attached to a porous surface.

Troubleshooting: Children do not acquire "bad habits" by being allowed to write before they can officially write correctly. Children will typically be excited to use the sign-up sheet, and given the opportunity to practice in a meaningful way, they will develop understanding about words and letters.

Think Sheets   **E10 F9 E8 C8 T8 I7 V9 +9 T = 8.5**

Reference: Baker, Gersten, & Graham, 2003.
Goal: Think Sheets are used as a planning tool to help students improve the quality of the content of their written stories and essays.
Age Group: Elementary or Secondary.
Materials: Think Sheets. A sample Think Sheet is listed in Appendix A.
Steps:

1. The use of Think Sheets is an instructional approach that involves teaching students writing strategies and providing students with a planning tool to guide them through the brainstorming, outlining, and writing process. This intervention includes direct teaching of writing skills through text analysis, modeling the writing process, and providing several opportunities for guided student practice. This instruction is part of a comprehensive writing program that provides students with many opportunities to practice the strategies.

2. The teacher provides instruction about the steps involved in the writing process. The acronym POWER can be used to teach the steps of: Plan, Organize, Write, Edit, and Revise. The POWER steps can be visibly displayed on a class chart or poster. Students are asked to practice the POWER acronym until they can recite it accurately.

3. The teacher provides an example of a Think Sheet to the students and explains that Think Sheets can be used as a note-taking tool for them to use as they brainstorm, outline, and write an essay or a story. The Think Sheets are not simply a "worksheet" to fill out, but a guide to help them become a competent writer.

4. A teacher-created Think Sheet can be designed or modified from the example provided. The Think Sheet should include the following information:

   Title or essay topic
   Who am I writing for?
   Why am I writing?
   What do I know?
   How can I group my ideas?
   How will I organize my ideas?

5. Instruction begins with the teacher presenting and discussing a writing sample to provide students with an example of a final written product. The teacher can model the strategies used to brainstorm writing ideas and organizing the ideas by filling in the spaces on the Think Sheet presented on an overhead transparency.

6. Next, the teacher can guide students through the writing of a class paper, with students generating ideas using the POWER strategy and using a Think Sheet to organize ideas. The teacher can use a transparency to lead a discussion with the students as they collaborate to complete a brief composition together.

7. After students have had sufficient opportunity to review the steps and practice with teacher assistance, they can complete a written composition independently. Students can be asked to explain and share their Think Sheets with a peer prior to writing their essay.

Troubleshooting: It is important that the teacher provides extensive modeling and thinking aloud for students at each step of the writing process. Students with disabilities may need more guidance, feedback, and extended practice.

Word Counts   E9 F10 E8 C9 T9 I8 V8 +9 T = 8.8

Reference: Moxley, Lutz, Ahlborn, Boley, & Armstrong, 1995.
Goal: Word Counts is a strategy to encourage writing and increase productivity in students by having them self-record the number of words written during a time-limited written language activity.
Age Group: Elementary.
Materials: Individual journals for each student, pencils, recording sheets, timer, writing calendar (optional).
Steps:

1. Self-recorded word counts are a strategy that provides students with frequent writing experiences and opportunities to self-evaluate their progress in increasing writing production and fluency.

2. Each student is provided with an individual journal to use for the writing activity.

3. The teacher may give the students a free choice of what to write about or specific topics may be designated for each writing activity. The teacher may provide students with a monthly calendar, with a writing topic listed for each day. Students color the box on the calendar when they have written about the topic in the box.

4. Students are instructed to write in their journals for approximately 15 minutes, two or three times per week. At the beginning of the writing activity, the teacher sets the timer and instructs the students to begin writing.

5. At the end of the timed period, students are instructed to count each word written, regardless of whether the word is spelled correctly or not. The purpose of the word count activity is to increase the rate of writing fluency (the amount of words written on the paper), rather than the mechanics of writing or revising and editing that may follow.

6. After the students have counted each word written, they are instructed to record the number of words they have written on a line graph or a bar graph in their journals, with teacher assistance as needed. A sheet of graph paper may be kept in the front of the journal to record word counts, if desired. The teacher may need to instruct younger children on how to self-record on their graphs. Students should also record each date along with the number of words written.

7. The class can also keep a class chart (a single large bar graph displayed in the front of the room) to record the total number of words written by the class as a whole. The whole class may receive a reinforcer (a certificate of the group accomplishment, class applause, class party, extra recess time, etc.) when they reach a predetermined class goal (e.g. 1,000 words). The teacher may also provide individual reinforcers (e.g., stickers) when a student reaches a specified number of words or shows improvement in word counts over time.

8. To provide modeling, students should have an opportunity to voluntarily share their writing with other students, by reading aloud to the class, reading aloud to a friend, or having a friend read it silently.

9. The teacher may need to periodically spot-check the reported scores for reliability.

Troubleshooting: In the initial stage of this intervention, some children may be reluctant to write if the teacher focuses on errors in writing. However, the teacher may need to create a rule against counting immediately repeated words, to discourage writing sentences containing "very, very", etc. The focus should be on individual and group progress over time, rather than emphasizing comparative rankings among students.

Writing Assessment Rubrics   E9 F9 E8 C8 T8 I7 V9 +9 T = 8.5

Reference: Schirmer & Bailey, 2000 and Jackson & Larkin, 2002.
Goal: Rubrics are a systematic method used to teach students the performance expectations of an assignment and to guide students in assessing their own and their peers' writing.
Age Group: Upper Elementary or Secondary.
Materials: Teacher developed rubric, Rubric Strategy Poster.
Steps:

1. A rubric is defined as a grading guideline to use in assessment of a student's work. A rubric is a scoring tool used to teach and identify important criteria or qualities, provide a definition of each criterion, and indicate the level of performance with a rating scale. Rubrics can be used to assess various subjects or curriculum areas; however, the example presented here is developed to assess students' writing performance.

2. There are several benefits to using rubrics: (a) Teachers can use the rubrics to teach students the important rules, conventions, and qualities of writing, (b) Students know prior to beginning the assignment what the performance criteria will be, (c) Students can monitor their progress as they work on the writing assignment, and (d) Students can use the rubric as a self-assessment tool when the writing is completed.

3. Rubrics can be developed or modified to accommodate individual differences or ability levels. To develop a writing assessment rubric, the teacher identifies the qualities (traits) of writing, creates a scale (i.e., 1–3), and defines each quality by describing the performance level of each point on the scale. An example of a self-assessment rubric used to identify the important writing qualities could include the following qualities and definitions. Students self-evaluate by rating their performance of each quality on a scale of 1 to 3 (i.e., 1 = many errors or lack of detail, 2 = adequate, and 3 = few errors, variety of detail).
   (a) Ideas—main ideas are well supported and explained.
   (b) Organization—presentation of ideas is logical.
   (c) Word Choice—use of vocabulary to convey meaning, good imagery.
   (d) Sentence Fluency—sentences are easy to understand.
   (e) Mechanics—punctuation, spelling, and capitalization.

4. Before using the rubric strategy, students will need to have an opportunity to learn the concept of rubrics and the steps for using them to self-evaluate. The teacher may need to spend one or more class periods explaining the qualities, discussing the criteria, and providing numerous examples. The students can be divided into teams and each team given a sample of writing to evaluate together, using the rubric.

5. After students are familiar with how to use the rubric, students can be asked to self-evaluate and evaluate with a peer, by rating their performance on each quality on a prepared rubric form. Students can add up their total score and turn their ratings in to the teacher. To self or peer-evaluate, students can be taught these Rubric Strategy Steps: **R**—read the rubric before beginning, **U**se the rubric and get a score, **B**—bring a friend to help you check it, **R**—review the rubric together, **I**—identify the score together, and **C**—check scores again.

Troubleshooting: Before developing a rubric, the teacher can assess students' work to determine the appropriate criteria to target. Rubrics can be used to assess stages in the writing process, steps in writing research reports, or various forms of writing (i.e., biographies, letters, etc.).

MATH—COMPUTATION

DRAW E9 F9 E9 C8 T8 I9 V9 $+9$ T $= 8.8$

Reference: Morin & Miller, 1998.
Goal: This intervention is a math strategy used to teach multiplication facts to students using a concrete-representational-abstract teaching sequence.
Age Group: Elementary or Secondary.
Materials: Multiplication Facts 0 to 81, manipulative items for each student (e.g., paper plates and small wooden blocks or other small objects such as buttons or beads), a poster board listing the four DRAW steps, and multiplication practice worksheets.
Steps:

1. This procedure involves a systematic teaching format that includes use of concrete manipulative devices to teach conceptual understanding of multiplication, representational lessons using pictures of objects, and mnemonic instruction to help students follow a sequence of problem solving steps.
2. The teacher models and demonstrates each of the processes used to solve problems while students watch and listen. While doing so, the teacher asks questions and solicits responses from the students. Next, the teacher provides guided practice while students complete practice problems on their own. Then the students practice completing problems independently.
3. The concrete lesson is used to teach conceptual understanding of multiplication with the use of manipulative items. Each student is provided with small paper plates used to represent groups, and small blocks

(or other items) used to represent the objects in groups. For example, in the problem 3×5, the students are taught to look at the first number (3) and count out that many groups (i.e., plates). Next, the students look at the second number (5) and place that many blocks in each group (i.e., on each plate). Then the students count all the blocks to determine the answer. They are taught that three groups of five blocks equal fifteen blocks all together. This process should be practiced with many multiplication facts over several lessons.

4. In addition to teaching conceptual understanding of multiplication, students are also taught two multiplication rules. The first rule is any number times zero equals zero. The second rule is any number times one equals the original number.

5. Following the concrete lessons, the students are taught to use pictures of objects during the representational lessons. Students can draw boxes containing dots, or circles containing vertical lines to represent the groups and objects in each group. For example to represent 2×3, the student draws two groups (circles) each containing 3 objects (lines). Next they count all the lines inside the circles to determine the answer.

6. Students are taught to use a mnemonic device to solve problems. The mnemonic, DRAW includes the steps listed below. The teacher can place a large poster listing each step in the classroom or provide each student with a cue card listing the DRAW steps. The students should practice and memorize the steps using verbal rehearsal.

   *D*iscover the sign. (Students look at the sign to determine the operation.)
   *R*ead the problem. (Students read the problem aloud and to themselves.)
   *A*nswer, or draw and check. (Students either know the answer or draw boxes and dots to solve the problem.)
   *W*rite the answer. (Students write the answer in the correct space.)

Troubleshooting: Students with math deficits may need more practice at the concrete levels before moving to the representational or abstract levels.

The 4 Bs   **E8 F10 E8 C9 T9 I8 V9 +9 T = 8.7**

Reference: Brown & Frank, 1990.
Goal: This intervention is a self-management procedure used to increase math skills through use of a mnemonic checklist.
Age Group: Elementary.
Materials: Math worksheets, 4 Bs checklists printed on laminated cards.
Steps:

1. The teacher introduces the self-monitoring strategy to the students. This strategy involves use of a checklist to help students remember the

procedure and steps needed to solve math problems, such as addition and subtraction of numbers involving regrouping.

2. The teacher prepares math worksheets containing 8–10 subtraction problems involving regrouping (commercially prepared worksheets may also be used). A brief description of the self-monitoring strategy including the four key words and their definitions—referred to as the "4 Bs" is written at the top of each page.

   (a) *B*egin (In the right column).
   (b) *B*igger (Which number is bigger?).
   (c) *B*orrow (If the bottom number is bigger, I must borrow), and
   (d) *B*asic facts (Remember them or use Touch Math).

3. The four key words (or beginning letters of each of the four words) are written next to each problem on the worksheet in a checklist format.

4. The teacher discusses the 4 Bs and models the use of the strategy for the students on the blackboard, verbalizing each step as it is completed. Students should practice the strategy by saying each step to themselves as they work through a problem and also practice saying each step from memory.

5. As the students work the problems and complete each step, they place a check mark next to each key word during the self-monitoring process. A laminated copy of the 4 Bs printed in a checklist format can also be made and provided for each student to place on their desks. They then check-off each step with an erasable marker as it is completed. The laminated checklist would be used instead of reproducing the checklist on each worksheet.

6. The same procedure can be used to assist students in working through addition problems involving regrouping with a similar mnemonic strategy, called SASH. The SASH strategy is written at the top of worksheets or on a separate, laminated self-monitoring card. The SASH descriptions include:

   (a) S (Start in the right column).
   (b) A (Add the numbers together).
   (c) S (Should I carry? Only if the number is above 9), and
   (d) H (Have I carried the right number?).

7. As with the 4 Bs, students place a check mark next to each step or letter as they work through the problems.

8. Once students demonstrate understanding of each step, and are consistent with their responses, the laminated cards can be used to serve as reminders while the checklists on the worksheets are gradually faded or removed.

Troubleshooting: Initially, the teacher may need to monitor students' responses and completion of each step by checking the checklists. Students may need reminders to check off each step.

Math Scramble (Interspersal technique)   **E10 F9 E9 C9 T9 I8 V9 +9 T = 9.3**

Reference: Johns, Skinner, & Nail, 2000.

Goal: This technique is used to increase student performance and preference for completing math assignments by interspersing easier math problems with more difficult math problems.

Age Group: Elementary or Secondary.

Materials: Math worksheets containing math problems consisting of both brief (easy) and more time-consuming problems.

Steps:

1. This technique is used to increase rates of active, accurate responding for students with low rates of math work completion. Some students with math difficulties may misbehave to avoid mathematics assignments or react passively by simply not doing the assignments. By interspersing briefer math problems with more difficult math problems, students may actually complete more problems on a worksheet than they would on a worksheet containing only difficult math problems. This procedure can influence student preference and academic engagement because during independent seatwork, problem completion serves as an immediate reinforcer.

2. The teacher prepares math worksheets for students to complete during independent work periods. The problems should be appropriate for each student's current learning goals and ability levels. For example, if students are learning to compute two-digit by one-digit multiplication problems (problems involving carrying), the worksheets might contain a ratio of 4 to 1. For example, four two-digit by one-digit multiplication problems (e.g., 23 × 4, 2 × 48, etc.), to one one-digit by one-digit multiplication problem (e.g., 2 × 3, 4 × 6, etc.).

3. The teacher can provide students with a choice of math assignments; either worksheets containing fewer, but only difficult problems (standard worksheet), or worksheets containing more problems, but also including easy problems (interspersal worksheet) along with difficult problems.

4. Teachers instruct the students that they will earn credit (or points) for the number of problems completed during each independent work period. Students who complete either the standard worksheet or the interspersal problem worksheet receive points for all problems completed, including the easy ones.

5. For students with very low rates of work completion, the ratio of difficult to easy problems can be adjusted (e.g., 2 difficult to 2 easy problems) and gradually increased as academic responding increases. A random ratio can also be used so that on some occasions, the worksheets include only a few difficult problems, and other days include only a few easy problems.

Troubleshooting: It is important that students receive instruction on how to compute math problems prior to completing work independently and possess sufficient math skills to complete all problems without assistance.

Number Lines   **E9 F9 E9 C8 T8 I8 V9 +9 T = 8.8**

Reference: Fueyo, & Bushell, 1998.
Goal: This intervention involves small group instruction to improve students' math skills in solving addition, subtraction, or missing addend arithmetic problems using the number line.
Age Group: Elementary.
Materials: Worksheets containing math problems selected from the classroom text or from grade level basic math curriculum, laminated cardboard number lines for each student.
Steps:

1. The teacher prepares individual number lines for each student. The number lines are approximately 1 inch by 12 inches, with the numerals from 0 to 10 written along a horizontal line. The line should be drawn with an arrow at each end. A minus sign is drawn over the arrow pointing to the left, and a plus sign is drawn over the arrow pointing to the right. The number lines should be laminated or plastic-covered for repeated use.
2. The number line is a manipulative that provides a concrete model for students to use to solve math problems such as addition, subtraction, story problems, and to solve missing addend problems (e.g., __ + 4 = 6).
3. The teacher instructs the students in how to use the number line by teaching the following procedure for addition or subtraction problems.
   (a) What is the sign? (The student names the operational sign, addition or subtraction).
   (b) Which way do I go? (The student points in the correct direction, either plus or minus).
   (c) What is the first number? The first number tells you where to start. Where do I start? (The student puts his or her finger or pencil on the first number of the problem).
   (d) What is the second number? This is how many jumps I make along the number line. (The student says the second number and moves his or her pencil that many jumps on the number line either right or left depending on the operation, counting the number of jumps along the number line in sequence until they have moved the correct number).
   (e) What number did I land on? (The student says the answer and writes the correct numeral on their worksheet. The student then reads the whole problem).

4. To use the number line procedure to solve a missing addend problem (e.g., $3 + \_\_ = 5$), the student also asks, "Is the blank before or after the equal sign?" and if so, states, "It's a tricky one." To solve, the student counts the jumps along the number line in sequence from the first number to the answer (e.g., from 3 to 5). This is the numeral that is written in the blank space on the worksheet.

5. To use the number line procedure with a small group or with peer tutoring, each student is given a worksheet or page containing single digit addition, subtraction, and missing addend math problems. The teacher, peer-tutor, or teacher assistant models the number line procedure and instructs the students to begin working on the daily assignment, providing assistance and feedback as needed.

Troubleshooting: To provide an additional visual cue, students can draw an arc with a wipe-off marker or crayon, between each numeral on the number line as they count.

Time Trials (Counting Periods)   E10 F10 E9 C10 T9 I8 V9 +9 T = 9.1

Reference: Miller, Hall, & Heward, 1995.
Goal: Daily Time Trials are an effective way to build students' fluency with basic math skills by providing drill and practice in a short period of time while increasing academic engagement and on-task behavior.
Age Group: Elementary or Secondary.
Materials: Math packets consisting of worksheets containing 50 mixed math fact problems (multiplication facts, addition facts, subtraction facts, etc.), and a timing device or stopwatch.
Steps:

1. Daily Time Trials consist of a series of short (1–10 minute) timed periods in which students complete as many problems on a page or worksheet as they can. Time Trials provide students an opportunity to practice their math facts within a short period of time, consistently and repeatedly on a daily basis. Time Trials also increase levels of on-task behavior compared to untimed work periods of equal duration. Daily time trials with self-correction can be conducted in 10 minutes or less.

2. The teacher instructs the students on how to complete the time trial procedures using a sample sheet. Prior to setting the timer or stopwatch, the teacher gives instructions, such as, "It's time for our time trials. Please clear your desk except for a sharp pencil. Do not begin to work until I tell you to start. When it is time to work, I want you to work hard and try your best. Answer as many problems as you can. Don't worry if you can't finish all of them. There will be more problems than you can finish.

Just try and do your best work. When the timer beeps, you will need to stop."

3. When the students are ready to begin, the teacher gives a signal (e.g., "Hold up your pencils to show you are ready"), then says, "Ready, Begin" and starts the timer.

4. While the students work, the teacher monitors the classroom, circulating around the room, but not interacting with the students.

5. When the timer beeps, the teacher says, "Stop. Draw a line after the last problem that you completed."

6. After each time trial (two 1-minute time trials can be conducted) a teacher-directed feedback and self-correction procedure can be implemented. The teacher instructs the students to pick up a red pen or marker and says; "Now we'll mark our papers." Using an overhead projector, the teacher progressively discloses each problem and answer from a completed worksheet. After the teacher reads each problem, the students read the problem and answer in a choral response fashion, until all of the problems attempted by the students have been corrected. Each student self-corrects his or her worksheet using a red pen or marker, placing an X over incorrect answers and writing the correct answer below it. This will provide students with immediate feedback on their performance, while eliminating the need for teacher scoring.

Troubleshooting: A performance feedback system in which students record and post their daily time trial scores may provide additional motivation for students and provide the teacher with ongoing access to student progress. The emphasis should be on individual progress to reduce competition between students. If the term Time Trials evokes a negative reaction from students and parents, the term "Counting Periods" can be used instead.

MATH—PROBLEM SOLVING

Word Problems   **E9 F9 E8 C9 T8 I7 V9 +9 T = 8.7**

Reference: Landi, 2001.
Goal: This intervention is an effective 4-step problem solving strategy used to help students make sense of math word problems and express the problems in mathematical terms.
Age Group: Elementary or Secondary.
Materials: Poster board listing the 4-step problem solving strategy.
Steps:

1. The activities and examples can be used to train students to use a cognitive strategy to improve math problem solving skills.

2. The 4-step problem solving strategy includes the following steps: (a poster listing the 4-steps can be placed at the front of the classroom).
Step 1: *Paraphrase* (put in your own words). The students practice underlining important information and retelling the problem in their own words.
Step 2: *Visualize* (a diagram or a picture). The students make a drawing or a diagram of the information.
Step 3: *Hypothesize* (number of steps, operation, and equation). Students decide how many steps are needed, decide which operation, and write the math problem.
Step 4: *Estimate* (predict the answer). Students estimate the answer.

3. To teach the steps, the teacher should present a word problem to the students, or have students make up their own word problems. An example might be, "My name is Tyler and I am 9 years old. Our class is going on a fieldtrip to the zoo. I need to bring $1.50 for the bus, $1.25 for lunch money, and $2.00 for admission. How much money do I need?"

4. To practice Step 1, the teacher reads the problem aloud and asks, "What am I trying to find out? I will circle the question to remind myself. What information will help me?" The teacher circles the question, underlines the important information, and models the process by thinking aloud, while discussing the meaning of important and unimportant information contained in the paragraph. The teacher asks students for a good way to restate the problem in their own words. After the teacher has modeled the steps, the students should create their own problems and practice circling the question, underlining important facts, and restating the problem in their own words.

5. Depicting word problems in drawings or diagrams will help students visualize the underlying structure. To practice Step 2, the teacher should begin with easy problems. The teacher models the process by thinking aloud while creating a drawing or diagram.

6. To teach Step 3, students are asked to practice identifying the type of problem (e.g., addition or subtraction) and how many steps are involved. Two-step problems can be color-coded. Students can practice reading problems and identifying the operation required. Students should then practice reading problems and telling or writing the correct math expression, rather than solving the problem yet.

7. Step 4 involves asking students to estimate the answer. The teacher can plot all the estimates on a number line and discuss them. For example, the teacher might state, "Remember, when you estimate, there is never one right answer. It's just getting pretty close to the right answer." After plotting all the estimates, the class can solve the problem and discuss how the solution compares with the estimates.

Troubleshooting: This procedure is offered as a suggestion for teaching word problem solving skills, however, to use this strategy, students should have the basic reading skills and vocabulary to read and understand the word problems.

ORGANIZATIONAL STRATEGIES

Cut and Paste   **E9 F9 E8 C8 T8 I7 V9 +9 T = 8.6**

Reference: Porte, 2001.
Goal: Cut and Paste is a notetaking strategy used to help students produce notes through manipulating and organizing pieces of written information about a topic, rather than writing it themselves.
Age Group: Secondary.
Materials: Notebook paper, glue or tape, photocopies of teacher prepared notes.
Steps:

1. This activity can be adapted for almost any subject area or curriculum, particularly history, science, social studies, or language arts. It can also be implemented in cooperative learning groups. The cut and paste activity encourages the acquisition of complete notes for students who may have writing speed and processing difficulties and it increases active student engagement in the learning process.
2. The teacher creates a set of notes containing the information desired for discussion and review of a particular topic. The notes may be handwritten or typed, however, the information should be well spaced and easy to read, with space reserved for numbers to be added later. For younger students or students with learning problems, the notes can be simplified or adjusted to the appropriate reading level. A photocopy of the notes is made for each student.
3. First, the notes are cut apart (with a paper cutter) into separate note strips, each one containing a heading, or an idea or piece of information (i.e., "The American Family of the 1800s", or "The American family of the 1800s had four basic features."). The copies (strips of paper) of each heading or piece of information are clipped together and placed in an envelope.
4. Each student will need a blank piece of paper, or a teacher prepared blank chart divided into columns. The teacher provides directions for the notetaking activity and models each step by talking out loud and demonstrating how students will attach each piece of information to their blank sheet.
5. Next, students are given the column headings and with teacher direction they determine the best order for the headings to be placed on the page

(the paper may need to be turned sideways). When the group has decided on the best order, the students affix the headings to the page.

6. Then, the students take turns selecting pieces of information that have been placed in the envelope. Each student takes a turn selecting a note, distributes copies to the group, and reads it as everyone in the group listens and follows along. The group then discusses the information and decides under which heading it should be placed.

7. The procedure for selecting and distributing notes continues until all of the separate notes are placed in the correct columns. Next, the notes under each heading are numbered for the best sequential order. Students can number the notes after all the notes are read and placed under the correct headings. The teacher should confirm that the placement is correct before the students affix it to the page with paste or tape.

8. After students have completed the notetaking activity, the notes can be used for study or review or to provide students with an outline for writing an essay about the topic.

Troubleshooting: If students have difficulty with organizing the notes on their page, the teacher may wish to use a prepared graphic organizer, strategic notetaking form (refer to interventions in this chapter), or provide a blank chart already divided into columns.

Daily Calendars E8 F9 E9 C9 T8 I8 V10 +9 T = 8.8

Reference: Flores, Schloss, & Alper, 1995.
Goal: Daily calendars are a method used by individual students to structure their school day, organize and plan activities, and self-monitor completion of activities and tasks.
Age Group: Elementary or Secondary.
Materials: Commercially made appointment calendars, or teacher-made weekly calendars for each student, class chart with a list of students' names.
Steps:

1. Daily calendars are used by students to schedule and self-monitor their completion of day-to-day personal responsibilities. Calendars can also be used to develop a student's reading and writing skills and communicate school information to parents.

2. The teacher can prepare teacher-made weekly calendars (a sheet containing a week on each page with space to write activities for each day), by placing several pages in individual student binders or notebooks, or purchase commercially made appointment-calendar books. Calendars should be easily portable and not overly cumbersome. Older students may prefer calendars that are less obvious and embedded into a multipurpose

notebook. Depending on the student's age and individual needs, calendars or schedules can be designed to include pictures or symbols with words.

3. Before using the calendars, the students are instructed to make a list of the daily, weekly, biweekly, and monthly events in which they participate. The list can also include activities across the day (i.e., lessons, homework time, sports/recreational activities, chores, vocational responsibilities, etc.).

4. Each student is provided with his or her own calendar and they are instructed to record the activities that are included on their lists onto their individual calendars. During a class discussion, the teacher and students discuss the importance of recording events to help remember and complete daily activities. The teacher demonstrates recording the daily activities in the calendar and provides students with an opportunity to practice recording with teacher supervision and assistance if necessary. Students are instructed to review their calendars throughout the day to monitor and check off completion of responsibilities.

5. The teacher instructs students to carry their calendars with them at all times. During the first two weeks, the teacher checks each student's calendar daily (calendars can be checked in a variety of settings and at various times of the day). If the student has their calendar with them to present upon request, and scheduled events are recorded in the calendar, they receive two points on the class chart. If a student does not have their calendar, they receive zero points on the class chart (the teacher can reward one point if the student has the calendar, but the daily activities are not recorded for that day).

6. After the first two weeks, the teacher can reduce the daily calendar checks to one time per week, or as frequently as needed to maintain student use. Random checks at various times will help to maintain consistent use.

7. The students can exchange weekly points for back-up reinforcers, or points can be entered as credit towards their grade for a particular class.

Troubleshooting: It is important that the teacher encourage students to record activities in their calendars and provide students the time and opportunity to make calendar use a part of their daily routine (e.g., allow a few minutes at the end of the period to record information).

Directed Notetaking   **E10 F10 E9 C8 T8 I7 V10 +9 T = 8.9**

Reference: Evans, Pelham, & Grudberg, 1995.
Goal: Directed Notetaking is an intervention used to teach notetaking skills, target passive learning, and reduce disruptive behaviors of students during classroom instruction and lecture periods.

Age Group: Secondary.
Materials: Student notebooks, overhead projector.
Steps:

1. Directed notetaking is a procedure in which the teacher provides the students with a model of the notes they should write in their notebooks during a lecture-format class and through direct instruction, teaches students how to write notes containing the main idea and details in an outline format. Increasing student notetaking can directly target problems of student attending and on-task behavior as well as improve comprehension of lecture information. Although initially, teacher time is required to train students in the notetaking strategy, these techniques can be used over a long period of time and in multiple class settings.

2. This intervention can be used with the entire class and with various subject areas. The teacher presents the lecture to the class and provides the modeling of the notetaking as the notes are to appear in the students' notebooks, although a co-teacher, teacher aide, or a student can also provide the notetaking modeling while the teacher presents the lecture.

3. Each student should have a notebook available to use during the notetaking sessions.

4. The teacher instructs the students that they will be required to have their notebooks each class period and that they will practice notetaking skills with teacher direction.

5. The Directed Notetaking strategy is conducted over several training sessions. During the initial training sessions, the teacher uses an overhead projector to present a model of teacher prepared lecture notes to the students while giving the lecture. The notes are divided into main ideas and details in an outline format. The teacher pauses during the lecture and instructs the students to copy the notes in their notebooks exactly as they appear on the overhead, explaining why some of the information is a main idea and other pieces of information are details. During the training the teacher or aide can assist and prompt students with the notetaking procedure.

6. After students have learned to copy notes correctly, the teacher asks the students to generate the ideas for the notes. Using verbal prompts, the teacher helps the students generate notes, and writes these notes on the overhead projector for the students to use as a model. Students are to copy the student generated notes in their notebooks.

7. The next step of Directed Notetaking is for the teacher to write only the main ideas on the overhead, and ask students to write the details on their own in their notebooks. The teacher can answer questions about the notes, repeat statements when requested, or ask students to report on the details they have written in their notebooks.

8. Finally, students are asked to generate the main ideas, which the teacher writes on the overhead projector for students to copy. The students are asked to complete the notes by writing the details on their own in their notebooks.

Troubleshooting: To encourage compliance, it is helpful to begin with short lecture periods (10–15 min.) and present simple, brief notes and gradually increase the information presented. Students may be allowed to use notes for tests and quizzes.

Graphic Organizers   E10 F9 E9 C8 T8 I8 V9 +9 T = 8.9

Reference: Baxendell, 2003.
Goal: Graphic organizers are visual representations used by teachers and students to help them organize information into meaningful concepts.
Age Group: Elementary or Secondary.
Materials: Graphic Organizer sheets. A sample Cause-and-Effect Graphic Organizer is listed in Appendix A.
Steps:

1. Graphic organizers are visual displays used to represent knowledge. Teachers can use them as an instructional tool and they can be used by students to help them organize information and make it easier to understand. Graphic organizers provide a visual picture of information or concepts. Graphic organizers can be used at any grade level and with a variety of subjects. Some examples of common graphic organizers include Venn diagrams, Semantic webs, Story Maps, and Genealogy trees.
2. The teacher can use a graphic organizer while presenting information to the class, by drawing on the board or on an overhead projector. Students can also draw their own graphic organizers, or the teacher can create a blank graphic organizer sheet for a particular subject, which students then complete by writing in each section. Graphic organizers can be used for classification (animals, foods), math problem solving, illustrating science concepts, explaining key concepts in a story, sequencing events, and cause-and-effect diagrams.
3. To use graphic organizers, consistency is important. The teacher should create a standard set of graphic organizers and establish a consistent routine for students to follow in the classroom. To create any graphic organizer, the teacher should (a) select the information to present to the students, (b) decide on the key components necessary for understanding, (c) create a graphic representation of the information and illustrate the link between key elements, and (d) help students understand the connections by demonstrating and discussing the graphic organizer.

4. For example, the Cause-and-Effect Diagram presented in the appendix can be used when performing science experiments, when discussing major history events, when discussing social or behavioral problems, or when reading fiction and nonfiction stories to demonstrate the effects or results of an individual's actions.

5. After reading a story, the teacher selects a main event, and demonstrates to students how to write this information in the center box labeled "Main Event." Next, the teacher discusses various causes or antecedents that contributed to the main event. Each cause is written in one of the ovals to the left of the center box, labeled "Causes." Finally, the teacher discusses what followed the main event (the result of the action or consequence) and writes each effect in one of the ovals labeled "Effects." Arrows can be drawn to help students visualize the link between causes, main event, and effects.

6. After the teacher has demonstrated how to use the graphic organizer, students can complete them during an independent reading or study period, during a class discussion, or in pairs. Students can also be given partially completed graphic organizers to fill in, or can use pictures to illustrate the ideas represented in the diagram.

Troubleshooting: Most students benefit from graphic organizers, however, students with special needs learn best when they are used consistently, they are presented in a clear organized manner, clear labels are provided, and the number of ideas is limited.

Homework Graphing E9 F10 E9 C9 T8 I9 V10 $+9$ T $= 9.2$

Reference: Trammel, Schloss, & Alper, 1994.
Goal: Homework Graphing is a self-monitoring procedure used to increase the completion of daily homework assignments.
Age Group: Secondary.
Materials: Assignment sheet (or weekly or daily planner), self-recording graphing sheets. Refer to Computerized Self-Graphing intervention in Chapter 5 for additional information.
Steps:

1. The teacher creates a weekly assignment sheet for students to record each assignment for a particular school day. The sheet includes a row adjacent to the day of the week (i.e., Monday through Friday). Next to each day of the week is a column numbered for each class period in which homework is typically assigned and a space by each period for students to record each assignment. A weekly planner can also be used if available.

2. The teacher demonstrates how to complete the assignment sheet through modeling and guided practice. Students are asked to record their assignments in the appropriate column associated with each class period. The teacher should write the assignment on the board for students to copy onto their sheet. If no homework is assigned for a particular class, the student can write "No Homework", NH, or mark an O in the space.

3. Each Friday, students obtain a weekly assignment sheet for the coming week. Students carry the assignment sheet to each classroom and write that day's homework assignment on their sheets. If an assignment is due at a later date, the due date should be recorded next to the assignment.

4. Initially, the teacher may need to review assignment sheets at the end of the class period or day to check that students have recorded all assignments. The teacher can provide verbal praise or small reinforcers (i.e., piece of candy, etc.) to students who have recorded assignments accurately.

5. When homework assignments are completed, students are to draw a diagonal line across the box to indicate that the assignment is complete. When the assignment is turned in, students are to draw a diagonal line going the opposite way across the box (forming a large X across the box). To be accurately recorded with an X, the assignment should be judged by the teacher to be at least 70% accurate.

6. The teacher instructs students on how to graph their homework completion data. Students are provided individual graphing sheets. Simple graph paper can be used or the teacher can create a graphing sheet containing the days across the horizontal axis, and the number of class periods or possible homework assignments (i.e., 1–7) on the vertical axis. At the end of the day, students count the number of completed assignments (the number of Xs), and mark their graphing sheet with the correct number for that day.

7. Students can be required to set individual goals for homework completion at the beginning of each week. Goals should be reconsidered each week and should be equal to or above levels obtained for preceding weeks. Students who meet their goal can earn small reinforcers or earn points towards secondary reinforcers. Individual graphs may also be publicly displayed in the classroom.

Troubleshooting: It is important that teachers discuss and provide feedback to students about their homework assignments. Homework assignments should have specific objectives and be used to practice or review material covered in class.

Homework Steps—PROJECT   **E9 F9 E8 C8 T8 I8 V9 +9 T = 8.6**

Reference: Hughes, Ruhl, Schumaker, & Deshler, 2002.

Goal: This intervention involves teaching students a self-managed assignment completion strategy comprised of the steps required for independent completion of any assignment.

Age Group: Secondary.

Materials: Student assignment notebooks containing a Monthly Planner, weekly Study Schedule, and Assignment Sheets. A sample Assignment Sheet is listed in Appendix A.

Steps:

1. The teacher explains the strategy to the students, discussing where, when, why, and how it can be used. The strategy includes seven sequential steps to cue specific overt and cognitive behaviors required to complete any assignment. The first letters of each step forms the mnemonic PROJECT, which is used to help students remember the steps.

2. The teacher presents the PROJECT steps to the students, on a poster, handout, or overhead projector. These steps include a sequence of behaviors (i.e., recording the assignment, analyzing the time needed, planning when to work on the assignment, working on the assignment, checking the assignment, and turning it in). The teacher should present each step by thinking out loud and modeling for students.

   Prepare your forms—students fill in monthly planners and weekly study schedules.

   Record the assignment and ask any questions—students record assignment on sheet.

   Organize by: **B**reaking assignment into parts. **E**stimate the time and sessions needed. **S**chedule the time, and **T**ake materials home (these sub-steps form the mnemonic BEST)—students complete these steps after all assignments have been recorded.

   Jump to it—students get out materials and check the requirements of the assignment.

   Engage in the work—students work on the assignment, recruiting help if needed.

   Check your work—students review work for accuracy, neatness, and completeness.

   Turn in your work—students turn in the assignment on time.

3. Each student is given an assignment notebook that contains several copies of three forms, the Monthly Planner—a blank calendar students can use for long-range planning, Weekly Study Schedule—a weekly planner page containing days of the week and time periods that students can use to record the time periods they will work on assignments, and an Assignment Sheet—a form on which students record the assignment.

4. When using the first step, "Prepare your forms", the students fill in numbers for each day of the month on the Monthly Planner, writing in any special activities. Next they mark the Study Schedule by blocking out time periods for completing homework. The second step is used when the teacher gives an assignment. Students record the assignment on the Assignment Sheet, noting the due date.
5. After students have learned each step they are provided an opportunity to practice each step on simulated assignments, with teacher guidance and corrective feedback.
6. Students can use the PROJECT steps as a checklist to self-monitor use of the strategy steps for assignments. Students can earn points for completing each step, with points contributing to the final grade or exchanged for secondary reinforcers.

Troubleshooting: It is important for teachers to spend adequate instructional time explaining each step, and encouraging students to fill in monthly calendars, study schedules, and assignment sheets by designating a few minutes during each class period to record the information.

Learning Logs   **E9 F9 E8 C9 T8 I6 V9 +9 T = 8.6**

Reference: Carr, 2002.
Goal: This intervention involves a technique that students can use to think about and record steps involved in higher-level thinking and problem solving skills. These techniques help teachers and students assess the thinking processes that students engage in as they read, write, and problem solve.
Age Group: Upper Elementary or Secondary.
Materials: Learning Log sheets or student journals. A sample Learning Log sheet is listed in Appendix A.
Steps:

1. Student learning logs or journals serve as a record of progress and provide information about students' learning processes. Students use the Learning Logs to record key ideas learned, record predictions, ask questions, summarize information, and make connections. Teachers can review Learning Logs to assess students' understanding of concepts, as well as students' misconceptions and questions they may have. The information obtained also provides information on the effectiveness of the teachers' instruction.
2. Learning Logs involve a short, objective, written entry that students complete on a regular basis following an instructional lesson or reading assignment. The entries are written on prepared Learning Log sheets or in student journals. Learning Logs can be used for any subject area; science, social studies, math, language arts, or reading.

3. To teach students how to use Learning Logs, a direct instruction approach is recommended. The teacher explains the purpose of the activity and demonstrates a sample entry (i.e., the teacher can explain the steps and thinking process while completing a Learning Log sheet on the overhead projector or on the board).

4. The Learning Log can be adapted for different ages and grade levels. The teacher can prepare Learning Log sheets with the questions listed below or adapt the format to include questions that will elicit the information desired.

5. The Learning Logs should include the name, date, topic and questioning statements for example;
   (a) The most important ideas I learned from today's discussion are:
   (b) Some things I already knew about this topic are:
   (c) Some things I don't understand are:
   (d) Some things I want to know more about:

6. Students may also record feelings, opinions, and personal experiences about a topic on Learning Logs (e.g., "What I like best about the story", "Two important ideas", "Two ways I could use this information", or "What I need to work on").

7. Students will become more proficient at writing entries and Learning Logs will be more effective if they are used on a regular, consistent basis (e.g., 15 minutes for 6th graders writing in Learning Logs twice a week, or 10–20 minutes daily).

8. Teachers also should review and respond to students' entries on a consistent basis; however, they do not need to respond to every entry. Responses should be brief and encouraging. Teachers can make a schedule so that review of student logs is manageable (i.e., review once per week) or have students share entries with a partner.

9. Teachers can assess entries based on the number of descriptive words, the length of entry, etc., rather than based on spelling or writing skills.

Troubleshooting: It is important for the teacher to model the process for the students, and show them that their thoughts, ideas, and questions are valued.

PACE 1,2—(Prompt, Arranged,   E10 F9 E8 C8 T8 I7 V9 $+9$ T $= 8.7$
Complete, Edited)

Reference: Rademacher, 2000.
Goal: The PACE 1,2 procedure is a scoring guideline or rubric used to teach students to self-check finished assignments with a standard set of work criteria.
Age Group: Secondary.
Materials: None.

Steps:

1. PACE 1,2, is a simple scoring rubric involving self-or peer-assessment to rate a student's finished work against predetermined standards. This procedure provides an opportunity for active student involvement and teacher feedback in the evaluating process. Because rubrics provide clear expectations, they help students see a specific way to improve achievement, thus increasing motivation.

2. The teacher explains that students will learn how to check the quality of work on their assignments. The teacher demonstrates by showing examples of assignments that represent "nonquality" and "quality" work, pointing out the differences.

3. The teacher explains the meaning of PACE as a way for students to remember the requirements for "quality" assignments, and shows the students an example of a "quality" assignment with the word PACE marked at the bottom of the page.

4. PACE is a mnemonic which refers to four basic criteria required of all assignments,

   (a) **P**rompt—assignment is completed and turned in on time.

   (b) **A**rranged neatly—well organized, neatly written.

   (c) **C**omplete—the entire assignment is finished, all sections completed.

   (d) **E**dited—the assignment has been checked for accuracy and proofread.

   (e) The 1, 2 following the word PACE refer to any number of additional criteria that may be required of a particular assignment (i.e., illustrations, note cards, outline).

5. The teacher models, while thinking out loud, how students should write the letters PACE and a series of numbers (1,2 . . .) in a designated place on their assignment. Next to each number, students write a word to indicate the additional requirements (i.e., 1—date, 2—picture). Under each letter and number, students are instructed to draw two short lines.

6. When students are finished with an assignment, they review their completed work. After review, students are to place a check mark or a zero on the top set of lines to indicate whether or not they met each requirement for the assignment. A check mark indicates that the requirement was met. A zero indicates the requirement was not met. The second set of lines is for the teacher to also evaluate with a check mark or zero whether or not each requirement has been met.

7. The teacher can provide an example of a "quality" assignment with clearly specified grading criteria for students to practice using the PACE procedure. After students have practiced marking the assignment the teacher and students can discuss and compare their evaluations.

8. When students demonstrate understanding and proficiency using PACE on a practice assignment, they can use this procedure on their own assignments or a partner's assignment.
9. After the teacher has marked and returned completed assignments, positive and corrective feedback can be given to students on their use of PACE.

Troubleshooting: It is critical to involve students in discussing the importance of evaluating their own work and to let them know that their input is valued. Individual feedback can be given to specific students as necessary, particularly if teacher and student evaluations significantly differ.

SQ3R   E10 F9 E9 C9 T8 I8 V9 +9 T = 8.8

Reference: Adams, Carnine, & Gersten, 1982.
Goal: The SQ3R method is a study skill strategy used to teach students specific steps to increase retention of reading material, particularly in content areas.
Age Group: Elementary or Secondary.
Materials: Grade level textbooks in any content area, list of SQ3R steps.
Steps:

1. The SQ3R strategy was first developed by Robinson (1941) in *Diagnostic and Remedial Techniques for Effective Study* as a study method to use with content area textbooks. SQ3R consists of a systematic metacognitive strategy in which the student is aware of the purpose of the strategy and taught to monitor use of the strategy. The steps of SQ3R include:
   (1) Survey—preview the passage by reading headings and subheadings before actually reading the text to get an overall idea about what you will be studying.
   (2) Question—ask yourself what is the subheading? What will I be studying? (Students are instructed to look up and try to say the subheading without looking and then check to see if correct). Ask yourself questions about what might be important to remember regarding the subheading.
   (3) Read—the information under the subheading to find important details.
   (4) Reread—the subheading to insure that it will become a retrieval cue. Then recite important details including answers to the questions asked in step 2 and any other important information.
   (5) Rehearse—review each subheading and recite important details and try to recall the information. Not recalling important information indicates additional study is necessary.

2. The teacher instructs the students on how to use the SQ3R study method, by providing a rationale for learning the study skills strategy, direct instruction of each step, modeling the use of each step, and guiding students through practice sessions and giving appropriate feedback. Initially, students learn to recite and apply the steps while studying one textbook passage together as a class. Students can also be given a list of the steps to keep at their desk for reference.

3. After students have demonstrated use of the steps, they are given a specific time period (20–40 minutes) to study independently and practice using the steps. Following the study period, the teacher can give students a 10-question quiz to complete without looking at their book. When reviewing the questions with the class, the teacher praises students for correct answers and provides correct answers when there is an error. The teacher can prompt students before each study period, by challenging them to study better so the next quiz score will be higher.

Troubleshooting: The initial emphasis is on learning an effective strategy—not a focus on grades or quiz scores. While learning the steps and practicing the study strategy, students should not be penalized for mistakes or low quiz scores, just encouraged to use the strategy to help them learn.

Strategic Notetaking   **E10 F10 E9 C9 T8 I8 V10 +9 T = 9.1**

Reference: Boyle & Weishaar, 2001.
Goal: Strategic Notetaking is a method that students can use to become more proficient notetakers during classroom lectures by using a form with written prompts.
Age Group: Secondary.
Materials: Strategic Notetaking Form, overhead projector. A sample Notetaking Form is listed in Appendix A.
Steps:

1. Strategic notetaking is a technique used to help students with learning or behavior difficulties take more efficient notes. This technique promotes active student engagement during lectures and increases attention to lecture material. Notes also serve as a written document that assists students during review and test preparation. Although initially, teachers must spend time teaching students the notetaking strategy, these techniques can be used over a long period of time and can be used in multiple class settings.

2. The teacher trains the students how to use the strategic notetaking form by providing a brief description of strategic notetaking, modeling the technique, and guiding students through practice sessions and giving appropriate feedback. The teacher tells the students the purpose of strategic

notetaking is to help them become proficient notetakers by organizing lecture information, identifying the main points, and helping them decide what information is the most important to record. Students without specific training often record notes in a verbatim fashion, which is inefficient and usually difficult for students with handwriting and spelling skills deficit.

3. The teacher reviews the Strategic Notetaking Form with the students, pointing out the cues on each page. The teacher can model the use of the sheet by having the class watch a short subject area video and the teacher demonstrate writing the notes on the form (using an overhead projector). The teacher can use a "think aloud" technique while writing notes on the form. The teacher should point out to students how important words and phrases should be recorded rather than recording the lecture verbatim. The teacher also emphasizes less concern with spelling or grammar. Following the teacher demonstration, the students practice filling in a Strategic Notetaking Form, with teacher assistance and feedback.

4. The Strategic Notetaking Form is a sheet that includes written prompts to help students organize and summarize lecture information. Students should review the sheet and fill in some of the information before the lecture. An example of a Strategic Notetaking Form can include the following cues with space for students to write notes after each cue; however, the teacher can develop a personalized form based on the class subject and grade level.

   (a) Before the lecture—What is today's topic?
   (b) Describe what you already know about this topic.
   (c) During the lecture—name three to seven main points with details of today's topic.
   (d) Summary—describe briefly how the ideas are related.
   (e) New vocabulary or terms.
   (f) The third step, (name three to seven main points with details), and the fourth step (new vocabulary or terms) can be repeated as necessary, depending on the length of the lecture.
   (g) At end of lecture—write five main points of the lecture and describe each.

Troubleshooting: Students may need several practice sessions to learn to use this technique before doing on their own. Once the technique is learned, use of the forms could be replaced by having students write the prompts on a note card to use as a cue card, or having the teacher write prompts on the board.

Chapter 7

Interventions for Social Skills

Social development is inextricably linked to a student's school success and his or her long-term social acceptance and adjustment. While most children develop social skills by observing the real-life modeling of parents, siblings, extended family, and teachers, as well as daily interactions with their peers; children with behavioral problems often have not developed or do not satisfactorily demonstrate these important skills. In fact, inability to establish and maintain satisfactory peer and teacher relationships is a key defining characteristic of behaviorally disordered children—unfortunately resulting in profound implications throughout their lives. Many students with attention problems, oppositional or defiant behaviors, aggressive behaviors, or those who annoy and bother other students are disliked or rejected by their peers. In addition, students with learning disabilities, autistic disorders, or internalizing disorders are sometimes teased by peers and may have significant difficulties making and keeping friends.

It is important to distinguish between social skills deficits and performance deficits. Students with social skills deficits have not acquired the necessary skills to interact with others in an age-appropriate manner. For example, these students have not learned how to read social cues and nonverbal cues in their environment, or have not yet learned conversational and listening skills or how to join into peer activities. Students with performance deficits, on the other hand, are those students who have learned the skills and have previously demonstrated these skills, however do not perform them consistently or at appropriate times. Students with performance deficits may lack motivation or the opportunity to use the skills or may be somehow reinforced for their inappropriate behaviors.

The social skills interventions described in this chapter are different strategies and activities that include the basic components of a behavioral intervention:

direct teaching, adult and peer modeling, opportunities for students to practice the skills, and positive reinforcement programs to encourage skill performance. These interventions can be implemented in the classroom with all students or modified for individual or small groups; however, social skills instruction is most effective when it occurs in the natural setting. Many of the procedures described in this chapter also share the same characteristics of a direct and systematic instruction model that is effective in teaching academic skills, including planned systematic teaching of specific skills through demonstration and modeling, guided and controlled student practice (role-playing), independent practice, opportunity for generalization to various settings and situations, and contingent reinforcement for successful skill performance.

When selecting social skills for intervention, the student's age and developmental level should be considered, as well as which skills most likely lead to increased acceptance by peers and adults. There are numerous social skills training programs that are commercially available and are appropriate for use with students with behavior problems. Regardless of the program used or the specific skill targeted, these basic considerations for implementing a social skills intervention are recommended.

1. To promote social competence for all children, it is important that the classroom climate encourages caring, respect, tolerance, and cooperation. In fact, teaching social competence is not an isolated lesson, but should be an integral component of the entire schooling process.
2. For specific social skills interventions, select skills that will maximize student success and lead to increased peer acceptance.
3. During instruction and practice, use relevant examples and situations that reflect what is actually occurring in the classroom or on the playground.
4. Provide sufficient supervised practice and extend practice by providing homework assignments.
5. Include student self-management or self-monitoring to enhance skill acquisition and to evaluate progress.
6. Ask other teachers, school personnel, and parents to support and reinforce the skill to enhance generalization to the real world and across settings.

SOCIAL SKILLS

Bibliotherapy   **E9 F9 E7 C8 T7 I9 V9 +10 T = 8.6**

Reference: Forgan, 2002.
Goal: Bibliotherapy is a strategy that involves teaching students social problem-solving skills and relating skills to problem situations identified in stories found in children's literature.

Age Group: Elementary.
Materials: Selected stories from children's literature. Examples are listed in Appendix A.
Steps:

1. Bibliotherapy is a technique used to help students solve problems through reading and discussing stories or books in which the character experiences problems similar to those encountered in childhood. Bibliotherapy is useful because students can identify with the character in the story, understand that others have similar problems, and discuss and plan solutions to a problem.

2. Bibliotherapy can be used in small group or whole class settings. The teacher selects stories containing experiences students are likely to encounter in school or social situations, such as teasing, anger, bullying, friendships, or self-esteem. It is important for the teacher to select topics that are developmental in nature. Stories should be chosen that allow students to identify with the main character. Stories can be selected from children's literature available at the library or bookstore. Refer to the appendix for a sample listing of appropriate stories and topics.

3. The first step in bibliotherapy is *prereading*. During prereading, the teacher displays the cover and title of the book and asks students to talk about and predict what might happen in the story, stating, "The story we are going to read today is about teasing. How many of you have ever been teased before?" Students are given an opportunity to discuss what they already know about the topic.

4. The second step is *guided reading*. During this step the teacher reads the story aloud to the students. Most children's literature can be read aloud during one class period.

5. Next is the *postreading discussion*. The teacher asks the students to retell the story sequence and discuss the character(s) feelings. The teacher can ask questions to help students think about their feelings and help them identify with the characters and events in the story (i.e., "How do you think ___ was feeling when the boy was calling him names? Why do kids say mean things?" etc.).

6. The final step is the *problem solving activity*. The I SOLVE mnemonic problem-solving strategy can be used and should be pre-taught through modeling and guided practice: (a) **I**—Identify the problem, (b) **S**—Solutions to solve the problem? (c) **O**—Obstacles to the solutions? (d) **L**—Look at all the solutions and choose one. (e) **V**—Very good. Try it. and (f) **E**—Evaluate the outcome.

7. The teacher guides the students through the problem-solving steps by identifying the main problem for discussion, asking students to list all

solutions the story characters considered as well as generating additional solutions, examining each solution and thinking of possible obstacles, choosing the best solution, trying the solution, and evaluating the outcome to decide if it worked.

8. The students can be given opportunities to role-play story problems and solutions.

Troubleshooting: To promote generalization, students should be reminded to use strategies throughout the day. It is important to practice using I SOLVE steps with several different stories to provide sufficient understanding and practice.

Buddy Skills   **E9 F9 E8 C8 T8 I8 V9 +9 T = 8.6**

Reference: English, Goldstein, Kaczmarek & Shafer, 1996.
Goal: This intervention involves a buddy system in which peers are trained to use "Buddy Skills" in a planned social interaction with students with social skills deficits.
Age Group: Preschool or Elementary.
Materials: Stickers, stamps, or other token reinforcers.
Steps:

1. The Buddy Skills activity is a peer-tutoring model used with young students to increase social interaction skills in students with low rates of social involvement or social skills deficits. It can be implemented in a classroom setting with an entire class (i.e., preschool classroom), with a small group, or with individual students. The Buddy Skills activity can be implemented across the day, during a recess or playtime period, or scheduled on a weekly basis.
2. To pair students, the teacher should make a list of potential peer buddies in the classroom, evaluating factors such as social maturity, communication skills, shared interests, and willingness to participate. The teacher then pairs the peer buddy students with the targeted students. Pairing should be considered a long-term match and if possible, students of the same gender should be paired.
3. The teacher determines a specific time period in which to implement the Buddy Skills activity. For example, the peer buddy may be asked to be a buddy for 5–10 minutes during the daily free play period or during a structured activity such as snack time.
4. The teacher introduces the Buddy Skills to the peer buddies through discussion and training. During the training session(s), three Buddy Skills are taught to the peer buddies: to STAY, PLAY, and TALK with their assigned buddy. Students are instructed to stay near their buddy during the activity. The teacher explains that to STAY with their buddy means to

"stick close." If during the activity their buddy moves to another area, they are to follow them. When beginning the activity, the peer is instructed to get their buddy's attention, say hi or hello, use the buddy's name, and ask the buddy to play with them.

5. The teacher explains that to STAY and PLAY with their buddy means: while they "stick close" to their buddy, they join in the activity in which their buddy is participating, bring a toy to the buddy, or ask the buddy to join in with them.

6. The third step includes STAY, PLAY, and TALK with their buddy, which means: while playing with their buddy, peers talk and interact with their buddy. During the training sessions, students should have an opportunity to practice using the three steps in role-play situations prior to using with their assigned buddy.

7. During the Buddy Skills activity, the teacher may use reminders or prompts to encourage peer buddies to use the steps correctly. The teacher may give verbal or visual prompts such as, "Remember to talk to your buddy while you're playing" or give a thumbs-up signal.

8. At the end of each activity, peers can be positively reinforced with verbal praise or receive stickers or stamps on a chart for "staying, playing, and talking" with their buddies during the classroom activity. Both peers in a pair receive the reinforcer.

Troubleshooting: Although training sessions can be conducted for the nondisabled peers, it is important to convey to both members of the pair that they are expected to interact together.

Cooperative Learning   **E9 F9 E9 C8 T7 I8 V9 +9 T = 8.6**

Reference: Rutherford, Mathur, & Quinn, 1998.
Goal: In Cooperative Learning, students are placed in heterogeneous learning groups to provide opportunities for positive social interactions.
Age Group: Elementary or Secondary.
Materials: Team cue cards (listing target skills).
Steps:

1. The teacher assigns students to cooperative learning teams based on ability level, random assignment, or by grouping students who work well together. To create heterogeneous teams that include socially competent and less competent students, the teacher can rate students on their level of social competence and rank order from highest to lowest. Starting from the top of the list and working down, each student is assigned to a team, (i.e., the student ranked first is assigned to Team A, the student ranked second is assigned to Team B, etc.) until each team has one member. The

second member is assigned by starting from the bottom of the list and consecutively working up (i.e., the last student on the list is assigned to Team A, the next to last is assigned to Team B, etc.). The third member of each group is assigned by returning to the top of the list of remaining students, and moving down, and so on until all students are assigned to a team.

2. The teacher instructs all students in three or four target social communication skills they will need to use in social interaction during cooperative learning. Target skills should be specific, observable, and measurable and can include (a) Conversational questions—questions used to elicit information from another group member or to encourage another member to participate (i.e., What is the problem? What do you think? What would you do?), (b) Positive comments to others—statements that include positive feedback, compliments, or manners words (i.e., Please. Thank you. That's a good idea, I think that would work), and (c) Positive self-references—statements that include positive references about one's preference, opinions or ideas (i.e., I think, I prefer, I suggest, or I understand). Target skills should be taught over several sessions, using direct instruction, teacher modeling, and opportunity for students to practice through role-play situations.

3. After students have had sufficient opportunity to practice the target skills with teacher feedback, students are asked to engage in a problem solving activity within their cooperative teams. This activity can be scheduled on a regular basis (i.e., two times per week for 10 minutes). The teacher reads a different short problem situation, and students are asked to listen carefully to the description of the problem and engage in a 10-minute discussion in their group on how to solve the problem. Each group can be given a cue card to use as a prompt to remind them of the target skills to use.

4. One group member from each group can be assigned the role of team recorder, and make tally marks on a notepad, every time a team member performs a target skill. After the 10-minute cooperative activity, a member of each group is asked to answer follow-up questions and report on the group's discussion of the problem.

Troubleshooting: The teacher can encourage use of skills and positive group interactions by awarding points toward a weekly or monthly snack party (e.g., 20 points = snack party). Points are awarded based on the team's responses during follow-up, and if every team member performs the target skills. For example, in 5-member teams, each team could earn 5 points toward the snack party if all members participated during the activity.

FAST and SLAM   **E9 F9 E7 C7 T7 I7 V9 +9 T = 8.1**

Reference: McIntosh, Vaughn, & Bennerson, 1995.

Goal: This strategy involves use of a mnemonic device to help students increase social problem-solving skills, and improve social interactions with peers.
Age Group: Elementary.
Materials: Poster or chart listing skill steps.
Steps:

1. FAST and SLAM are mnemonic devices used to teach students interpersonal problem-solving skills. Through direct instruction, modeling, and role-playing the teacher provides skills training to students on both strategies, either with the entire classroom or with small groups. The teacher may select a small group of students (which can include students with behavior or social disabilities) to be the class's "social skills trainers." Student trainers meet several times to learn the strategies and practice skills. Student trainers can then present the information to the entire class. By designating students with disabilities as "trainers" who will present information to the other students, the peer acceptance of these students can be elevated.

2. The teacher presents the first strategy, "FAST" to the "trainers". The following steps are explained to the students and visually presented on a chart or poster.
   (a) **F**—Freeze and Think (Students ask themselves, "What is the problem?" "Can I restate the problem?").
   (b) **A**—Alternatives (Students ask themselves, "What are some things I can do to solve this problem?" Students think of and list several alternatives).
   (c) **S**—Solution (Students decide on the best alternative, asking, "Is it fair?" "Is it safe?").
   (d) **T**—Try it (Students try out the solution and ask, "Did it work?" If the solution doesn't solve the problem, return to step two and pick another alternative).

3. The SLAM strategy is another mnemonic device students can use to accept negative feedback or respond to negative comments. As with FAST, the SLAM steps are explained to the "trainers" and visually presented on a chart or a poster.
   (a) **S**—STOP (The student should stop what they are doing).
   (b) **L**—LOOK (The student looks at the other person).
   (c) **A**—ASK (The student should ask the person a question to clarify what is meant).
   (d) **M**—MAKE (The student should make an appropriate response to the person).

4. The teacher provides opportunities for "trainers" to practice the steps of FAST and SLAM by constructing a "problem-solving box" and asking

students to write down social problems on a slip of paper and place them in the box. During training sessions, students can select a problem and practice the steps to solve the problem in a role-play situation.

5. After "trainers" have practiced the steps, they can present a social skills training session in the classroom to provide the information to the other students through skits designed from selected problems.

Troubleshooting: The student trainers can meet outside the classroom to learn the strategies and practice skills before presenting to their classmates. The class should perceive "trainers" as providers of new information. One way to encourage this is to form the "trainer" group by pairing less-accepted students with higher-accepted students.

Good Friendship Game   **E9 F9 E8 C8 T8 I9 V9 +9 T = 8.7**

Reference: Cashwell, Skinner, & Smith, 2001.
Goal: The Good Friendship Game is a classwide game that combines interdependent group reinforcement and public posting to help students identify and report peers' prosocial behaviors.
Age Group: Elementary.
Materials: Small 3 × 5 index cards, class container, and poster board.
Steps:

1. The teacher instructs the students that they will be participating in the Good Friendship Game to help them improve helpful and prosocial behaviors and to reduce tattling. The Good Friendship Game includes teaching students to identify prosocial behaviors, helping students record and report instances of peers' prosocial behaviors, and a group contingency reinforcement when the class meets a predetermined goal.

2. Through direct instruction, modeling, and role-play, the teacher provides a definition of prosocial or helpful behaviors and provides examples and nonexamples of specific behaviors. Examples of prosocial behaviors should be discussed and solicited from the students. Examples include, invite someone to play with you, let them go first, be a good sport, offer to share, offer to help someone, stick up for someone, give a compliment, apologize, smile and say "Hi" to a new kid, etc. These specific behaviors can be listed on the bulletin board or written on a large chart.

3. The teacher instructs students on how to record examples of peers' prosocial behaviors and defines the criteria. The criteria include: (a) behaviors of another student, (b) the behavior is a specific helpful or prosocial behavior listed on the chart, and (c) the behavior occurred at school. Students are taught how to record an instance of a prosocial behavior on a small index card by writing the name of the student, what they did, and who

they were with (i.e., "Billy asked Austin to play with him at recess", or "Jacob shared the legos with Skyler").

4. The teacher and students generate a list of possible group-oriented activity or tangible reinforcers (i.e., class party, popcorn and movie, game time, etc.). The teacher and students select a reinforcer and determine a cumulative goal (i.e., 50–100 reports). The goal is posted on a large poster board divided into 50–100 squares, or a ladder drawn on a poster board containing 50–100 steps. The poster is displayed in a visible location in the classroom.

5. Each day, all students are given an index card that is taped to their desks. They are instructed to record all incidents of peers' prosocial behaviors observed during the day. At the end of the day students put their index cards in the classroom container. A specific time should be scheduled each day for the teacher to review the cards and announce how many peer reports were made. An icon is moved up the steps of the ladder or a square is colored in the poster for each positive report, to provide students with cumulative progress feedback.

6. When the class reaches their cumulative goal, the entire class receives the predetermined reinforcer. A new goal and new reinforcer can be selected and the process begins again.

Troubleshooting: Younger children may verbally report peers' positive behavior and move the icon up the ladder during a scheduled group period. The teacher may also incorporate "mystery motivators" (randomly marked surprise squares or steps on the ladder) to provide intermittent reinforcement (smaller rewards) along the way.

Positive Peer Reporting   **E9 F9 E9 C9 T8 I8 V9 +10 T = 9.0**

Reference: Moroz & Jones, 2002.
Goal: This intervention involves the use of structured peer praise to increase the positive social interactions of students with social skills or behavioral problems.
Age Group: Elementary.
Materials: Poster listing steps for giving praise statements, jar, and cotton balls or marbles.
Steps:

1. Positive Peer Reporting (PPR) involves teaching and rewarding students for providing descriptive praise to students with social problems or students with low rates of social involvement.

2. The teacher provides a rationale and description of PPR by introducing the activity to the class. The teacher informs the students that they are going to work on peer relations and that each week a different student

will be chosen as the "class star." One student at a time will be the "class star" and other students in the class will have an opportunity to praise the star's good behavior.

3. During the introduction to the activity, the teacher should present the steps to use when making a praise statement. These steps can also be displayed in the classroom on a poster or a bulletin board. The steps to giving appropriate praise include:
    (a) Look at the person.
    (b) Smile.
    (c) Describe what the person said or did.
    (d) Say something nice, such as "good job" or "Wow, way to go."

4. After learning the steps, students are given an opportunity to practice giving examples of appropriate praise statements to each other.

5. The teacher selects a student to be the "class star" for the day and announces the name at the beginning of the day or week. During each day, a scheduled time period of 5 to 10-minutes is allocated for the PPR session. The period should be scheduled after the recess period. During the PPR session, the teacher announces that students will be given the opportunity to praise the "class star." The teacher reviews the steps in giving appropriate praise statements. Students are allowed to give the praise statements on a voluntary, random basis. The teacher encourages the group to give praise statements by asking for example, "Would anyone else like to say something?" The teacher praises students for giving appropriate comments.

6. The teacher can determine the length of time each student is the "class star." One or two week durations work well so that by the end of the school year all students will have a turn as the "class star."

7. The teacher can include a group contingency reward component by placing a cotton ball or a marble in a jar for each appropriate praise statement given during the PPR session. When the jar is full, the teacher can provide a classwide reward (i.e., popcorn, treats, class party, root beer floats, etc.).

Troubleshooting: The students should have sufficient opportunity to practice giving descriptive praise statements. The teacher may need to remind students to focus praise statements on something the student said or did that was socially or behaviorally appropriate, rather than praising how the student looks or what he or she is wearing (i.e., "Good job playing the game", rather than, "Nice shirt.").

Puppet Script Training   **E7 F9 E8 C7 T7 I10 V9 +9 T = 8.3**

Reference: Gronna, Serna, Kennedy, & Prater, 1999.
Goal: In this procedure, puppets enacting sociodramatic scripts are used to teach social skills to young students.

Age Group: Preschool or Early Elementary.
Materials: A variety of large, colorful puppets (paper puppets can also be used), and teacher created story scripts, or commercially available social skills curriculum.
Steps:

1. The teacher selects specific social skills to target for instruction based on individual or class assessment of skills needed. Examples of skills suitable for young children include: greetings, responding to a greeting, initiating a conversation, asking to join, making a request, asking a question, etc.
2. During puppet script training, students sit in a semicircle in the classroom or on a carpeted floor facing the teacher. Sessions can be conducted daily, or weekly in 15-minute periods.
3. Commercially available puppets work well, or large, colorful, paper puppets can be created. A variety of animal or people puppets can be used.
4. Commercially available curriculum containing social skills lessons can be used, such as *Cool Kids* (Kemp, Fister, & Conrad, 1998) or *The Tough Kid Social Skills Book* (Sheridan, 1995) or the teacher can custom-design a sequence of steps for any desired prosocial behavior. For example, specific skills for a giving a greeting typically include establishing eye contact, smiling, saying the other child's name, and saying, "Hello", "Hi", or "Good Morning" in a nice voice.
5. The teacher explains to the students that they will play a puppet game in the classroom. The teacher uses the puppets to model one skill per session. The teacher uses the puppets to introduce the social skill by telling students they will be watching and listening to the puppets act in a story (i.e., "Greetings from Billy Bear"). The teacher introduces the skill and discusses the importance with the students, outlining necessary components. The teacher then models the skill by enacting a sociodramatic script using the puppets. For example, the teacher can tell a simple story about Billy Bear meeting another animal while walking in the forest, and the animals stop to greet each other. While enacting the story, the teacher can pause the puppet performance to restate the skill steps needed (e.g., face the person, look at the person, smile, say "hello" in a nice voice).
6. Following the teacher demonstration using the puppets, the students are assigned to puppet roles, and given the opportunity to role-play the skills during a guided practice session. Students can face the puppet held in his or her hand, and practice the skill, as well as practice having their puppets respond (speaking in a normal voice) to a puppet held by another student. Teacher prompts and feedback should be used as needed and faded during the training sessions as students demonstrate competency. After each puppet script training session, the teacher leads a discussion

with the students on how the skill was performed and eliciting comments from other students.

Troubleshooting: Stickers can be given to students as reinforcers for correct performance and participation during the training sessions or if they are observed to perform the skill in the natural setting. Following training, students should be reminded and encouraged to practice the skills during free-play activities or other opportunities throughout the day.

Recess Partners   **E6 F8 E8 C7 T7 I7 V9 +7 T = 7.7**

Reference: Nelson, Smith, & Colvin, 1995.
Goal: Recess Partners is a peer- and self-management procedure combined with positive reinforcement to reduce children's aggressive behaviors and/or negative social interactions with adults and peers during recess or playground periods. This intervention can be used with a few students or with several students.
Age Group: Elementary.
Materials: Individual point cards, back-up reinforcers.
Steps:

1. The teacher explains and reviews rules for appropriate behavior during recess or playground periods. The teacher models examples and nonexamples of each behavior and students are provided opportunities to practice appropriate behaviors in role-play situations.
2. Examples of positive peer social behaviors include, talking nicely to another student, inviting someone to play, taking turns, smiling at others, sharing playground equipment, or asking to join a group of students. Examples of negative peer social behavior include, touching other students in a negative manner (hitting, pushing, shoving, kicking), throwing objects in a negative manner, verbal insults, taunts, ridicules, attacks, or name-calling.
3. The teacher instructs the students on how to rate their behavior on a daily point card using a scale of 0 to 3.
   (a) 0 = Unacceptable—violated one or more rules during the entire rating period
   (b) 1 = Poor—Violated one or more rules most of the period
   (c) 2 = Average—Violated only one rule with no serious aggression, and
   (d) 3 = Excellent—No rule violations—only positive social behaviors.
4. Students are paired into teams of two. Students with high rates of negative behaviors and disciplinary referrals should be paired with a student with high rates of positive behaviors and willingness to participate in the intervention.
5. The teacher provides each student with a daily point card. Point cards should have a space to rate their behavior and a space to rate their partner's

behavior during the recess period. Students practice rating their own and their partner's behavior during role-plays.

6. At the end of the recess period students mark their point card on the 0 to 3-scale using the above criteria. Each member of a team also independently rates their partner's behavior, using the same scale. The two partners then compare their ratings. If a student's self-rating matches the peer-rating exactly, each student earns the number of points corresponding to their self-rating (e.g., a rating of 3 = 3 points) plus a bonus point for the match. If a student's rating was within 1 point of the partner's rating (higher or lower), the student earns the number of points corresponding to the rating, but receives no bonus point. The recess period can also be divided into two intervals, and students add their points from the two intervals at the end of the period.

7. At the end of the day (or week) students can exchange their points for back-up reinforcers (e.g., free time, computer time, video games, music, snack, etc.).

Troubleshooting: The recess supervisor should review self-ratings frequently at first, to check for accuracy. Verbal warnings or removal from recess may be required for serious rule violations (refer to Sit and Watch).

Self-Monitoring Social Skills   **E8 F9 E9 C8 T8 I7 V10 +9 T = 8.6**

Reference: Gumpel & David, 2000.
Goal: This intervention is a self-monitoring and performance feedback procedure used to cue individual students to use their social skills in a recess setting.
Age Group: Elementary.
Materials: Individual timers or stopwatches, small pocket-sized memo pads, and felt-tip pens.
Steps:

1. This intervention can be used with an individual student or a few students who exhibit performance deficits in self-regulatory behavior leading to social interaction problems in unstructured settings, such as recess and playground periods.

2. The teacher can determine target skills based on a functional assessment of student behaviors. This intervention should be used with those students who exhibit performance deficits (inappropriate use of behaviors already in the student's repertoire of social skills), rather than with students who are unable to perform such skills.

3. The teacher meets with selected students individually to explain the activity. The student(s) are given a small electronic kitchen timer or an individual stopwatch. Students are instructed in how to set the timer for

a 4-minute interval and turn off the timer bell at the end of the interval. Prior to the self-monitoring procedure, students can be given the timers for an entire recess period during which they can practice using them.

4.   The teacher determines target behaviors for self-monitoring. Each student is given a small pocket-sized memo pad, or note card with three (or fewer) target behaviors printed on the card. Target behaviors should be stated in positive terms and be measurable and observable. Examples of target behaviors include, "I succeeded in playing without hitting", "I asked a friend to play with me", or "I used friendly words while playing." Target behaviors can be individualized depending on student needs.

5.   The teacher explains to the students that they will be practicing their target behaviors during recess and monitoring how well they do by marking in their memo pad or on their note cards. The students are instructed to set the timer for 4-minute intervals, listen for the timer to ring, turn off, reset, and reactivate the timer, and mark down on the memo pad or note card whether or not they were engaged in each of the target behaviors at the moment the timer rang. Students can make + marks or check marks on the pad for each example of target behavior and record 0 for nonexamples. For example, if a student exhibits three target behaviors appropriately when the timer rings, he or she would make three check marks on the note card. If a student is not exhibiting the target behaviors they would record three 0s.

6.   The teacher may provide an opportunity for the students to practice using the timer and keeping track of their behavior by marking on the pad or note card during a supervised play period with teacher feedback and assistance.

7.   During each recess period, students are given their memo pad and timer and instructed to keep track of their behaviors. At the end of the recess period, the student should return the equipment and show their note card with that day's self-monitoring to the teacher. The teacher may respond with verbal praise or provide reinforcers based on the number of check marks recorded.

Troubleshooting: To encourage accurate self-recording, the teacher can supervise recess behaviors and compare teacher ratings with the student's rating, awarding extra points for matches.

Stop and Think   **E10 F9 E8 C8 T8 I7 V9 +9 T = 8.7**

Reference: Rosenthal-Malek, 1997.
Goal: Stop and Think is a metacognitive strategy used to help students learn social skills and use them in social interaction situations.
Age Group: Preschool or Elementary.

Materials: Poster or chart listing skill steps.
Steps:

1. Social Metacognitive Strategy Training is a method used to train students in using social metacognitive strategies to plan social interactions, and identify and use social problem-solving skills in social situations. This strategy involves teaching young students self-questioning strategies through direct instruction, then providing opportunities for students to practice the skills in student-directed free-play situations.

2. The Stop and Think strategy can be used during any free play, recess, or activity period with the entire class. During a direct instruction session, the teacher introduces the strategy to the students, explaining that they will learn a new way to help them play with friends by asking themselves some questions during free-play periods. These questions will help students choose whom they want to play with and what they want to play.

3. During training sessions the students are taught six general steps and self-directed questions that will help them think about playing with friends:

   (a) Stop and think! (The teacher tells students to "Stop and think" at the beginning of the play period to remind them to use the following questions).

   (b) Who or what do I want to play with? (The teacher tells students this will be the first question they ask themselves during playtime. Students are to think about whom they might play with and what game or activity they would like to play. Students are instructed to also answer the question and decide what or who to play with before they begin playing).

   (c) What will happen if ___? (Students are instructed to think about the consequences of their choices by answering this question. For example, "If I play with Joey, we can play with legos.").

   (d) How do I feel? (Students think and answer, "Am I happy, sad, or angry when I am playing?").

   (e) How does my friend feel? (Students ask and answer, "Is my friend happy, sad, or angry when they play with me?").

   (f) Who or what else can I play with? (Students should always ask themselves this question before choosing a new activity or student to play with).

4. The students practice each questions by orally repeating the questions, reading the questions from a chart or the board, discussing examples, and role-playing examples of each question.

5. Each day, immediately prior to the free-play period, the teacher can review the steps and encourage students to use the new strategy. During the free-play period, students are instructed to choose what or whom they

would like to play with. The teacher monitors and encourages student self-questioning by using reminders and verbal praise.

Troubleshooting: To promote generalization of social skills, students should be encouraged to use the strategies throughout the day. Teachers can remind them with prompts and verbal praise.

The "Talking Game"   **E8 F9 E8 C8 T8 I8 V9 +9 T = 8.3**

Reference: Spohn, Timko, & Sainato, 1999.
Goal: The "Talking Game" involves the use of placemat pictures used to encourage social interaction skills at the lunch or snack table.
Age Group: Preschool or Kindergarten.
Materials: Laminated picture placemats for each student, index cards with each student's picture and name printed on them.
Steps:

1. This activity can be implemented as a classroom-wide intervention involving all students in a small class or with a small group of students seated around a table. The "Talking Game" is a structured intervention during mealtime involving placemats used to facilitate communication between students and effectively teach social interaction skills. This activity can be conducted during a typical snack or meal activity that is routinely scheduled during the day.
2. The teacher creates picture placemats for each student who will be seated at the table. Picture placemats consist of colorful, large, paper placemats containing four pictures each. A variety of pictures can be used that would be of interest to young children, such as animal pictures, children's cartoon characters, people, food items, or something funny. Each placemat should include a picture from each category and should be laminated. The placemats are distributed daily by rotating them so that students have a different placemat each day. The teacher also creates index cards with each student's picture and name attached.
3. At the snack table, the teacher introduces the "Talking Game" to the students and models the procedure with another adult. The "Talking Game" consists of students taking turns verbally interacting with one of their peers at the snack table. Each student is seated in front of a picture placemat. The index cards containing each student's picture and name are shuffled so that students interact with a different student each day. The game begins with the student whose card is on top of the deck of index cards. The first student takes a card from the top of the deck to indicate with whom he or she will interact. The student is to look at the student pictured on the card, say the student's name, and make a comment or ask

a question of the student. The second student verbally responds to the statement or question with a relevant comment or answer. The first student should then respond back to student number two, so that the interaction includes a minimum of three steps. Students can initiate conversations on any topic of their choosing or be prompted to talk about their placemat if they cannot think of anything to say.

4. After the first student has engaged in the three-step interaction, the second student chooses a card and directs a comment or question to the student pictured on the card. These steps are continued until every student at the table has had an opportunity to participate by playing the game as both the initiator and the recipient of a verbal interaction. If students do not initiate or respond, the teacher gives prompts or cues, individualized to each student's specific level and needs.

Troubleshooting: Verbal and edible reinforcers (raisins and cereal) can be given to the students intermittently for listening and interacting appropriately. To assist with generalization, parents can be encouraged to play the "Talking Game" at home during mealtimes.

Teaching Recess   **E10 F9 E9 C7 T7 I8 V10 +9 T = 8.6**

Reference: Todd, Haugen, Anderson, & Spriggs, 2002.
Goal: This intervention involves an instructional strategy to teach recess routines and expectations to reduce behavioral incidences during recess periods.
Age Group: Elementary.
Materials: Rule charts, tickets, back-up reinforcers.
Steps:

1. This procedure can be implemented on a class or schoolwide basis to teach, reinforce, and routinely monitor appropriate social behaviors outside the classroom setting (i.e., playground, cafeteria, hallways, and arrival and dismissal areas. Teaching recess includes three components to reduce behavioral incidences, (a) defining and teaching behavioral expectations, (b) reinforcing appropriate behaviors, and (c) regular practice and monitoring of appropriate behaviors and routines.

2. The teacher or school team develops three or four positively stated classwide or schoolwide rules designed to emphasize appropriate behaviors (i.e., be safe, be respectful, and follow teacher or adult directions). Within the context of classroom instruction, the teacher explains the rules and provides opportunities for students to practice the rules in various settings (class, hallways, playground, etc.).

3. A recess workshop is developed to teach specific recess expectations and routines. At the beginning of the school year each class or combination

of several classes participates in the recess workshop by attending a 30 to 45-minute outdoor recess workshop. During the recess workshops the students begin in the classroom with the teacher providing and reviewing a map of the playground with the boundaries outlined and playground equipment and grade level play areas labeled. After reviewing the map, the class lines up and walks to the playground, walks around the playground boundaries, and rotates through equipment and game areas to discuss names of equipment. At each equipment or game area the teacher demonstrates examples and asks students to demonstrate examples of rules and behavioral expectations (i.e., taking turns, sharing equipment, including others, cooperating, etc.). The students spend about 3 to 5 minutes at each area. After visiting each specific area, the students line up, return to class, and participate in a brief follow-up discussion with the teacher.

4. A 30-minute indoor recess workshop is conducted at the beginning of winter. During the indoor recess workshop, the teacher focuses on classroom routines for free play indoors. Specific routines such as getting started, participating in recess, and cleaning up are discussed and practiced by the students.

5. During recess periods, the teacher or adult supervisors provide specific feedback to students with a 4:1 ratio of positive comments to corrective comments. Positive comments can be randomly and intermittently paired with colored stickers or tickets that are given to individual students who demonstrate appropriate behaviors. The class may pool their stickers or tickets to earn a classroom choice activity.

6. The teacher corrects inappropriate behaviors by reviewing the behavioral expectations with the student, asking the student to demonstrate the appropriate behavior, and a verbal agreement by the student to follow the rules.

Troubleshooting: Chronic or serious behavior may result in an office referral, loss of recess, or a parent conference (refer to Sit and Watch in Chapter 5 or Structured Recess interventions in Chapter 8). Recess workshops may be repeated periodically, as needed.

The Turtle Trick   **E8 F10 E7 C9 T10 I8 V9 +9 T = 8.8**

Reference: Eddy, Reid, & Fetrow, 2000.
Goal: This intervention is a self-management technique that is taught to young children to improve self-control and to reduce aggressive behavior and to use as an alternative behavior for responding to teasing by tattling.
Age Group: Preschool or Early Elementary.
Materials: Animal puppets (including a turtle puppet).

Steps:

1. The teacher explains to the students that they will be learning a new technique to use when they are angry and upset or when classmates tease them.

2. The teacher uses animal puppets, including a turtle puppet, to demonstrate (role-play) teasing situations that frequently occur on the playground, or in the classroom. In the first example, one puppet teases, the other puppet responds negatively, and both puppets become angry, upset, or sad. The teacher asks the students to think of other alternatives they could do to respond to teasing, without becoming angry and upset or without tattling.

3. After discussing different responses to teasing, the teacher should stress that it's OK to feel angry, but it is important to calm down so that no one is hurt and so that they might think of other solutions to teasing. The turtle puppet explains the "turtle trick" to the class. For example, the puppet might say, "The turtle trick is a good trick to use to help you calm down when someone is teasing you. When someone teases you or calls you names, just pretend you are a turtle and go inside your shell. In your shell you are safe and calm, and no one can get hurt. In your shell you can think of what to do about the teasing without getting upset." The teacher has the turtle puppet demonstrate pulling its' head and legs inside its' shell to think and be calm.

4. The teacher instructs the class to imagine they are turtles that are being teased and imagine pulling into their shell where it is safe and calm. The students can practice closing their eyes, putting their heads down, and pulling their arms in close to their bodies while they relax their muscles to calm down. While they are in their shell they can stop and think of other solutions to the problem and decide how they will respond when they come out of their shell.

5. After the teacher explains the "turtle trick" and the students imagine being a turtle, the students are asked to think of various situations when the "turtle trick" could be useful. Students are selected to role-play some of the situations and practice using the "turtle trick" when provoked. The teacher can assist students in pretending to go into their turtle shell and calm down. Several or all students should be given an opportunity to practice the "turtle trick" in role-play situations.

6. Prior to recess or playground activities, the teacher may wish to review and remind students to use the "turtle trick" when they need to calm down.

7. After recess, students are asked to review their use of the "turtle trick" and the teacher verbally reinforces positive behaviors observed on the playground.

Troubleshooting: Teachers may need to provide individual and class rewards based on the display of positive behaviors during the recess period.

Videotape Feedback   **E6 F8 E9 C7 T6 I8 V10 +9 T = 8.2**

Reference: Kern-Dunlap, Dunlap, Clarke, Childs, White, & Stewart, 1992.
Goal: Videotape Feedback combines videotaping peer activity sessions, self-evaluation, and feedback and reinforcement to increase desirable peer interactions.
Age Group: Elementary or Secondary.
Materials: Video equipment (camera, television, VCR), self-monitoring tracking sheets, games (age-appropriate board games or card games), and small rewards (candy, pencil, small prizes).
Steps:

1. The use of videotape provides an opportunity for students to self-monitor and self-evaluate their peer interactions during an activity period in the classroom. Prior to implementing this procedure, the students are informed that they will be participating in an activity to help improve positive peer interactions in the classroom. Parents are informed and permission is obtained to use the videotaping procedure.

2. Prior to beginning the activity sessions, the teacher discusses the importance of desirable peer interactions when playing games. The teacher provides examples of positive verbal interactions such as praise statements (e.g., "Good job," "Good try"), helping statements (e.g., "It's your turn," "You get another turn") or neutral statements or questions (e.g., "I like this game"), or desirable nonverbal gestures (e.g., thumbs up). The teacher should also discuss inappropriate interactions such as insults, demands, or harsh voice tone (e.g., "You're stupid," "Give me that"), or nonverbal gestures (e.g., grabbing, interrupting), asking students to correctly differentiate desirable from undesirable examples.

3. The videotaped activity is conducted weekly with a small group of students in the classroom or in another location in the school. Video equipment should be available and ready to use when the activity begins (i.e., a portable camcorder stationed on a tripod in the corner of the classroom). Students are videotaped as they interact together while playing a game during a 15–20-minute activity session. Games can include age-appropriate board games or card games randomly selected prior to the session. During the game activity students should be supervised by an adult although adult interactions should be limited to rule clarifications or questions pertaining to the game.

4. During feedback sessions, students view approximately 5–10 minutes of the videotape from the activity session held the previous day. At each 30-second interval students respond to the statement, "I had desirable peer

interactions," by either marking a + or a 0 on a self-monitoring tracking sheet (sheets can consist of a row of blank boxes or spaces corresponding to each 30-second interval). A + is marked if no undesirable interactions occurred during the interval. A 0 is marked if any negative or undesirable interaction occurs. Following the self-evaluation, the teacher can review the results with the students, asking for suggestions for alternative behaviors when undesirable interactions occur.

5. Students can be awarded 1 point for exhibiting desirable peer interactions throughout each 30-second interval. Points can later be exchanged for a small reward (e.g., a pencil, a piece of candy, etc.) at the end of the feedback session.

Troubleshooting: To encourage accuracy in self-evaluation, the teacher can randomly select a student and also record the occurrence of desirable and undesirable interactions. Students can be awarded extra points for matching the teacher's response.

Chapter **8**

School-wide Positive Behavioral Intervention and Support

School-based interventions may be much more effective when incorporated as part of a milieu in which the majority of children and adults within an entire school are working together to create a proactive, positive environment, while reducing the opportunities and conditions that trigger behavior problems. A program in which the school responds proactively and consistently to provide effective behavioral support to all teachers and students is referred to as a school-wide intervention, or positive behavior intervention and support program. A school-wide intervention plan should be an essential component of the primary goal of schooling—to ensure all students achieve academic success and receive instruction in a school environment conducive to learning.

WHAT IS A SCHOOL-WIDE INTERVENTION?

Increasingly, administrators, teachers, and researchers have found that a school-wide approach is more effective than any single classroom program in addressing the challenges of maintaining discipline and reducing problem behaviors in the school setting. With recent legislation mandating that schools are accountable for improving achievement levels for all students, schools are encouraged to develop and use positive behavioral interventions and supports. School-wide intervention and positive behavioral support refers to programs used to assist schools to more effectively prevent or reduce problem behaviors and increase student learning across the school environment. Most importantly, a school-wide intervention and support plan is *preventative*. It is a plan that includes a comprehensive framework or philosophy that is consistently followed to proactively teach and reinforce appropriate behaviors, prevent the occurrence of potential misbehaviors, and manage problem behaviors effectively. In such systems, a building based team is usually established to develop and monitor a school-wide discipline plan, with an emphasis on a creating a proactive plan that will build student success, provide instruction in pro-social skills, and reduce the number of negative or punitive consequences. School-wide interventions should be developed based on an assessment of the most problematic behaviors occurring at the school and a consideration and review of interventions that have proven effective elsewhere. A school-wide intervention can include one or several components such as,

- Establishing unified school rules,
- Direct teaching of behavior expectations to all students,
- Focus on the *prevention* of problems,
- Developing clear consequences for inappropriate behaviors and positive reinforcement for appropriate behaviors,
- Implementing a school-wide system for early identification and of students "at risk" for learning and/or behavioral problems, and providing strategic intervention to these students, and
- Ongoing monitoring of data and program evaluation.

School-wide interventions can also include an emphasis on school-wide instruction in social skills, reducing bullying behavior, or improving academic skills. To be effective, school-wide interventions must be supported and implemented by all staff in the school and should be designed to meet the needs of all students, including students with behavior problems.

DEVELOPING A SCHOOL-WIDE INTERVENTION PLAN

School administrators and teachers may choose from a variety of commercial, packaged programs for use on a school-wide basis or the school staff may develop a customized program based on the needs of their particular student population and student needs. Four key factors are critical for success of a school-wide intervention plan: (a) the principal or school leadership provides active involvement and support, (b) all staff members work together, (c) an overall framework or philosophy is developed, and (d) a specific step-by-step plan is written and followed. In developing a customized school-wide intervention plan; the following guidelines may be useful.

1. An important key element of a school-wide approach is active involvement and support from the school leadership. The principal or other school administrator must take a visible and active role in planning and implementing any school-wide intervention. Prior to or at the beginning of the school year the principal or school administrator meets with the school staff to discuss the need for and enlist staff agreement in supporting a school-wide intervention plan.

2. It is important at this stage to provide a rationale for developing a school-wide program and to include all teachers and support staff in the process by giving staff an opportunity for their input of ideas and concerns. Although some teacher time is required to develop such a program, a school-wide intervention plan should be presented as a means to enable academic instruction and learning to occur and a necessary component in achieving school-wide instructional goals—not as an extra duty that simply interferes with a teacher's valuable time.

3. A small team or committee of school staff members is formed (e.g., Behavior Support Team). The team can be comprised of administrators, teachers, and other school personnel (master teachers, school psychologists, counselors, social workers, playground supervisors, lunchroom managers, etc.) Membership should be voluntary and team members must be willing to be actively involved in this process. The purpose of this core team is to function as a Behavior Support Team who will expand on ideas, develop the program, and assist the other staff members in implementing the school-wide plan. This core team will meet on a regular basis at least 1–2 times per month.

4. After getting input from the school staff, the team will meet and list all problem behaviors of concern and determine the needs of the school. Specific settings in which high rates of inappropriate behaviors occur should be considered (i.e., playground, hallways, cafeteria, gym, auditorium, classrooms, bus and bus area). The team should also consider the time of day when most problems occur (i.e., before school, transition periods, during assemblies, after school, etc.). The students who are most at risk (those 7%) should be identified. This information can be obtained by review of office referrals, teacher logs, or commercially developed programs such as *Discipline Tracker* (EduSoft Solutions, 2001), a software program developed to track student infractions.

5. Clearly described school and classroom rules are developed which will apply across all locations and activities in the school. Rules typically address such areas as student movement within the class or school, student-student or student-teacher interactions, and student work behaviors. Rules should be stated in the positive and be limited to about five specific rules. Unified reinforcement that will be available to all

students who follow the rules should be identified and used consistently by all staff (e.g., teacher praise, token reinforcers, group rewards, etc.).

6. Unified correction procedures (consequences) should also be identified and used consistently by all staff (e.g., verbal reminders, loss of privileges, other-class time out, office referral, etc.). A continuum of correction procedures should be determined and implemented. Severe behaviors that threaten the safety of others and could result in suspension or expulsion should also be identified.

7. Prior to implementing a school-wide intervention plan, staff development and training should occur to ensure that staff will work together effectively and that the plan is implemented consistently and uniformly.

8. The first few days of a new school year can be designated as training days in which all staff and students participate in training activities to teach the school-wide rules and expectations. Training activities can include developing short skits to demonstrate examples of rule following behaviors, rotating students through different areas to discuss and practice appropriate behaviors (refer to Teaching Recess), and initiating a token reinforcement system during the first few days to increase compliance.

9. The Behavior Support Team can also develop direct interventions to promote generalization of appropriate behaviors across settings. Direct interventions can include individual reinforcers and group contingencies (refer to Recess Tickets, Recess Wristbands). Active supervision by school staff should also be conducted in targeted settings and during transitions.

10. While a school-wide intervention plan will most likely meet the needs of 90% of the students in the school, a more structured program will be needed for those 7–10% of students who are identified as most at-risk. Individual interventions and student tracking systems (refer to Daily Homenotes, Behavior Contracts) can and should be developed for these students.

11. A final step in implementing a school-wide intervention is ongoing data collection and program evaluation. Objective and measurable data should be the basis for program evaluation. Data can include staff and student surveys, number of discipline referrals, computer entries, review of individual daily tracking forms, frequency counts of problems (e.g., rates of peer conflict), or teacher logs. Program changes can and should be made in response to these data.

The following interventions in this section are selected as promising school-wide interventions designed to support administrators and school staff in developing a positive behavior support system in their school. These are programs that can be used independently, adapted to meet specific school needs and concerns, or incorporated into existing school-wide programs.

SCHOOL-WIDE INTERVENTIONS AND POSITIVE BEHAVIORAL SUPPORT PROGRAMS

The High Five Program

Reference: Taylor-Greene, Brown, Nelson, Longton, Gassman, Cohen, Swartz, Horner, Sugai, & Hall, 1997.
Goal: The "High Five" Program is a comprehensive positive school-wide approach to school discipline developed by the teachers at a middle school to define, teach, and reward appropriate student behavior.
Age Group: Elementary or Secondary.
Materials: High Five Rules, High Five Tickets, reinforcers, individual tracking forms.
Steps:

1. A core committee is formed and designated as the Behavior Support Team. The first functions of the team are to secure support from the school administrator and determine school needs by collecting data (e.g., rates of student discipline referrals).
2. At a staff meeting for all school staff, the Behavior Support Team presents the idea of a school-wide program to improve student behavior, invites staff suggestions, and enlists staff support and participation.
3. After review of behavioral data, the team identifies problem areas in the school where most inappropriate behaviors occur (hallways, gym, auditorium, cafeteria, etc.). These areas are labeled the target training areas. The team also identifies five school rules and expectations that will apply to all students in the school. Rules should be specific and stated positively (refer to Give Me Five or Stoplight Rules in Chapter 5).
4. All of the school staff participates in developing specific examples of the rules in each targeted area. Staff training provides teachers an opportunity to discuss and endorse a unified set of rules and expectations.
5. The first two days of school are designated as "High Five" days. All students participate in training to learn and practice the school rules. Students are organized into groups of 35–40 students (e.g., homerooms). In their group, students rotate to each targeted training area. Teachers, staff, or parent volunteers are stationed at each area to instruct students. Each training session lasts 30–45 minutes. Students can be given cards (listing each session) to carry with them as they rotate through the target

areas. At the end of each session, their card is stamped as an indication they have successfully completed the session. At the end of the day, students return to their homeroom or classroom. Students with completed cards (stamped at all sessions) receive a treat (e.g., Popsicle, ice cream sandwich, candy, etc.).

6. Beginning with the first day and over the next several days, students also have opportunities to receive token reinforcement for demonstrating appropriate rule-following behaviors. All staff members are provided with High Five tickets. Teachers and staff use the tickets to immediately and frequently reinforce students as they participate in training and as they continue to follow rules after the first day. At the end of the week, students are given the opportunity to exchange the tickets for reinforcers (e.g., raffles, student store items, small candies, etc.). This token reinforcement program can be ongoing and continued throughout the year. Students can exchange tickets to attend a monthly activity (e.g., class party, open gym—a 30-minute period where students may play basketball, socialize, etc., or purchase items such as a bag of popcorn with 5 tickets).

7. Students identified as most at-risk (e.g., students with chronic, inappropriate behaviors) may be referred for an individualized behavior and tracking program. Data are collected for these students on an individualized basis. Prior to implementing an individualized behavior program, the student, parents, teacher(s), and school psychologist or administrator meet together to discuss the plan.

8. The "High Five" Program individual plan consists of students checking in at the counseling center at the beginning of each school day. Students are greeted by an assigned adult (counselor, teacher, secretary, etc.) and asked if they have their necessary school supplies ready. Students pick up a daily tracking sheet that they will carry with them as they go from class to class throughout the day. At the beginning of each class, they give the form to the teacher, and pick it up as they leave class. Forms should include a space for teacher signatures, parent signature, and points for each class period based on student behavior. At the end of the day, students return to the counseling center and review their signed daily tracking sheet with the assigned adult to determine if they have met a predetermined goal for the day (e.g., 80%). If they have met their goal, students receive a small treat and verbal praise. If they have not met their goal they are encouraged to keep trying. Students take their signed form home, to be signed by a parent and return it the next day at check-in.

Troubleshooting: As with any school-wide intervention program, it is important to collect data and evaluate the program. Program changes should be made in response to the data. To implement the individual behavior plan, support from the teachers and parents is necessary. Several adults may be needed to assist with the daily check-in and check-out sessions, as there may be 15–20 students in a school who are on individual plans. It is also important to recognize success and show appreciation to students and staff for their support and participation (e.g., intercom announcements, school newsletters, staff celebrations, etc.).

Principal's 200 Club

Reference: Jenson, Rhode, Evans, & Morgan, in press.
Goal: The Principal's 200 Club can be used as a positive support program as part of any school-wide intervention plan.
Age Group: Elementary or Secondary.
Materials: A large laminated poster divided into 200 squares, plastic poker chips or tickets numbered from 1–200, erasable marker, student coupons or certificates, and an envelope containing the name of a mystery reinforcer (i.e., Mystery Motivator).
Steps:

1. Refer to *The Tough Kid: Principal's Briefcase* (Jenson, Rhode, Evans, & Morgan, in press), for a complete description of the Principal's 200 Club, and additional school-wide intervention and support programs.
2. A large laminated poster divided into 200 squares (e.g., 10 rows of 20 squares each) is prepared and posted in a visible location in the school. The blank squares are large enough for a student's name to be written in each square. The poster can be placed in the main office, by the principal's door, on a prominent location on the cafeteria wall, or in a hallway near the main entrance to the school. The poster can be titled, "Principal's 200 Club" or any other name selected by the principal or school Behavior Support Team. Plastic chips, round tags, or tickets numbered from 1–200 with a magic marker are placed in a container in the office or somewhere near the poster. The chips should be in a secure location with limited student access unless supervised.
3. A large, sealed envelope with a big question mark drawn on the front is attached to the principal's door. Inside the envelope a piece of paper with a selected reward written on it is placed (e.g. lunch with the principal, root beer float, pizza party, choice from prize box, video rental coupons, etc.).
4. The staff or a school Behavior Support Team develops and creates unified school rules. All students within the school are instructed and provided practice in following school rules. Rules should be posted in a prominent location in the school as well as in every classroom.
5. Each teacher or staff member in the school is provided with coupons to present to students who are observed to be following the school rules. It is recommended that each teacher be provided with about 10 coupons

per day. These can be placed in teachers' boxes daily or weekly. Specific, observable behaviors may be targeted for the coupon reinforcement. Different specific behaviors may be targeted each month (e.g., standing up for someone, friendly behaviors, responding to adult directions politely and immediately, etc.). Teachers and staff may reward coupons during class, in the hallway, cafeteria, or playground when a student is observed to display a clear example of the target behavior. Teachers should be encouraged to watch for target behaviors and give coupons consistently and frequently, several times per day or week. Teachers should make extra effort to give coupons to unknown students or those students who don't typically receive recognition.

6. Students who receive coupons are instructed to go to the office (or other location) at a specific time of the day (e.g., the last or first 5 minutes of the day or on their way to the lunchroom) with their coupon. Under supervision, the student randomly selects a plastic chip from the container. The student writes his or her name on the poster in the square corresponding to the number drawn (an erasable or water based pen is needed so the poster can be reused). Each numbered chip drawn is placed in a separate container so that each number is only selected one time.

7. Students continue to randomly fill in the squares with their names as coupons are rewarded. When ten consecutive names are filled in (the ten names can be across, down, or diagonal—any ten names in a row), all of the students whose names are included in the row of 10 are called down to the office (an announcement over the school intercom can be made). These students are the Principal's 200 Club winners. The mystery envelope is opened and those students in the winning row receive the reward specified on the paper. After the winning row is announced, the poster is cleared and the process is started over again.

8. The winning students can receive additional recognition and reinforcement by calling the parents to inform them or by writing student names in a Good Behavior Book that is displayed in a prominent location for parents to review during parent conferences.

Troubleshooting: Although the remaining students whose names are not on the winning row do not receive the mystery reward, all students who earn a coupon can be provided with a small treat when they exchange it for a number. The coupons may also be publicly posted on a bulletin board or sent home to inform the parent of the student's good behavior.

School-Wide Bully Prevention

Reference: Heinrichs, 2003 and Milgliore, 2003.
Goal: The Bully Prevention program is a school-wide plan to reduce and prevent bullying problems within a school environment.

Age Group: Elementary or Secondary.
Materials: No Bullying Rules poster for each classroom.
Steps:

1. Several key components are important in developing a school-wide bully prevention program, including;
   (a) increasing staff and student awareness of bullying behavior,
   (b) gathering information from staff and students about the prevalence and incidence of bullying behavior in the school,
   (c) identifying high-risk areas where bullying occurs,
   (d) developing school and class rules against bullying,
   (e) increasing supervision in high-risk areas,
   (f) establishing consistent consequences for bullies, and
   (g) providing social skills training for students (both targets and bullies).

2. At a staff meeting for all school staff, the school administrator or school Behavior Support Team presents the idea of a school-wide plan to reduce and prevent bullying behavior. It is important to invite staff suggestions and participation in determining the needs of the school and developing the plan. Information should be gathered from the staff about when, where, and how frequently bullying behavior occurs in the school. Information can be obtained through a staff survey or group discussion. The group discussion should also include information and consensus about what constitutes bullying behavior. Bullying is defined as a continuum of behaviors in which a power imbalance is present with intent to harm and the behaviors occur repeatedly. Bullying is unfair and one-sided and the targeted victim usually feels helpless to respond effectively. Bullying includes low-level and moderate-level behaviors—teasing, name-calling, and ridicule as well as high-level behaviors—physical aggression, or sexual harasssment.

3. The team or school staff identifies specific school rules against bullying that will apply to all students in the school. Bullying rules usually include statements related to three general principles (a) Do not bully others, (b) Try and help others who are being bullied, and (c) Include all students—no one is left out.

4. Students should also be surveyed to obtain data about their perceptions regarding the frequency and types of bullying problems in the school. An anonymous questionnaire is often the most efficient method of obtaining student input.

5. The teacher provides students with examples of specific behaviors and expectations associated with each rule. During a teacher-directed class discussion, students have an opportunity to discuss bullying problems and ways they can follow the No Bullying Rules. Role-playing different situations can be an effective method of instruction for teaching rules

and expectations. Students can also write or draw about their experiences. It is important for each teacher to create a class environment where teasing and bullying are not acceptable. Teachers should always model respectful behavior toward students and be aware that intimidation, sarcasm, and put-downs are subtle forms of bullying behavior. At the beginning of the school year, or any time throughout the year, students can participate in no-bullying activities, such as making No Bully posters to display around the school or performing skits or presentations at school assemblies.

6. Consequences for bullying behavior should be pre-determined and followed uniformly and consistently by all school staff. Consequences for bullying should be discussed with students during the presentation of the No Bullying Rules. Students are encouraged to report bullying behavior and help other students who are being bullied. A clear procedure on when and how to report bullying should be discussed with the students and can be publicly displayed on a wall poster.

7. The school Behavior Support Team or school leadership develops specific strategies to use when bullying situations occur. Reports of bullying should be taken seriously and all students who bully receive specific consequences. Consequences should be pre-planned and uniform throughout the school. Consequences can include a firm, calm statement such as, "Those words are offensive. We don't say those words here" for some low-level behaviors, or loss of privileges along with some activity that promotes awareness and empathy for the victim for aggressive behaviors or high-level behaviors (refer to Structured Recess). Some incidents may require that the bully make an apology or do something helpful for the victim.

8. Increased adult supervision should be provided in those areas identified by staff and students as high-risk areas for bullying. Scheduling similar age groups for recess or after lunch periods is sometimes recommended to avoid having older students mix with younger students during unstructured times. Class schedules should be organized to minimize problems and conflicts. Adult supervisors should be trained to respond immediately and consistently to student reports of bullying. Adults should also reinforce students who demonstrate responsible, friendly behaviors whenever possible. A positive behavior reinforcement plan such as the Principal's 200 Club may be implemented to reinforce students who are demonstrating appropriate behaviors or who are making extra effort to include others.

9. Students should be taught strategies to avoid being a victim and what to do if they are bullied. Different approaches that can be discussed during a class meeting include, assertive statements such as, "Stop doing

that", joining a group of friends or students, avoiding the bully, or using positive self-statements. Students should also be taught to report bullying whenever someone is unsafe, afraid, or they have tried other things and the bullying continues. Students who repeatedly bully others can be provided social skills training to teach them more positive behaviors.

10. When implementing a school-wide bully prevention plan it is also critical to involve parents and enlist their support. Parent-Teacher organization meetings or conference days can provide a forum for disseminating the information to parents. The No Bullying policy should be included in the school handbook sent home at the beginning of the year. Parents should be informed when their student is involved in a bullying incident and parents should be listened to when they express concerns about incidents involving their child. Some schools include parent-teacher organizations (PTA) as part of the Behavior Support Team or ask for PTA assistance with a positive behavior reinforcement plan.

Troubleshooting: Stigmatizing or retaliation towards students who report bullying should not be allowed and should be addressed immediately. Students who report should be praised and told that by reporting they can help prevent other students from being bullied. A confidential comment box can be used if students are hesitant to report bullying in person.

School-Wide Bus Intervention

Reference: Neatrour, 1994 and Greene, Bailey, & Barber, 1981.
Goal: A school-wide bus intervention plan is used to teach students school bus rules and regulations and to reduce disruptive student behavior while riding the school bus and while waiting at the bus stop.
Age Group: Elementary or Secondary.
Materials: Poster listing Bus Rules, tickets, reinforcers.
Steps:

1. While not all students ride the bus to school, school transportation is the largest single system of public transportation in the United States. Many schools will need to address the issue of bus discipline to increase bus safety.

2. To implement a bus intervention plan, the administrator and school team (e.g., Behavior Support Team) should identify all problems of concern that occur on the bus or at the bus stop, and develop a list of alternative appropriate behaviors and expectations that will be incorporated into the bus rules. It is important to ask bus drivers and bus staff for their input on problem behaviors. Commonly reported problem behaviors that occur on the bus include; out of seat while the bus is moving, noise

outbursts, roughhousing—pushing or shoving other students, and waving arms, legs, or objects out of the bus window.

3. A list of about 5 bus rules are developed and posted in a visible location in the school. Students can be taught the rules and examples of expected bus behavior. It is important that all students know the rules and they have an opportunity to practice the rules. Lessons can be conducted in the bus waiting area and also on the bus (refer to Teaching Recess).

4. Examples of bus rules include: Take your seat quietly, Remain seated when the bus is moving, Keep your feet and hands to self and inside the bus, Be courteous to the bus driver, and Talk in a conversational voice tone. It is important that the bus driver and bus staff also know the rules and the expected student behaviors.

5. Specific procedures and routines for waiting at the bus stop, lining up, and getting on and off the bus should also be developed and enforced. An assigned school staff member should monitor students who are waiting at the bus pick-up location. Students should be instructed to stay in a specific location while waiting for the bus, and board the bus together in a single file line. Some schools designate assigned bus seats and give the bus driver a clipboard with the assigned seat and name of each student. Teachers and bus staff can remind students to follow bus rules and provide verbal praise to students who are exhibiting appropriate behavior.

6. Depending on student age and grade level and severity of bus behaviors, a variety of positive reinforcement programs or consequences can be used to encourage positive behaviors and respond to problem behaviors. The Behavior Support Team can develop a continuum of consequences for misbehavior as well as incentives to encourage appropriate behavior. Consequences can include verbal reminders or corrections, positive practice with a simulated bus ride and watching a safety video, assigned bus seating or assigned waiting spots, debriefing (refer to Chapter 5), administrative referral, temporary loss of riding privileges, and individual behavior contracts.

7. In situations where several students with behavior problems are transported to the school, an individual positive intervention program or group contingency reinforcement program may be used. One example of a positive reinforcement program is the use of "Bus Tickets." With "Bus Tickets," students have the opportunity to earn a ticket for each bus ride (to and from school equals two tickets per day). The driver or bus aide gives the tickets to each student who has followed the bus rules as they exit the bus each morning (students are given their afternoon ticket the next morning). Students place their tickets in an envelope that is kept in the classroom. At the end of the week, students have an opportunity to spend the tickets on secondary reinforcers purchased at the "Bus Store"(treats,

school supplies, small prizes, etc.). The tickets required to purchase "Bus Store" items can range from 5–100, depending on the value of the item. Students can elect to save up tickets for a larger-valued item. If a student misbehaves, the bus driver fills out a "pink slip" with the students' name and a description of the behavior, which is given to the teacher. Students who receive a "pink slip" do not earn a "Bus Ticket", and they must pay two tickets to the "Bus Store" at the end of the week for every "pink slip."

8. A group contingency reinforcement program can be used in which music is available to the students if there are no rule violations or excessive noise levels. A cassette tape player or CD player with speakers is placed or installed in the front of the bus. Students can list music selections or choose a local radio station (music should be preapproved by the teacher or school team). Music can be taped by the teacher or supplied by the students. If noise levels are excessive or rule violations occur, the music is not available to students on the next day's bus ride.

Troubleshooting: Most interactions between bus staff and students should be friendly and positive. Verbal reminders or corrections are more effective if they are made in a firm, respectful voice, stating the rule and what the student should be doing instead. Severe behaviors should be referred to the school administrator or teacher for parent notification and other consequences.

School-Wide Cafeteria Intervention

Reference: Sprick, 1995 and Lewis, Sugai, & Colvin, 1998.
Goal: A school-wide cafeteria intervention plan is used to structure the cafeteria environment, consequences for misbehaviors, and implement a reinforcement program to increase appropriate student behavior.
Age Group: Elementary or Secondary.
Materials: Large posterboard for the cafeteria wall for reinforcement program, poster containing Cafeteria Rules.
Steps:

1. Disruptive student behaviors frequently occur in the cafeteria or lunchroom setting. Some problems are related to student congestion, lack of supervision, unclear cafeteria rules and procedures, and inconsistent enforcement or consequences for misbehaviors.

2. Refer to *Cafeteria Discipline: Positive Techniques for Lunchroom Supervision* (Sprick, 1995) for a complete program to manage and improve behavior in the cafeteria.

3. To develop a school-wide cafeteria plan, the administrator, school staff, or Behavior Support Team (with staff input) should identify all problem behaviors of concern that occur in the cafeteria setting. After listing

problem behaviors, the team should develop a list of alternative appropriate cafeteria behaviors and expectations that will be incorporated into the cafeteria rules. Problem behaviors commonly reported to occur in the cafeteria are, touching others, pushing or cutting in line, out of seat, running, yelling or loud noises, roughhousing, taking food from other students, and misuse of food or utensils.

4. The Behavior Support Team should also consider the environmental structure in the cafeteria setting that may contribute to behavior problems. For example, variables such as student movement into the cafeteria, formation of lines, time scheduling, length of the lunch period(s), student seating arrangement, age groups, clean-up procedures, exit traffic patterns, and what students do after lunch should be considered.

5. Cafeteria rules and procedures are developed and posted in a visible location in the cafeteria. Rules may vary depending on the age group and school, however, it is important that all students know the rules, and the rules are consistently enforced with preplanned consequences.

6. Examples of cafeteria rules are: Wait in line quietly, Use a quiet voice, Walk, Keep hands and feet to self, Clean up after yourself, etc. During classroom lessons or at a school-wide assembly, students are taught the rules and procedures. Students should have sufficient opportunity to learn the routines and procedures with teacher or student modeling of examples and nonexamples and guided practice. It is important to teach appropriate behaviors for entering and exiting the cafeteria, waiting in line, choosing a seat, socialization during lunch, and cleaning up procedures. These lessons can be conducted in the cafeteria setting (refer to Teaching Recess). It is also helpful to teach students a "signal" for immediate attention (e.g., lights out for 5 seconds, three short whistles).

7. School staff members must actively supervise students during the lunch period to encourage appropriate behaviors through praise and positive reinforcement and to respond to problem behaviors consistently.

8. The Behavior Support Team develops a continuum of consequences for misbehavior as well as procedures to encourage appropriate behavior. Consequences can include verbal reminders or corrections, positive practice, assigned seating, brief time-out at another table, administrative referral, or assist with lunch clean up (refer to Debriefing and Structured Recess). The consequences for misbehavior should be explained to students at the time rules and procedures are being taught. It is important that adult supervisors respond to misbehaviors calmly, consistently, and in a timely manner and follow the procedures determined by the Behavior Support Team.

9. Procedures to encourage positive behaviors can include positive attention, verbal praise, and school wide announcements or rewards. A whole

group contingency strategy can be implemented to encourage appropriate behavior. For example, the lunchroom supervisor places a large posterboard on the wall. Using a variable interval schedule (random bell or beeper sound), the staff member marks a point on the poster if the majority of the students in the cafeteria are following the cafeteria rules (or if no problem behaviors have occurred during the preceding interval). When a predetermined number of points are earned (e.g., 100 points), all of the students earn a special treat (e.g., ice cream or root beer party) during an afternoon recess or other time period.

10. Another reinforcement strategy is to award a "Good Behavior Banner" (or flag) at the end of the week to a table or class exhibiting positive cafeteria behavior throughout the week. The banner is displayed in a prominent location in the classroom the following week, and the winning class is announced over the school intercom congratulating the winning group at the end of each week.

Troubleshooting: Most interactions between adult supervisors and students should be friendly and positive. Verbal reminders or corrections are more effective if they are made in a firm, respectful voice, stating the rule and what the student should be doing instead. Punitive consequences or administrative referrals should be reserved for dangerous behaviors or continued refusal to follow directions. Throughout the school year, teachers and staff should periodically review the rules and procedures. Staff should evaluate the plan periodically and meet to discuss any problems and share ideas about what works and doesn't work.

School-Wide Social Skills Training

Reference: Fister, Conrad, & Kemp, 1998 and Jones, Sheridan, & Binns, 1993.
Goal: A school-wide social skills training program is used to provide in-class social skills training for all students to teach important prosocial skills identified by teachers and to increase opportunities for student practice and reinforcement of these skills on a consistent basis.
Age Group: Elementary or Secondary.
Materials: Skill posters for each social skill taught.
Steps:

1. Although social skills training can be conducted in individual classrooms, school-wide implementation provides a program where all students receive instruction in a core set of important skills, and students are given opportunities throughout the day for reminders, practice, and reinforcement, thus increasing the generalization of skills.

2. The *Cool Kids* (Fister, Conrad, & Kemp, 1998) program is one example of a commercially published social skills curriculum to use with an

individual classroom or on a school-wide basis. The *Cool Kids* program is a complete program that includes 36 skills suitable for elementary or secondary school students, as well as guidelines, lesson plans, skill cards, planning calendar, skill posters, and additional fun activities and materials. This program includes detailed instructions on how to implement on a school-wide basis.

3. To develop and implement a school-wide social skills training program, data are collected from teachers, staff, and students to identify specific social problems within the school and determine which skills to teach. Data collection can include direct observations of student behavior across settings, teacher ratings, sociometric measures, or student surveys.

4. A program that includes support and leadership by a school administrator and a building behavior support team composed of staff members willing to help plan and work with the school staff is essential. All teachers and school staff are involved in implementing the social skills program. An initial staff training session is conducted to inform staff of the purpose and general procedures. The school staff is instructed in the correct procedures for teaching skills, modeling skills, providing cues, and reinforcing students for appropriate social skills outside the training sessions.

5. A written plan is developed which can include a school calendar listing a specific skill for each month along with related activities. At least one new skill should be taught each month. Each staff member is provided with the materials needed to teach the skills (e.g., class posters listing each skill and steps, and a general outline of instruction).

6. Once a detailed plan is developed, the students can be introduced to the social skills program at an assembly, at which staff or selected students can introduce the first skill. A school bulletin board can also be used to highlight the skill of the month.

7. Teachers and staff follow the plan by teaching the skill at the beginning of the month, posting the skill in a visible location in the classroom, and reviewing and reinforcing the skill throughout the month. Classroom based skills training involves a 20–30 minute lesson conducted in the regular education classroom. The skills training should follow a general outline which includes (a) introducing the lesson and discussing the rationale, (b) teaching the skill steps, (c) modeling the steps, (d) student practice of steps through role-playing, and (e) questioning students for understanding.

8. A positive school-wide reinforcement program, such as the Principal's 200 club, or High Five program described in this chapter can be used to reward students who demonstrate appropriate social skills or who can name the steps when quizzed by a teacher or staff member. Students may

be given tokens (tickets or coupons) when they are observed demonstrating one of the skills spontaneously or when prompted by the teacher. Tokens are entered into a weekly drawing or are redeemed weekly or monthly for tangible or edible items at a school store. Other positive reinforcers might include stickers, rubber stamps, or compliment notes to take home.

Troubleshooting: A counselor or school psychologist might present the first lesson in each classroom to provide a model for the classroom teacher to follow. Throughout the school year, teachers and school staff should keep reviewing and reinforcing the targeted skills. After the program has been in effect for a few months, a brief booster session can be held for teachers to discuss any problems and troubleshoot difficulties as well as share ideas about what worked.

Structured Recess

Reference: Jones, Wilson, Binns, & Wasden, 1992.
Goal: The structured recess program is a school-wide behavior management program used to teach appropriate recess behaviors and reduce aggressive and inappropriate recess behaviors. Students with aggressive or chronic recess problems receive small group instruction and remediation of behavior problems.
Age Group: Elementary.
Materials: White slips or small tickets.
Steps:

1. The Structured Recess (SR) program is a structured opportunity for students who exhibit aggressive behaviors to learn appropriate playground behaviors during the lunch recess period. It provides training in the natural setting for individual students. This program is available to all students but primarily targets those 7–10% of students in the school with more problematic behaviors. SR is not intended to be punitive but rather, emphasizes prevention and assist students in learning effective strategies for solving conflicts.
2. The Behavior Support Team in the school or school staff identifies five recess rules and expectations that will apply to all students in the school. Rules should be specific and stated positively. Recess rules should include behaviors incompatible with aggressive behaviors or fighting (e.g., "I will be nice to others", "I will solve playground problems by talking, not hitting," or "I will use playground equipment in a safe and fair way").
3. All students in the school participate in training to learn and practice the recess rules. This can take place within each individual classroom, and/or presented at a beginning of the year assembly. Behaviors that are

not allowed should be discussed, such as hitting, play-fighting, throwing objects, yelling, swearing, pushing, etc.

4. While teaching recess rules and expectations, the teacher explains that students who violate the recess rules and engage in aggressive or inappropriate behaviors will be placed on SR, if they receive three white slips. A teacher, adult aide, administrator, or other staff person on duty at recess can give a student a white slip for a rule violation. The white slip is filled out by the person on duty with the name of the student, date of violation, and a brief description of the inappropriate behavior. The adult filling out the white slip is responsible for turning the white slip in to the student's teacher at the end of the recess period. The teacher keeps the white slips for students in his or her classroom. If a student has received three white slips, they are automatically placed on SR. A letter may be sent to inform parents that their child has been placed on SR. The principal can also place a student on SR at his or her discretion if a student engages in a severe violation.

5. A teacher, recess aide, administrator, or other staff person is needed to supervise the SR program. This program is highly flexible, but involves a student spending from 3 to 10 consecutive days in a supervised recess setting.

6. Each day the student is assigned to SR they must report to a SR table in the lunchroom. No talking is allowed at the SR table. The SR table is a designated table that is supervised by an adult in the lunchroom. The remainder of the lunch recess is spent in a supervised area.

7. On the second day of SR, the student again reports to the SR table for lunch and then goes to the supervised room for an assignment. The assignment should be age-appropriate and include writing or drawing about the problem behavior and thinking of an appropriate alternative behavior.

8. On the third day of SR, the student reports to the SR table and goes to the supervised room for a social skills lesson. During this activity, students practice and role-play target playground social skills (e.g., Solving Problems, Using Self-Control, Using I Messages).

9. On the fourth and any additional days required, the student plays a SR recess game inside or outside. During this activity students must play an organized game with adult supervision appropriately prior to being allowed to resume the typical unstructured recess. Students who are compliant and participate can earn early release from SR.

Troubleshooting: If it becomes problematic to provide sufficient staff to conduct a SR on a daily basis, the program can be modified to a weekly SR, in which students must attend a session each Friday over a three-week period. This program, referred to, as "Friday School" requires that a student receiving three white slips will report to the SR table in the lunchroom the following day. The student must then report to "Friday School" for the next three Friday lunch periods. The "Friday School" takes place in one designated classroom or location in the school. One adult (teacher, counselor, school psychologist, or other staff trained to conduct the lesson) implements the lunch activities (writing assignment, social skills lesson, and supervised game) each Friday during the lunch period.

Unified Discipline

Reference: White, Algozzine, Audette, Marr, & Ellis, 2001.
Goal: Unified Discipline is a proactive school-wide program used to reduce and manage problem behaviors by establishing uniform school rules, expectations, and correction procedures.
Age Group: Elementary or Secondary.
Materials: Rule poster for each classroom, a poster board with pocket for each student in the class, green, yellow, and red tickets or cards.
Steps:

1. The need for a Unified Discipline plan is discussed at a staff meeting prior to the beginning of the school year. It is important that the school administrator take an active role in communicating the importance of a school-wide plan to the rest of the school staff and enlists their support. A core team or Behavior Support Team composed of staff members is selected to work with the staff to develop a specific discipline plan and assist in implementing it.
2. After review of behavioral data to identify the primary needs of the school, the team develops 4–5 clearly described school rules that will apply in all locations within the school. Rules should be specific, simple to understand, represent basic expectations, and stated positively, if possible. Examples of rules appropriate for an elementary school include: (a) Follow all teacher instructions promptly, (b) Speak in a quiet, calm voice, (c) Keep hands and feet to yourself, and (d) Stay in your assigned spot.
3. The team also develops and trains the staff in the unified correction procedures that will be applied consistently throughout the school. The following procedures are suggested when a rule is violated: (a) The teacher or staff member states the problem behavior and states the rule that is violated, (b) The teacher or staff states the consequence, and (c) The teacher or staff encourages the student to follow the rule in the future.
4. Each teacher is provided with a rule poster to place in a prominent location in the classroom. Each teacher is also provided with a laminated poster board with a pocket for each student in the classroom. Each student's name is printed on the pocket. In each pocket are placed three colored tickets, green, yellow, and red (refer to Stoplight Rules). The poster board

is placed in the front of the classroom or somewhere easily accessible to the teacher. Each morning all pockets contain the three colored tickets, with the green ticket in front and visible to the students and teacher.

5. On the first occasion of a rule violation, the teacher gives a calmly stated verbal reminder to the student to follow the rule (e.g., "Joey, you need to follow directions promptly"). On the second occasion of a rule violation, the teacher follows the unified correction procedure, by stating the behavior and the rule violated, and removing the green ticket from the pocket (leaving the yellow ticket visible). If the student is noncompliant or continues to violate the rule, the teacher removes the yellow ticket and the student is escorted to a "thinking-spot" chair or an exclusion area in the classroom for a short time period to calm down (e.g., 3–5 minutes).

6. If a student violates the rule a fourth time, they may be sent to another classroom (refer to Other-Class Time Out) for a 20–30 minute period or given some other consequence that has been determined by the school plan (e.g., sent to the office for a discipline referral, call to parent, loss of privileges, etc.).

7. When the student returns to class, they are to rejoin the group and resume participation in classroom activity. The ticket sequence is restarted each day so that all students begin the day with a green ticket in front of their pocket.

Troubleshooting: The key feature of a Unified Discipline plan is that all teachers and staff attend to misbehaviors and follow through with the identified correction procedure in a consistent, calm manner. Although the correction procedures suggested here have been found to be effective, any other correction procedures determined and agreed upon by all staff could be used.

Appendix A
Student Forms

- ABC Functional Assessment Sheet
- Anger Log
- Assignment Sheet
- Bibliotherapy Book List
- Contract
- Debriefing Form
- Graphic Organizer
- Daily Home Note
- Learning Log
- Mediation Report Form
- Monitoring Sheet (Good Student Game)
- Partner Reading Checklist
- Story Map
- Story Planner Form
- Strategic Notetaking Form
- Think Sheet

ABC Functional Assessment Sheet

Student's Name:_____Date:_____

Teacher's Name_____Setting:_____

A Antecedent—Something Before the Behavior

Time _____

People _____

Places _____

Events _____

Other Behaviors _____

B Behavior—Specific, Observable, Objective

Behavior Excesses (to decrease) _____

Behavior Deficits (to increase) _____

C Consequence—Something that Follows the Behavior

Punishment _____

Positive Reinforcers (attention, tangibles, sensory) _____

Negative Reinforcers (escape, avoidance) _____

R Replacement Behavior

Comments _____

_____

Anger Log

Student Name: **Date:**

1. What was your trigger? (describe what triggered your anger)

2. Where were you?

3. How angry were you?
    ☐ 1 = Not angry ☐ 2 = A little angry ☐ 3 = Angry ☐ 4 = Pretty
    angry ☐ 5 = Furious

4. What did you do?
    ☐ Yelled ☐ Hit or pushed ☐ Threw something ☐ Cursed ☐ Broke
    something
    ☐ Talked about it ☐ Ignored it ☐ Walked away
    ☐ Other_____

5. How did you do?
    ☐ 1 = Poor ☐ 2 = Not good ☐ 3 = OK ☐ 4 = Pretty good ☐ 5 =
    Super!

6. Did your anger work for you?
    ☐ Yes—I stayed in control, respected people and property, and resolved
    the problem.
    ☐ No—I did not use self-control, hurt someone or something, and did
    not solve the problem.

Assignment Sheet

Name:_____Partner:_____Phone:_____

Subject:_____

Read:_____

Answer:_____

Write:_____

Other:_____

_____

_____

_____

_____

_____

# of parts_____   # of study sessions_____

Due:_____   Done:_____

Bibliotherapy Book List

Bang, M. (1999). *When Sophie Gets Angry—Really Really Angry*, NY: Blue Sky Press. (Anger)

Choi, Y. (2001). *The Name Jar*, NY: Alfred A. Knopf. (Friendship, Diversity)

Cohen, M. (1996) *Will I Have a Friend?* NY: Aladdin Books. (Friendship)

Crimi, C., & Munsinger, L. (1999). *Don't Need Friends*, NY: Dragonfly Books. (Friendship)

Heide, F. P., (2000). *Some Things Are Scary*, MA: Candlewick Press. (Feelings)

Henkes, K. (1987). *Sheila Rae, The Brave*, NY: Greenwillow Books. (Problem Solving)

Henkes, K. (2000). *Wemberly Worried*, NY: Greenwillow Books. (Feelings)

Hoffman, M., & Binch, C. *Amazing Grace*, NY: Dial Books. (Self-concept)

Lovell, P. (2002). *Stand Tall Molly Lou Melon*, (Teasing)

O'Neill, A., & Huliska-Beith, L. (2002). *The Recess Queen*, NY: Scholastic Press. (Bullying)

McCain, B. R. (2001). *Nobody Knew What To Do*, IL: Albert Whitman & Co. (Bullying)

Nickle, J. (1999). *The Ant Bully.* NY: Scholastic. (Bullying)

Rafe, M., & Shannon, D. (1992). *The Rough-face Girl*, NY: G.P. Putnam's Sons. (Self-concept)

Shepard, A., & Edelson, W. (1995). *The Baker's Dozen: A Saint Nicholas Tale*, NY: Atheneum Books. (Sharing)

Steptoe, J. (1998). *Mufaro's Beautiful Daughters*, NY: Lothrop, Lee & Shepard Books. (Self-concept)

Van Allsburg, C. (1988). *Two Bad Ants*, MA: Houghton Mifflin Co. (Problem Solving)

My Contract

Name:_____

I agree to:_____

_____

If I am successful by:_____**(date),**

I will earn the following privilege(s):_____

_____

_____

If I am not successful:_____

_____

Student Signature:_____

Teacher Signature:_____

Today's Date:_____

Debriefing Form

Student Name:_____ **Grade:**_____

Adult Name:_____ **Date:**_____

1. What was the problem behavior?

2. Where, when, and why did the problem behavior happen?

3. What will you do next time instead of this behavior?

4. What will you do when you finish completing this form?

5. Do you need to discuss this problem further with someone?

Student Signature:_____

Adult Signature:_____

Cause and Effect Graphic Organizer

Name:_____ Date: _____

Causes   Effects

The

Main Event

Daily Home Note

Name:_____ Date:_____

Target Behaviors or Subjects	Rating	Teacher Initials
1.		
2.		
3.		
4.		
5.		
6.		
7.		

Rating Scale: 0 = Poor, 1 = OK, 2 = Good

Teacher Comments_____

_____

Teacher Signature:_____

Parent Signature:_____

Learning Log

Name:_____ Date:_____

Topic:_____

1. The most important ideas I learned from today's discussion are:

2. Some things I already knew about this topic are:

3. Some things I don't understand are:

4. I want to know more about:

Mediation Report Form

Date:_____

Student Names:_____

Mediator Names:_____

Referral made by:_____

1. What was the conflict about?

    Student 1:_____

    Student 2:_____

2. What strategies were used or considered during the conflict?

    _____

    _____

    _____

3. Was the conflict resolved?_____

4. What is the agreed-on solution?_____

    _____

    Student signature:_____

    Student signature:_____

    Mediator signature:_____

    Mediator signature:_____

Monitoring Sheet

Date:_____

	Yes	No
1		
2		
3		
4		
5		
6		
7		
8		
9		
10		

Group:_____

Monitor:_____

Partner Reading Checklist

Coach_____   Reader_____

Role	Yes	No	Comments
Coach—pick up folder.			
Reader—push desks together.			
Partner Reading—First reader reads the text.			
Identify errors—"Stop, you missed that word."			
Wait 4 seconds to correct the reader.			
Correct reader—"The word is ____."			
Prompt reader to read sentence again.			
Raise hand if neither partner knows the word.			
Second reader reads the same text.			
Paragraph Summary—retell what was read.			
Ask—"What was the first thing you learned?"			
Ask—"What is the most important thing about it?"			
Ask—"What happened next?"			
Ask for summary sentence.			
If incorrect—"That's not quite right. Try again."			
Reader answered correctly and stated summary sentence in 10 words or less.			
On Task—Coach			
On Task—Reader			

Story Map

Title of Story:_____

Main Characters:

Setting:

Problem:

Major Events:
1.
2.
3.
4.

Story Outcome:

Group Members:_____

Story Planner Form

Name:_____ Date:_____

Essential Story Elements	Write as I Plan	Check as I Write
Main Character:		
Supporting Characters:		
Setting—Place story occurs:		
Problem:		
Plan (action):		
Ending		

Strategic Notetaking Form

Before the lecture begins, fill in this portion.

Write the title of today's topic and describe what you know about the topic.

Topic:

What I know:

During the lecture, fill in this page to take notes about the lecture.

Today's topic?

Name three to five main points and details while the teacher is discussing them.

1.

2.

3.

4.

5.

Summary—briefly describe how the ideas are related.

New Vocabulary or Terms learned today:

Think Sheet

Name _____ **Date** _____

Topic _____

WHO am I writing this for? (who is my audience)

_____

WHY am I writing this? (what do I want the reader to know)

_____

WHAT do I know? (brainstorm ideas I want to include)

1. _____

2. _____

3. _____

4. _____

HOW can I group my ideas? (conceptual categories)

HOW will I organize my ideas?

Appendix B
Least Restrictive Behavioral
Interventions (LRBI)
(Evans, Jenson, Rhode,
& Striefel, 1990)

Description of Strategies and Intervention Procedures

Preliminary Strategies for Positive Behavioral Supports–Effective Educational Practices

Procedure
1. Appropriate and Motivating Curriculum
2. Assistive Technology
3. Environmental Engineering
4. High Rates of Positive Responses From Teachers
5. Home Notes
6. Instructional Pacing
7. Monitoring Performance
8. Parent Conference
9. Precision Commands
10. Rules
11. Staff Training
12. Structured Daily Schedule
13. Supervision

Positive behavioral supports and effective educational practices should be in place throughout the educational program and across settings, even when more intrusive procedures are selected by school teams to change a specific problem behavior.

Procedure	Definition	EXAMPLES P≫Preschool E≫Elementary S≫Secondary	Reminders
1. Appropriate and Motivating Curriculum	A curriculum which challenges students while enabling them to achieve success.	**P≫** Mr. Peabody makes the concepts being taught relevant to young children's interests by using colorful and engaging pictures to supplement his verbal explanations. **E≫** Maria is given independent reading materials at the reading level identified by her teacher as "instructional" or "easy" for her, never at her "difficult" level. She successfully reads these, improving her fluency. **S≫** Mr. Practical structures skill building in his ninth grade math classes around real life events such as balancing a checkbook and saving for a car. This provides his students with the opportunity to relate the skills they are learning to their own lives.	A curriculum that is too difficult or easy is likely to increase inappropriate behavior. Teacher testing and evaluation skills are important. To use the appropriate curriculum, teachers must know the level at which their students are functioning.
2. Assistive Technology	Any item, piece of equipment, or product system used to increase, maintain, or improve functional capabilities of students with disabilities.	**P≫** Mrs. Considerate tapes her read-aloud stories and allows students to take them home and listen to them again. **E≫** Mr. Engebretsen teaches Emily to use a communication board. By pointing to the letters to spell "I need some water," she gets a drink without having a tantrum. **S≫** Mr. Rapidity leaves material on the overhead projector for an extended period of time for students who have a difficult time keeping up with the pace of lecture presentations.	This may involve such items as large print material, a laptop computer, or augmentative communication devices required by the student to make progress on IEP goals.

3. Environmental Engineering	The process of arranging the physical environment of the classroom to enhance student learning and behavior.	**P≫** Mrs. Adams arranges her class so that she has visual contact with all parts of the room. For example, she uses low bookcases so students are in her line of sight. **E≫** Mr. Red (1) divides the classroom into areas for quiet reading, seat work, and small group work; (2) teaches rules on how quiet students must be; (3) arranges the room so students cannot easily look out windows or doorways into halls, and (4) places himself between the students and open areas if there are runners in the class. **S≫** Mr. Tolman strategically arranges student seating so that individuals prone to misbehave are adequately separated from one another.	The physical environment serves as a set of stimuli which influence appropriate and inappropriate behavior. Teachers can pay attention to such factors as basic layout of classroom space, wall displays, traffic patterns, and other aspects of the classroom.
4. High Rates of Positive Responses From Teachers	Frequent use of positive comments or actions to students who demonstrate appropriate behavior.	**P≫** Mr. Watson observes students playing appropriately and provides frequent verbal praise. **E≫** Mrs. Garcia tells the students "thanks for listening" and "nice effort" frequently as she monitors their creative writing behavior during second grade. **S≫** Mr. Skinner continuously makes a point to verbally praise those students who are on task and ready to work, while engaging in planned ignoring of mild off-task behaviors of other students.	Teachers create a positive environment by frequently praising the student for appropriate behavior and correct academic responses. Positive responses should be specific, so students can repeat the desired behaviors. If too general, students may not know which behaviors to repeat. The recommended ratio of positive to negative responses is at least 4:1.
5. Home Notes	An informational note that	**P≫** Johnny takes home his sticker chart at the end of the day and Mom praises him.	This communication should occur on a regular basis. Home

(*Cont.*)

provides clear, precise communication between school and parents about a student's academic and behavioral performance.

E≫ Ms. Wheeler sends notes home with five different students each day rating their academic work, study habits, and effort. By this method, each student in the class receives a home note once a week.

S≫ The student takes home a note indicating class performance, assignments completed, and upcoming test dates. The home note must then be signed by one of the parents and returned to the teachers. This ensures parent-teacher communication on a regular basis to avoid lengthy periods of academic non-productivity.

notes should emphasize positive information and also include information about areas of concern.

6. Instructional Pacing

The speed or rate at which the teacher presents instructional material and tasks to the learner.

P≫ Mrs. Weismuller moves from one preschool child to the next in quick succession, maintaining engagement with the activities during circle time.

E≫ Miss Zabriskie delivers direct instruction to the students at the rate of about nine learning tasks per minute, and asks for group responses from students frequently to check understanding.

S≫ Mr. Dynamic asks his twelfth grade students frequent questions to assess their understanding of the science material. Their responses serve as an indicator as to the possible need to repeat or review particular subject matter.

A brisk pace of instruction enhances student attention and increases the number of response opportunities. Appropriate pacing may decrease disruptive behavior.

7. Monitoring Performance

Collecting specific information systematically and

P≫ Mrs. Hansen keeps records for each preschool child showing data on current IEP goals and objectives, as well as behavioral concerns that may

Collecting information can help the teacher determine whether the program is effective. By

	consistently on a student's academic or behavioral performance.	require future intervention. E≫ Mr. Thomas conducts a running record on each student's reading quarterly and adjusts the student's skills instruction according to the results. S≫ Mr. Bandura keeps a copy of IEP goals and then tracks a particular student's reading progress. Based on those goals, the teacher assesses whether current instruction is effective with this particular student.	analyzing the data, the teacher knows when to make changes in both academic and behavior programs.
8. Parent Conference	A meeting (or other communi-cation) with parents to discuss the student's progress, successes and difficulties, and to involve parents in problem resolution.	P≫ Mr. Consequences meets with parents regularly to discuss the progress of the preschool children with whom he works. E≫ Miss Rigby calls Jim's mom twice during one week when he begins to stay out on the playground after the bell rings. Mom agrees to check with him daily on whether he returns to class promptly at the end of recess, and to praise him when he has a positive report. S≫ Mrs. Smith sends a brief e-mail message weekly to parents of students who are on academic tracking.	Parents may be involved via phone calls, e-mail, and home and/or school visits. Progress toward the annual goals of the IEP must be reported to parents at least as often as non-disabled peers receive progress reports. As appropriate, parent training may be included on a Behavior Intervention Plan.
9. Precision Commands	Precise verbal statements made by staff to enhance compliance of students.	P≫ When Sam runs in the classroom during free play time, his teacher says, "Sam, please use walking feet." (Five-second delay.) "Sam, I need you to use walking feet now!" (Five-second delay.) Sam is praised if he starts to walk. E≫ If Bill is not sitting down, the instructor says, "Bill, please sit down!" (Five-second delay.) "Bill, you *need* to sit	A precision command is clear, direct, and specific, without additional verbalizations or lectures.

(*Cont.*)

down *now*!" (Five-second
delay.) Consequate behavior
appropriately for compliance
or non-compliance.
S≫ If Lori is not wearing her
safety goggles as instructed
during a seventh grade science
experiment, her teacher says,
"Lori, please put on your
goggles!" (Five second delay.)
"Lori, I need you to wear your
goggles now!" (Five second
delay.) If Lori complies, the
teacher thanks Lori for
compliance with lab safety
procedures. If Lori refuses to
comply, she is instructed to sit
out of the lab and read the
safety manual.

10. Rules	Behavioral expectations for whole school, classroom, and transitional environments.	P≫ One of Ms. Allen's three preschool classroom rules is, "Use soft voices." The rules are posted in picture format along with the written rules, and children are verbally reinforced for compliance. E≫ Ms. Nakamura has five rules in her third grade classroom. She teaches and guides her students in practicing them until they follow the rules consistently. S≫ Every teacher in the high school holds students accountable for the rule that reads: "Be in your seat before the tardy bell rings." Each teacher establishes consequences for compliance and non-compliance with this rule.	Rules for each environment must be taught, posted, and frequently reviewed. General rules are made, supplemented by expectations for unique environments in the school such as the bus, lunchroom, and playground.
11. Staff Training	Personnel development activities conducted for	P≫ During an inservice, staff were instructed on the use of modeling. All staff then set a goal to use modeling five times	All staff training should emphasize research-validated procedures.

general and special educators, para-educators, and administrators to gain and maintain competencies in the strategies required for them to be effective.

a day for a week and record the results for a discussion in their weekly departmental meeting.

E≫ Mrs. Green, principal of Dogwood Elementary School, arranges inservice on the use of differential reinforcement. All teaching staff participate, practice the skill in the classroom, and then receive feedback from peer observers on their proficiency with the strategy.

S≫ A workshop is provided for the teaching staff in "self-management" procedures (i.e., self-monitoring, self-evaluation and self-reinforcement). The teachers brainstorm behaviors that would lend themselves to self-management procedures in their classrooms and select two students with whom to implement the strategy.

12. Structured Daily Schedule

A daily outline of classroom activities designed to maximize student learning.

P≫ During circle time, Josh's teacher previews the daily events using a picture schedule.

E≫ Ms. Adams, a second grade teacher, writes the daily schedule paired with visual aids on the board and highlights the weekly events and homework with colored chalk. She reviews the schedule with her students at the beginning of each day.

S≫ Mr. Alvarez, who teaches math in seventh grade, writes both the daily schedule and the weekly homework on the board. Students know what to start on when the bell rings each day, and they know the

Structuring time through a planned daily schedule of specific activities and transitions maximizes "on-task" behavior and minimizes students' inappropriate behavior.

(*Cont.*)

order of activities for
teacher-directed instruction,
guided practice, and
independent practice.

13. Supervision Systematic management and monitoring to promote academic and behavioral success of students.

P≫ Before snack and lunch, staff accompany preschool students to the restroom while they use the bathroom and wash their hands. Supervisors remain with students until all exit the restroom.
E≫ During recess, two teachers and a paraprofessional monitor the students' playground activities, as they had been trained to do in a yearly inservice on active supervision.
S≫ Between classes, teachers in the junior high stand in the halls by their doors and supervise students as they go to the next class. The presence of teachers in the halls has resulted in few students wandering the halls or stalling in the bathroom, and has reduced the number of fights.

Supervisors should be trained in the practices expected of them in each supervisory setting (e.g., playground, lunch room, halls). Adequate and appropriate supervision can guide students to succeed and prevent problems.

Level I-Positive Intervention Procedures

Procedure
1. Behavior Contracts
2. Behavior Momentum
3. Chaining
4. Contingent Observation

5. Differential Reinforcement
 	
   a. Differential Reinforcement of Other Behaviors (DRO)
   b. Differential Reinforcement of High Rates (DRH)
   c. Differential Reinforcement of Low Rates (DRL)
   d. Differential Reinforcement of Alternative Behavior (DRA)
   e. Differential Reinforcement of Incompatible Behavior (DRI)
   f. Differential Reinforcement of Functional Communicative Behavior (DRC)

6. Direct Instruction
7. Fading
8. Graduated Guidance
9. Group Reinforcement Response Contingency

10. Modeling/Differential Reinforcement of Another Person's Appropriate Behavior
 	
   a. Observational Learning
   b. Participant Model

11. Parent Training
12. Peer Involvement/Tutoring

13. Positive Reinforcement
 	
   a. Continuous Schedule of Reinforcement
   b. Intermittent Schedule of Reinforcement
     (i) Ratio Schedules of Reinforcement
     (ii) Interval Schedules of Reinforcement

14. Prompting
15. Redirection
16. Self-Management
17. Shaping
18. Social Skills Training
19. Stimulus Cueing
20. Structured Non-instructional Periods, including Recess
21. Teaching Interaction
22. Token Economy
23. Tracking

Positive behavioral supports and effective educational practices should be in place throughout the educational program and across settings, even when more intrusive procedures are selected by school teams to change a specific problem behavior.

Procedure	Definition	EXAMPLES P≫Preschool E≫Elementary S≫Secondary	Reminders & Potential Undesirable Side Effects
1. Behavior Contracts	Written agreements between school personnel and students, which specify expected behaviors, positive and negative consequences, time frame of the contract, and review dates.	P≫ The teacher says to Kelly, "If you pick up the toys, then you get to pass out the snack today." E≫ Having been tardy for school six days in a row, Sally agrees to be on time for the next week. Her mother agrees to help her keep a record of what time she leaves the house each day. The teacher commits to let Sally be the classroom leader on the fifth day of being on time to school. The contract is written and signed by all. S≫ Kevin is failing his Algebra class and his teacher puts him on a behavior contract. If he completes and turns in four consecutive assignments with 80% accuracy, he only has to do half of the assigned problems on the fifth day for full credit.	The contract is signed by all parties who are participating in the contract (student, teacher, parents, etc.). For preschool, an informal verbal contract is appropriate. Remember, contracting involves a delay or interval before a primary reward is given, which can result in decreased responding if the interval is too long. Positive consequences should be included in a well-balanced contract.
2. Behavior Momentum	Increasing compliance by identifying and then making a minimum of three requests with which the student has a high probability of compliance before making a low-probability request.	P≫ At lunch time, Ann is often reluctant to eat her lunch. In order to increase the likelihood that she will try her lunch, her teacher uses the following sequence of requests: "Ann, please sit down next to Shauna today! Ann, pass the napkins, please! Ann, look at the pretty shoes Shauna is wearing! Ann, have a bite of your sandwich!" E≫ Mr. Cleaver is working with nine-year-old Alison on compliance. After identifying high- and low-probability	Be sure to reinforce compliance with the low-probability request.

(Cont.)

behaviors for Alison, he uses the following sequence: "Alison, tell me your name. Alison, give me five. Alison, point to the dog. Alison, put your puzzle back on the shelf." If she puts the puzzle away, she receives a token.

S≫ Mrs. Evans teaches a high school history class. Reducing non-compliance is a goal on Calvin's IEP. She uses the following sequence of requests: "Calvin, please turn off the light. Calvin, hand this pencil to Julie. Calvin, mark two points on your card for listening and following directions. Calvin, please go to your seat, take out your assignment, and begin to work."

| 3. Chaining | Reinforcement of responses in sequence to form more complex behaviors. Chaining can involve both forward and backward steps. | P≫ Al can't put on his coat. First he is reinforced for taking his coat off the hook. Next he is reinforced for putting the coat on the floor in the prescribed manner and then for putting both arms in the sleeves. Last, he receives praise for flipping the coat over his head and having it on properly. E≫ Tom, a seven-year-old boy, is not toilet trained. First, his teacher praises him if he walks to the toilet. Next, he is reinforced when he walks to the toilet and pulls his pants down, and then for eliminating and pulling up steps, respectively. Lastly he is rewarded if he completes these four steps and washes his hands appropriately. S≫ Sharon is being taught to | As each new behavioral step is added, only the most recent step needs to be reinforced. *Note*: In conjunction with chaining and other behavior management techniques, a strategy known as task analysis must first be used. In task analysis, skills are broken down into concrete, specific component tasks, which in some cases may be very minute. If a child doesn't make progress on a task, it may be that it needs |

feed herself independently. First, she is handed the loaded spoon and reinforced for putting the food in her mouth. Next, she is rewarded for moving the loaded spoon from the tray to her mouth and putting the food in her mouth. Then, she is reinforced for loading the spoon, moving it to her mouth, and putting the food in. Finally, she is rewarded for picking up the spoon, loading it, moving to her mouth, and putting it in her mouth.

to be task analyzed further (broken into even smaller steps).

4. Contingent Observation	Telling a student who is doing some-thing inappropriate to step away from the activity, sit, and watch the appropriate be-havior of other students while the teacher intentionally reinforces them. After a brief period of observation, the teacher prompts the student to rejoin the activity, and reinforces the desired behavior.	P≫ The children are playing with blocks. The teacher says, "Stack your blocks." Robbie throws some of the blocks. The teacher says, "No, Robbie, that is not stacking. Watch Sally stack her blocks. Now, Robbie, stack your blocks." She reinforces him for stacking his blocks appropriately. E≫ During art, Tiffany hoards the paint at her table and won't let anyone else use it. Her teacher tells her to sit out and watch how students at other tables share the paint. After a few minutes, Tiffany returns to her table and is reinforced for sharing the paint with other students. S≫ Ms. Bodega, a science teacher, tells Adam and Steven, who have not read the lab procedures and are setting up the lab incorrectly, to sit out and watch other groups as they set up the experiment. Ms. Bodega then praises other groups for the steps they are performing correctly. Adam	The observation will usually be for a brief time. (One- to-five-minute periods are as effective as longer ones.)

(*Cont.*)

and Steven are then permitted to return to their lab station and set up, and are reinforced for following the procedure.

5. Differential Reinforcement	The reinforcement of one form of behavior, but not another; or the reinforcement of a response under one (stimulus) condition but not under another.		All of the differential reinforcement procedures take a substantial amount of time to be effective. If an inappropriate behavior is very disruptive or dangerous, use of a more intrusive procedure (that is, one higher in the LRBI intervention hierarchy) may be warranted to protect the student or other students in the classroom or work environment. Because an inappropriate behavior is ignored or not reinforced, there may be a dramatic increase or burst of the behavior before it decreases.
5. (a) Differential Reinforcement of Other Behaviors (DRO)	Reinforcement following any appropriate/ replacement behavior while ignoring the inappropriate/ target behavior in a defined period of time.	P≫ Nadia has a tantrum whenever she is asked to put her toys, supplies, and/or belongings away. Her teacher praises her and gives her a sticker each time she goes ten minutes without a tantrum, while ignoring her each time she has a tantrum. E≫ John is a student who scratches himself most of the time. The staff decides to smile, compliment, and give him points every two minutes	DRO always contains a predetermined length of time or interval. After each interval, the student is reinforced for *any* appropriate behavior, but never reinforced after the target/inappropriate behavior.

when he is not scratching. They ignore him and do not reinforce him at the two minute interval if he is scratching.
S≫ Tom likes to call attention to himself by talking out in class. His teacher ignores him each time he speaks out. The teacher verbally reinforces Tom each time he is not talking out at the end of a five-minute interval.

5. (b) **Differential** **Reinforcement** **of High Rates** **(DRH)**	Reinforcement given after performing some behavior at a pre-determined higher rate.	P≫ Kate does not interact with her peers. She is reinforced for spending increasing amounts of time in appropriate interaction with her peers. E≫ Diane receives a star for finishing three problems in five minutes. The next time she has to finish four problems in five minutes to earn a star. S≫ Lyle has a habit of being tardy to class. The staff decides to reinforce him with extra computer time each day he makes it to six of his ten periods on time.	
5. (c) **Differential** **Reinforcement** **of Low Rates** **(DRL)**	Reinforcement given after performing the target/problem behavior at a predetermined low rate.	P≫ When Jimmy decreases his talking during circle time by a predetermined amount, the teacher praises him. E≫ Sally talks out ten times every morning during the teacher's instruction. The teacher sets up a program specifying that if Sally reduces her talk outs to five, she can choose a privilege. This program continues to reduce the number of talk outs Sally can have until she gets to an acceptably low rate. S≫ Dale has a habit of swearing an average of six	This procedure is usually used for behaviors that occur at such a high rate, or are so ingrained into the student's behavior patterns, that a large immediate drop in occurrences is unrealistic.

(*Cont.*)

times during class. The teacher
sets a limit of three swear
words each day during the first
week. If Dale swears three or
fewer times during the class
period, he is reinforced. The
following week the criterion is
set at two swear words in a
given class, and the program
continues until the criterion is
zero.

| **5. (d) Differential Reinforcement of Alternative/ Replacement Behavior (DRA)** | Reinforcement of a replacement behavior while ignoring the inappropriate behavior. | P≫ Kit does not follow the teacher's directions. He is verbally reinforced each time he does comply and is ignored when he does not.
E≫ Sam's out-of-seat behavior in a kindergarten is targeted to be decreased. When he is out of his seat, he is ignored. But when he is in his seat, the teacher goes to Sam and praises him for being in his chair.
S≫ Tammy writes and passes notes during class. Whenever Tammy is taking notes from the lecture or paying attention and listening, the teacher stands near her desk and praises her for being on task. Whenever she writes notes, her behavior is ignored. | This procedure is commonly called differential attention and proximity praise. |
| **5. (e) Differential Reinforcement of Incompatible Behavior (DRI)** | Reinforcement of an appropriate behavior that is physically or functionally incompatible with the target behavior, while ignoring the inappropriate | P≫ Denise pokes students who sit next to her on the rug during opening time. She is reinforced for sitting with her hands folded together on her lap.
E≫ Jose, a first grader who is often lying on the floor, is reinforced when he sits on a chair.
S≫ Emily draws on her notebook and books during lectures. The teacher reinforces | |

		behavior.	her for writing notes about the lesson in her notebook.
5. (f) **Differential Reinforcement of Functional Communicative Behavior (DRC)**	Reinforcement of a functional communication skill leading to a needed reward, activity, or alternative, while ignoring inappropriate behavior.		**P≫** Sandra receives her snack each day as she displays successive approximations of an appropriate verbal request to the teacher. **E≫** Cade is having a tantrum and is ignored by the teacher. The teacher determines that the function of the tantrum is to obtain a glass of water. He is then taught the sign for water. When Cade signs "water," he is given a glass of water and praised. **S≫** Paul starts carving on his desk with his pen whenever he gets bored or distracted. The teacher teaches him to raise his left hand whenever he begins to feel restless. When and if the teacher acknowledges him with a nod, he is allowed to go and get a drink of water. Paul is allowed this privilege two times at most in a given period, and a time limit is established for his drink breaks.
6. **Direct Instruction**	Active teaching or explicit instruction, including explaining to students exactly what they are expected to learn, demonstrating the steps needed to accomplish a task, providing		**P≫** Ms. Day teaches the children to recognize and name two colors, red and yellow. She shows pictures of common objects in each color, then has the children identify objects in the room that are of each color. **E≫** The teacher explains to Dennis that the lesson is about long division. Then she demonstrates the steps on the chalkboard and watches while he tries to do a problem. Feedback is given to correct any errors and to reinforce him for following procedures

(Cont.)

		opportunities for practice, and giving feedback based on performance.	correctly. **S≫** In English class, Ms. Paulos teaches her freshman students how to diagram sentences involving subject, predicate, articles, adjectives, and adverbs. She demonstrates the procedure with a sample sentence and writes each step on the board. Then she puts a sentence on the board and asks the students to diagram the sentence in their seats while she walks around and gives assistance and corrective feedback. Finally, one student goes to the board and illustrates how to correctly diagram the sentence.	
7. Fading	The gradual elimination of cues, prompts, reminders, or suggestions that control a specific response.	**P≫** John is learning to feed himself. He, receives less and less physical guidance, and eventually eats independently using a spoon and fork. **E≫** Fewer and fewer dashes or dots are placed on the page on which Sarah is learning to print, so that she completes more and more of the task independently. **S≫** Sandy struggles in her freshman year to get to class on time. A program is implemented where she is escorted to the class for a week. Next, an adult observes her go to the classroom alone. Finally, the teacher comes to the door and watches her come to the classroom. She is reinforced for each instance of arriving in class on time.	If cues are removed too quickly, student's response will deteriorate.
8. Graduated Guidance	A systematic, gradual reduction of	**P≫** Mr. Stringham is teaching Connie to go to the rug for circle time promptly. He pairs	Use enough pressure to guide the movement, but never

manual guidance.

Manual guidance is gently touching the student for instructional purposes or redirection.

verbal instructions with a light hand hold, guiding her to her spot in the circle. As she moves toward the circle, he lessens the hold each day until she goes there alone.

E≫ Rita, who cannot hold a spoon to eat, is assisted by the teacher who covers her hand to help hold and guide the spoon. Little by little, the teacher moves the physical help to just resting her hand on Rita's hand. The next step is to gradually move to a slight tap on the back of the hand. The physical assistance is faded out until Rita can perform the behavior independently.

S≫ Jed cannot keep his hands in the proper keyboarding position. The teacher holds his wrists up until his hands are correctly positioned. She keeps her hands there until he types one page. Then, she moves her hands so that they are just lightly touching his wrists while he types the next page. Finally, she lifts her hands from his wrists and allows him to type on his own.

force it. If force is required, this becomes a more intrusive procedure-see "Forceful Physical Guidance," Level III (#1). Take caution to avoid injury to student or staff because a student may resist being touched or struggle when minimally guided through a procedure.

9. Group Reinforcement Response Contingency

Reinforcement of the entire group dependent upon the perform-ance of individual members.

P≫ Mrs. Bailey gave each child who put away the art materials correctly a smile and a thank you. (independent)

E≫ If Demetrius earns a score of 75% or better on each math test during the third quarter, the fourth grade class will all take a trip to the dinosaur museum in April. (dependent)

S≫ Mr. Miller's sophomore history class is allowed to watch a movie on Friday if all

A student may sabotage or ruin the reinforcement for the group to gain negative attention.

Extreme peer pressure may be placed on the individual who does not meet the group contingency criteria.

(*Cont.*)

of the students bring in their homework for the entire week. (interdependent)

Group-oriented contingencies may be of three types: (1) Dependent: the performance of one or more particular group members determines the consequence received by the entire group. (2) Independent: each group member receives a consequence if he meets the contingency. (3) Interdependent: each student must reach a prescribed level of behavior before the entire group receives a consequence.

10. Modeling/ Differential Reinforcement of Another Person's Appropriate Behavior

Learning through observation of a peer or adult model's behavior.

P⟫ Louie does not raise his hand to ask questions. The teacher stands near him and praises those students sitting next to him who raise their hands. She also puts a sticker on their name tags. When Louie raises his hand to ask a question, she praises him and gives him a sticker.
E⟫ Sharon is squirming in her seat. The teacher goes to Ron, the student next to Sharon, and gives him a plus on his point card for "sitting quietly." Sharon sees Ron get the plus and stops squirming. After 20 seconds of quiet sitting, the teacher puts a plus on Sharon's point card.
S⟫ Kent does not stay on task when given an assignment in

It is important to identify and state the desired behavior to the student when reinforcing it. There are a number of social skills and anger management programs that have videotaped examples and non-examples of behaviors to be taught. Self-modeling via videotaping the child performing a desired behavior is another variation of this strategy.

his health class. The teacher praises other students sitting near him when they are on task and completing their assignments.

10. (a) Observational Learning	After observing a modeled response, the observer exhibits that response.	**P≫** The teacher demonstrates to Billy how to sort the blocks by colors. He completes the task alone after observing her. **E≫** Lori watches the teacher demonstrate how to appropriately greet others. Then Lori greets peers on her own and receives verbal reinforcement from the teacher. **S≫** Brittany has trouble with multiple choice tests. Mr. Daniels sits down with a test and demonstrates how he approaches this kind of exam. He explains step by step, verbally expressing what he is thinking and how he is solving each test item.	Other steps and procedures may need to be used in conjunction with observational learning.
10. (b) Participant Model	Learning by both watching someone act and actively practicing the behavior observed.	**P≫** Jake cannot hang his backpack on the hook. His teacher shows him how to hang the backpack up, and instructs him to observe the other children. Next, she has him practice with guidance from her. Finally, he puts the backpack on the hook alone. **E≫** Lois is shy and not very assertive. A teacher models five different assertive responses, such as asking for a toy she wants and telling someone not to push her. Lois is then asked to role play the response and is reinforced for being properly assertive. She practices the responses at recess with her peers and receives feedback from her teacher.	Student may imitate inappropriate behavior as well as appropriate behavior.

(Cont.)

S≫ Katie has trouble solving math problems. A peer tutor is assigned who understands each step of the problem-solving process. He models his own work while Katie watches, explaining each step to her. Next they do a problem together. He gives her corrective feedback on the remainder of the assignment.

| 11. Parent Training | Training parents to use appropriate behavioral interventions with their child. | P≫ Nancy has temper tantrums that are a problem at school and home. The teacher trains the parent in effective procedures used at school for reducing the number of Nancy's tantrums.
E≫ The third grade classes at Mt. McKinley Elementary School are struggling to get their homework done regularly. The teacher holds a group parent training session on strategies to improve their homework completion rate.
S≫ Tyler has recently been arrested for shoplifting at a local convenience store. His parents are concerned and come to his high school for help. A counselor meets with the parents and teaches them some concrete ways to improve their supervision and monitoring of Tyler outside of school time. | Parent training is used when the student needs to have the same behavior interventions at home and school in order to improve generalization.
• School staff may invite parent to the classroom setting to observe the implementation of appropriate interventions.
• Handouts on specific behavior strategies are another option.
• Explain a specific intervention, such as a Picture Exchange Communication System, and give the parents a set of materials for home use. |
| 12. Peer Involvement/ Tutoring | The use of same- or cross-age peers for academic tutoring, structured social | P≫ Debbie has difficulty sitting on the rug during circle time in her preschool class. The teacher assigns Kathy to sit next to Debbie on the rug so that Kathy can model appropriate behavior. | |

	engagement, or as peer "buddies."	**E≫** Beth and Jean are struggling to remember to take their homework home in fifth grade. The school psychologist assigns them to check each other's backpacks at the end of the day to make sure they have the homework they need. **S≫** Kimberly walks next to Kyle in his wheel chair to the lunch room and carries his tray to a table of friends in the lunch area.	
13. Positive Reinforcement	Reinforcement of a student, contingent upon performing a specific behavior, to maintain/ increase a behavior.		If food is used, try nutritious food first. Be sure student is not allergic or diabetic.
13. (a) Continuous Schedule of Reinforcement	A schedule of reinforcement in which each occurrence of a response is reinforced.	**P≫** Sierra does not follow teacher directions very often in her preschool class. Every time she complies with a teacher request, she is given a piece of cereal. **E≫** Each time Joan takes a step unaided, her friends cheer. **S≫** Jack's teacher is trying to teach him to use better manners in his high school class. Every time Jack says "thank you" his teacher gives him a smile.	Continuous reinforcement is often used to begin a teaching sequence or to shape new behaviors. When continuous reinforcement is stopped, the behavior stops almost immediately. Students may stop responding or avoid the reinforcing stimulus because they have had too much of the stimulus.
13. (b) Intermittent Schedule of Reinforcement	A schedule of reinforcement in which some, but not all, of	**P≫** When Shawn uses appropriate communication skills with his preschool peers, he is reinforced with a sticker	Intermittent reinforcement increases the rate of response and makes

(Cont.)

	the occurrences of a response are reinforced.	on a random basis. E≫ When Laura walks down the elementary school halls, the teacher sometimes puts her hand on Laura's shoulder and tells her, "Good job walking in the hall." S≫ When John works on his math assignment the teacher gains eye contact and smiles at him on a random basis.	the established behavior more stable and habitual. Be sure the reinforcement immediately follows the desired behavior, not other behaviors the student exhibits. If the schedule of reinforcement is too infrequent, it may not produce the desired change in behavior.
13. (b) (i) Ratio Schedules of Reinforcement	A schedule in which reinforcement is made contingent upon a specific number of responses before being reinforced (fixed ratio) or upon the average number of responses (variable ratio).	P≫ Paul has to put five toys away in his preschool classroom when it is clean up time before he is reinforced. E≫ Every third time that Jose raises his hand before he speaks, the teacher tells him to give himself a point on his card. S≫ Sixteen-year-old Joe is reinforced, on average, after four correct answers. He may be reinforced twice in a row, then after eight correct, so long as the average remains four.	If the work requirement is too much, the student may stop working and become frustrated. If the schedule of reinforcement is too infrequent, it may not produce the desired change in behavior.
13. (b) (ii) Interval Schedules of Reinforcement	A schedule in which some specified amount of time must pass and then the next occurrence of one appropriate response is reinforced.	P≫ If Matthew stays engaged with a single activity for three minutes, the teacher rewards him as he continues the activity. E≫ Bob's first grade teacher praises him if he remains on task after a five-minute interval. S≫ Cassidy is a high school student who has poor attendance. If she attends six periods in a day, then when she shows up in seventh period the	Students may stop responding after being reinforced because they may think the procedure is over.

		teacher rewards her for attending a full day of school.	
14. Prompting	Presentation of a cue (visual, auditory, physical) in order to facilitate a given response.	**P**≫ When it is time to clean up at preschool, Mrs. Kindly turns the cleanup music on. **E**≫ While Sarah is learning to print in kindergarten, she is given papers on which there is a dot where each letter should start. **S**≫ When the teacher passes Martin's desk he is off task. She touches his shoulder softly to bring his attention back to world geography.	Overuse of prompting may result in a high level of dependency on prompts. Be conscious of students for whom a physical cue is aversive.
15. Redirection	Interruption of a problem behavior and redirection to an appropriate replacement behavior.	**P**≫ During rug time, Dallin stands up and leaves the activity. The teacher's aide touches him on the shoulder and tells him to come back to circle time. **E**≫ Veronica is running up the slides during recess. Mrs. Black approaches her, points to the swings, and says, "Look, there's an empty swing for you." **S**≫ Alonzo begins to talk to a high school peer during study skills class. The teacher taps his paper and points to his assignment.	A gentle touch or a light verbal statement may be used to interrupt the inappropriate behavior and direct student to the appropriate behavior.
16. Self-Management	Strategies which involve students' management and control of their own behavior through the systematic application of behavioral principles (e.g., self-	**P**≫ Mrs. Gough says, "If you're sitting on your carpet square, you may go wash your hands for snack." **E**≫ Sue records a check mark on her card each time that she comes in from recess on time. Her second grade teacher also keeps track of Sue's on-time behavior. At the end of the day, the teacher asks Sue to come up and compare her card with the teacher's. If their cards	The desired behaviors must be taught using other procedures. Young children may not respond well to self-management interventions.

(Cont.)

	monitoring, self-reinforcement, self-evaluation).	match, Sue is reinforced. **S»** Each time that Jim says something nice to a peer, he makes a dot on his card. The resource teacher reviews the card with him and buys him a pop if he has ten dots. Periodically, the teacher checks with the other students to verify his recording of points.	
17. Shaping	Developing new behaviors through the use of systematic reinforcement of successive approxima-tions of the behavioral objective.	**P»** Sharon is learning to request her favorite toy. She is first taught the sign which the teacher pairs with the word. If Sharon makes the sign for baby, she receives the doll. Next, she has to make a "b" sound to get the doll. Shaping continues until she says "Baby" to receive the doll. **E»** Jackie always sits by herself at lunch and does not interact with her fifth grade peers. She is first reinforced for sitting at the table where other peers are, then for sitting next to a peer and, finally, for engaging in conversation with a peer. **S»** In order to get Kevin to remain in his seat in his high school resource class, he is first regularly reinforced for entering the classroom, then for being near his desk, then for touching his chair, and finally, for being correctly seated in his chair.	
18. Social Skills Training	Individual or group instruction designed to teach appropriate interaction	**P»** Johnny often grabs toys from other children and makes them cry. He is given individual instruction and simple role-play situations on taking turns and playing cooperatively with others.	Modeling and practice of social skills to mastery is highly important. Teachers should take the time to teach them and review

with adults and peers.

E≫ Sarah's teacher reports that she makes frequent rude remarks to other students and this makes the other students dislike her. Sarah has small group instruction by the school counselor on effective communication and making friends.

S≫ Matt is experiencing problems with depression and anxiety since moving to a new school. He feels isolated and hasn't made any new friends. He is included in a small group run by the school psychologist that teaches skills for making friends, including initiating and sustaining conversations.

them until students can perform them consistently and independently. With school-age students, use of examples and non-examples of appropriate social skills clarifies the desired behavior.

19. Stimulus Cueing

Use of a random auditory or visual cue to prompt appropriate behavior.

P≫ Jean often looks around the room instead of paying attention to the story during circle time. A beeper tape with random beeps at 30 second to 1 minute intervals is played during story time to remind her to attend to the story.

E≫ Colby seems to be constantly out of his seat. His teacher begins using a timer set randomly from one- to five-minute intervals during seat-work time. The goal is for everyone to be in his or her seat when the timer rings.

S≫ Christopher is having trouble staying on task during class. When the teacher makes the statement, "Check what you're doing right now and mark your card if you're on task," he adds a point to his card. At the end of the hour, he is reinforced for having five or more points.

A beeper tape with a tone at random intervals is an example.

(*Cont.*)

20. Structured Non-instructional Periods, Including Recess	A systematic intervention program for a student who requires a high level of structure during non-instructional periods.	**P**≫ The preschool teacher notices that most of Johnny's conflicts with other children occur during free play. She decides that instead of free play, she will have Johnny pick between two activities. **E**≫ The other students are constantly complaining that Alex interrupts and interferes with their games at recess. A classroom aide teaches Alex the rules for kick ball. The classroom aide then goes to recess with Alex and prompts him to join the game. The aide monitors his play and interaction with other students. Alex is rewarded for playing by the rules and for getting along with the other children. **S**≫ Jacob purchases a candy bar and soda from the vending machine every day at lunch time, eats them quickly and then goes from table to table in the lunch room touching other people's food and bullying weaker students. The counselor teaches a group of students including Jacob a game to play after they finish eating. Each time Jacob shows up at the specified meeting place and plays appropriately, he is reinforced.	Students are taught specific game rules, as well as appropriate hall, lunchroom, bathroom, and playground behavior. Then they are reinforced for appropriate behavior during these activities.
21. Teaching Interaction	A short social skills teaching sequence: expression of affection, initial praise, description of inappropriate behavior, description of	**P**≫ When the teacher observes Susie grabbing a doll from Natalie, the teacher takes Susie aside and tells Susie how much she enjoys having her in the class. She rehearses with Susie how to ask Natalie if she can play with the doll. The teacher tells Susie what a good job she did and then sends her back to	

	appropriate behavior, rationale, acknowledgement, practice, feedback, consequences, general praise.	play. **E≫** Russell was teasing Jane about her new haircut. The teacher asks Russell to stay in and help her pass out art supplies at recess. During recess, she congratulates Russell accomplishing his reading goal. She then describes how she saw him teasing Jane and how that can really hurt somebody's feelings. She asks Russell to apologize to Jane and give her two compliments during the day. He promises to do that. The teacher pats him on the back and says she is proud of him. **S≫** Terri is a student in a self-contained classroom. When Ben is chosen as Student of the Week, she throws her books on the floor and starts to cry. The teacher takes her aside and tells Terri how well she is doing and reminds her that she was chosen as Student of the Week just two weeks ago. They practice how to congratulate Ben. Terry then goes over to Ben and says, "Good job!" Terry looks at the teacher, who smiles at her.	
22. Token Economy	A system of individual reinforcement of appropriate/ replacement behavior in which tokens are given (chips, check marks, paper money) and exchanged	**P≫** Elena forgets to wipe her saliva off her chin. The teacher shows her how to keep her chin dry. Then she gives her one piece of a three-piece non-interlocking puzzle each time she wipes. When the puzzle is complete, Elena gets five minutes of computer time. **E≫** Phyllis earns a point for being in her seat when the bell rings, for each assignment	Token reinforcement can be used for behavior that the student knows how to do. Successive approximations of behavior to be established may also be reinforced. Token systems may not deprive students of constitutionally

(Cont.)

	later for back-up reinforcers.	completed on time, and for appropriate behavior at recess. At the end of the day, the points are exchanged for backup rewards which Phyllis has pre-selected. S≫ Jordan does not turn in his English homework and is failing the class. Jordan and his parents agree to a token economy system where he earns one chip for every assignment turned in. Jordan then pays his parents one chip per day for phone privileges.	guaranteed rights. Token systems involve delay of giving or delivering reward, which can result in decreased responding if the delay is too long. Inappropriate lengths of delay may become punishing. Guard against token theft and counterfeiting by students.
23. Tracking	Monitoring of a student's academic and/or behavioral performance with regular feedback.	P≫ Jane is new in the preschool class. She whines and cries several times each morning. She is put on a tracking program where she gets to put a smiley face or a "frowny" face on a chart at the end of each block of time if she doesn't whine or cry. She receives a piece of fruity cereal for each smiley face she earns. E≫ Russell is moving from one seat to another on the bus. He now has a tracking sheet to monitor this behavior. The bus driver signs his tracking sheet at the end of each ride when he stays in his seat. Russell is rewarded every morning by the resource teacher if he has two signatures on his sheet. S≫ Bret, a middle school student, is required to have each teacher in his schedule rate his work completion each day. He turns the tracking sheet back in to his resource teacher at the end of the day and is reinforced for five or more high ratings.	Public posting violates confidentiality, as per the Utah Family Education Rights and Privacy Act. Be sure to follow district policies.

Level II–Mildly Intrusive Contingent Procedures

Procedure
1. Administrative Intervention
2. Detention, Before and After School ✐
3. Detention, Lunch ✐
4. Extinction*
5. Food Delay*
6. In-School Suspension (ISS)

7. Over-Correction
 	
    a. Restitutional Over-Correction
    b. Positive Practice Over-Correction*
    c. Neutral Practice Over-Correction/Contingent Exercise*
    d. Full Cleanliness Training*

8. Required Relaxation
9. Response Cost*
10. Startle
11. Time Out, Exclusionary
12. Time Out, Inter-Class
13. Time Out, Non-Seclusionary
14. Verbal Reprimand
15. Work Detail

*Caution must be exercised when using these procedures.**
✐ *Notify parent by phone or other method when student is detained, and document time and date of contact.*

Positive behavioral supports and effective educational practices should be in place throughout the educational program and across settings, even when more intrusive procedures are selected by school teams to change a specific problem behavior.

Procedure	Definition	EXAMPLES P≫Preschool E≫Elementary S≫Secondary	Reminders & Potential Undesirable Side Effects
1. Administrative Intervention	Interaction between student and designated building administrator regarding problem behavior, including procedures for de-escalating disruptive behavior, obtaining and maintaining instructional control, teaching alternative behaviors, and preparing student for classroom re-entry.	P≫ Not appropriate. E≫ Brittany swears and uses other inappropriate language in the classroom. The principal and teacher decide that each time this occurs, she will go to the principal's office. There Brittany is given five minutes to calm down, and then the principal discusses the problem with her, including appropriate alternative behaviors. Finally the principal accompanies Brittany back to her classroom where she apologizes to the class, sits down and starts to work. S≫ Two boys are caught engaged in a fistfight in the hallway. They are both escorted to the vice principal, who speaks to the students and evaluates the situation to determine the appropriate consequences.	Often used in conjunction with in-school suspension (ISS). Often includes steps in "Teaching Interaction," Level I(21). Administrative intervention should be used for a limited number of extreme behaviors. Classroom behaviors must be managed by the teacher to achieve behavior change in context.
2. Detention, Before and After School	A school-based intervention whereby a student reports to a supervised study hall for an assigned period of time (usually thirty minutes to two hours) before or after the normal school	P≫ Not appropriate. E≫ Chris, who is in sixth grade, is assigned one hour of after-school detention for fighting with another student. During detention, each child sits at a study carrel and works on homework. If the child does not bring any homework, the detention supervisor has worksheets appropriate for each grade level. S≫ Lorie is failing her history class because of not turning in	To be effective, the detention must occur in a non-reinforcing environment. The amount of time for detention should reflect the seriousness of the problem and the age of the student. Notify parent or guardian of a student *(Cont.)*

day.

assignments, according to her mid-term progress report. She is required to attend study hall after school for one hour per week. At the end of the term, she has improved her grade by turning in more of her assignments.

prior to holding the student after school on a particular day. (UCA 53A-3-415)

3. Detention, Lunch

Similar to before- and after-school detention, except that the time assigned is during the student's lunch period.

P≫ Scottie, a four-year-old, threw toys at a classmate. The class is going outside for a picnic snack. Scottie must remain in the room, with supervision, to eat his snack. **E≫** When Eric calls his second grade classmate names, he has to eat lunch in the classroom with the teacher and has to miss five minutes of his lunch recess. **S≫** Amber dumps the basket of homework papers onto the floor, so she is required to have her lunch and remain in the classroom for the entire lunch period.

Lunch detention is usually conducted in a isolated, quiet location, while still providing the student with the opportunity to eat his/her hot or cold lunch. To be effective, the detention must occur in a non-reinforcing environment, with no reinforcement from the adult supervisor.

Parental notification required!

4. Extinction

Non-reinforcement of a previously reinforced behavior.

P≫ Sue often cries to get attention at preschool. Her teacher stops giving her attention when she cries. At first Sue cries harder and longer. The teacher still ignores her. As the behavior is not being reinforced, the crying gradually tapers off. Sue periodically reverts back to crying to see if the teacher has "changed the rules." As the teacher ignores it consistently, the crying disappears completely. **E≫** Mike continually puts his hands in his pants. He receives attention from the teacher and the aide when they ask him to

Extinction is not appropriate when the behavior is dangerous to the student or others. In such an instance, extinction should be combined with other LRBI procedures. Extinction is a technical procedure that requires staff training.

Because an inappropriate behavior is ignored or not reinforced, there may be a dramatic

take his hands out of his pants. The teacher and aide begin to compliment Mike when he is sitting appropriately and do not attend to him when his hands are in his pants.
S≫ Barbara is a high school student who makes inappropriate remarks to her teacher. The teacher decides to withdraw his attention when Barbara makes inappropriate remarks by breaking eye contact, making no facial expression, and walking away. When Barbara is appropriate in her remarks to the teacher, he responds briefly and redirects her attention back to the classroom activity.

increase or burst of the inappropriate behavior.

5. Food Delay

Delay of food for a specified period of time, contingent on inappropriate behavior.

P≫ When Rachel does raspberries during a table top activity, her teacher says, "Rachel, please stop making those sounds." When Rachel continues, the teacher says, "Rachel, don't make those sounds at the table. You will have to wait for your snack." The teacher then delays her snack for three minutes.
E≫ Irene is very slow at clearing her desk before lunch time, although she is generally compliant. Mrs. Douglas usually has the class wait for her to finish, making the group late for lunch. Irene is told that if she is not ready to go, she must remain in the classroom for 10 minutes to finish cleaning up. Then she is dismissed to join her class in the lunch room. On the days when she is ready on time, she

Students cannot be completely denied a meal (e.g., lunch). Usually a delay is about fifteen minutes or half of the allotted lunch period. Delay should never be more than two hours. Check with parents regarding medical considerations related to food delay. Signed parental permission is recommended.

If food is delayed too long, the student may increase the misbehavior.

(Cont.)

is praised and goes to the lunch room with her classmates.

S≫ Josh is a high school junior who is continually late for fourth period, which is right before lunch. Each time he is late, his teacher makes him wait for fifteen minutes once the lunch bell rings before he is excused.

6. In-School Suspension (ISS)	Removal of a student from the classroom to a non-reinforcing supervised setting inside the school where the student works on assignments.	P≫ Not appropriate. E≫ All morning Erik is in an irritable mood and responds to his fifth grade teacher's directions with vulgarity. The instructor sends Erik to ISS with the day's assignments. The ISS supervisor reviews the in-house rules with Erik, then assigns him a desk facing the wall, where he remains for the rest of the day. S≫ Shauna comes to her ninth grade science class without the required supplies for the third time this week. Ms. Kopinski fills out an ISS request form and sends it with Shauna to the office. The school administrator approves the request, contacts Shauna's parents, and notifies her class instructors. Her instructors send assignments for two days to the ISS supervisor. Shauna reports to ISS.	In-school suspension is ineffective if avoiding scheduled classes is more reinforcing than participation. If ISS is an effective intervention, the inappropriate behavior should be decreasing. A pattern of ISS can become a change of placement (see Rule V.C). Services specified in the IEP must be provided, or the day counts as an out-of-school suspension. Teachers should not overuse this intervention; use Preliminary Strategies and Level I interventions before and in conjunction with this procedure.
7. Over-Correction	Performing an appropriate behavior intensely or repeatedly after the		For all over-correction procedures, forceful physical guidance is not permitted.

	occurrence of an inappropriate behavior.		
7. (a) Restitutional Over-Correction	Restoration of the environment to better than its original condition.	**P≫** Pedro eats play dough at preschool. He is required to clean out his mouth and pick up paper bits from the rug. **E≫** Fred spits on the desk. He is required to clean the desk he soiled, plus three others. **S≫** Jeff writes inappropriate names on some lockers at school. The principal has Jeff clean the lockers he defaced as well as all the lockers in the Senior Hall.	Restoring the environment must be possible with reasonable time and effort.
7. (b) Positive Practice Over-Correction	Intense practice of an appropriate behavior for a specified number of repetitions or a specified period of time.	**P≫** On the playground, four-year-old Trevor runs up the slide and steps on the fingers of two other preschoolers. The recess aide then requires Trevor to turn around and go down the slide properly three times. **E≫** Sylvia runs down the hall. The teacher then requires her to walk down the hall appropriately three times. **S≫** Jennifer throws a softball and hits other students during tenth grade P.E. She is told to throw the ball back and forth appropriately with another student for five minutes.	Positive practice may involve motor tasks or academic tasks. However, assigning large amounts of writing or math is not an appropriate over-correction procedure.
7. (c) Neutral Practice Over-Correction/ Contingent Exercise	Repetition of an action that is neither restitutional nor related to the desired behavior.	**P≫** While washing his hands in preschool class, Ryan throws water on his classmates. The teacher has Ryan do the stand-up, sit-down exercise ten times. **E≫** Every time Tony neglects to come in from recess at the appropriate time, he is required	This often takes the form of contingent exercise. Neutral practice must never be implemented to the point that it causes physical harm or pain.

(Cont.)

		to do 15 sit-ups. S≫ In P.E. class, Lee is required to run five laps around the gym every time she uses profanity.	Be aware of medical considerations for a specific student. A student may resist being touched or struggle when guided through this procedure.
7. (d) Full Cleanliness Training	Excessive cleaning as a result of wetting or soiling, used commonly in toilet training or in cases of feces smearing.	P≫ Jill is four and a half years old and has just soiled her underpants. She is required to wash out the underclothing in clean water for three minutes. Then she is required to assist in cleaning and changing herself. E≫ Stanley smeared feces on the wall of the toilet stall. His teacher requires him to clean the walls thoroughly with soap and then to clean himself. S≫ Arnold has soiled his underpants. He is required to wash out the underclothing in clean water for five minutes. Then he is required to bathe, shower or otherwise clean himself and properly take care of the soiled clothing.	Cleanup activity must be long enough to be uncomfortable but not harmful.
8. Required Relaxation	Spending a fixed period of time in relaxation following each occurrence of an upsetting behavior.	P≫ Julian occasionally has angry outbursts. When this occurs, an aide takes him to a quiet corner and they practice breathing slowly for four minutes. E≫ Nancy, who acts out by hitting other children, learns to identify when she is feeling frustrated. She is taught two relaxation techniques. When she lets the classroom teacher know she is frustrated, she is excused from the room to a designated place for a 10-minute period of relaxation. S≫ Alice periodically has	Teach relaxation techniques to the student under non-stressful circumstances. A student may resist being touched or struggle when guided through this procedure. If forceful physical guidance is needed to get the student to comply, this becomes the Level III (#1) procedure. The period is never more

panic attacks. She learns a progressive muscle relaxation technique that effectively calms her. When Alice feels highly agitated, she goes into the nurse's room and practices relaxation for fifteen minutes.

than one hour. No talking, eating, listening to radios, or playing with objects is permitted.

9. Response Cost

Contingent withdrawal of a specific amount of available reinforcers following an inappropriate response.

P≫ If Cathy finishes the table time activity without kicking the table, she gets a large ball of play dough. Each time she kicks the table, a portion of the play dough is removed. When the activity is completed, she gets to play with the remaining dough.

E≫ Steve is awarded ten points at the start of recess. Each time he breaks one of the playground rules, he loses a point. At the end of the recess period, Steve may bank all the points he has retained and exchange them after the last recess of the day for items listed on a menu of reinforcers.

S≫ Bart's preferred activity is computer time. He starts each class with ten minutes of computer time to use at the end of the period. Each time he spits on the floor, he loses one minute of his computer time.

Response cost must be less than the total amount or number of reinforcers available (i.e., never go in the hole). All students have civil rights to water, food, clothes and use of the bathroom which cannot be withheld.

Taking away a highly prized reinforcer or privilege can lead to aggression directed at the teacher, other students, or property.

A student may cry, whine, or pout when reinforcement is withdrawn.

10. Startle

Use of a sudden and loud verbal statement or physical action to gain student's attention.

P≫ Sally often picks her nose absentmindedly. Whenever this behavior is observed, Mrs. Miller loudly says, "Sally, no!" to make Sally aware of what she is doing.

E≫ Mrs. Gomez slaps Tommy's desk with her open hand loudly when he is off task.

S≫ When he sees Heather daydreaming and gazing out the window, Mr. Eisen moves

This procedure may be viewed as abusive by an uninformed observer. Use judiciously as these techniques interrupt instruction for the entire class.

(Cont.)

		in closer to her desk and claps his hands sharply once. This calls her back to the present task.	
11. Time Out, Exclusionary	Removal of student from a reinforcing setting into a setting with a lower reinforcing value, *but not a time-out room.*	P≫ Torie continually bothers her classmates while sitting on the mat during story time. She is put in a chair away from the group for three minutes. During this time, she cannot see the storybook pictures as well as before. E≫ Joey is giggling constantly in his second grade reading group. As a result, his chair is turned around, facing away from the group, for five minutes. The teacher continues to reinforce the other group members for appropriate attending behavior. S≫ Jake belittles other students' comments during a small discussion group in Health. He is removed from the group and seated near the teacher for a five- minute period.	Time out is used for a relatively short amount of time based on the age of the student, and is not effective unless the classroom is positively reinforcing. Time out must not be humiliating to the student. Inappropriate examples would be standing in a corner, nose on wall, and dunce caps.
12. Time Out, Inter-Class	Removal of student from a reinforcing setting into another classroom with a lower reinforcing value.	P≫ Not appropriate. E≫ When Jan keeps teasing her fourth grade peers, she is escorted to a first grade classroom, where she sits for ten minutes. S≫ May not be as effective for this age group.	Effective practice is to place student two or more grade levels away from his or her own. This procedure requires making arrangements with the other teacher in advance. Where the student sits in the other classroom is important. The student's response to the other classroom must be monitored. The student remains in the other room for

			a specified period of time, not until a particular assignment is completed.
13. Time Out, Non-Seclusionary	Removal of student from reinforcing activities in the instructional setting for a specified period of time.	P≫ Jordy's truck is taken away after he repeatedly runs it over the fingers of his playmates. The truck is placed on the shelf and the timer is set for four minutes. E≫ While the other third grade students continue to earn points toward a Friday activity, Sam's opportunity for reinforcement is removed for five minutes when he shouts out in class. S≫ Glen is removed from the P.E. soccer game for sixteen minutes after yelling obscenities at the goalie. He has to watch from the sidelines.	Forceful physical guidance is not permitted (e.g., forcing a student's head onto the desk). For the intervention to be effective, the student must be timed out from a reinforcing activity and/or from reinforcement during an activity.
14. Verbal Reprimand	A stern verbal statement or direction to gain attention and/or interrupt student behavior.	P≫ At the sensory table, Steven flips rice around the classroom with the shovel. Mrs. Delano says, "Steven, stop!" E≫ Ben is talking during seat-work time. Mrs. Yates stands three feet from his desk and makes eye contact with him. In a firm voice she then says, "Ben, back to work!" S≫ Susan is tapping her pencil on her desk while reading the geography chapter. Mrs. Newell says, "Susan, stop tapping your pencil!"	This may be reinforcing and should be used sparingly. Use judiciously as these techniques interrupt instruction for the entire class. This does not mean yelling at a student.
15. Work Detail	As a consequence of relatively serious misconduct, assigning a specific task of labor or	P≫ Not appropriate. E≫ Geoff, a fifth grader, sprays urine around the walls in the boys' restroom. He is assigned to pick up all the litter from the playground and to empty all classroom wastebaskets in the building	Note that the work detail is not related to the inappropriate behavior. Do not run afoul of child labor laws. Students should not be assigned to tasks such as

(Cont.)

engagement in a task for a specified period of time, under the appropriate supervision of a school staff member.

for two days.

S≫ Bart swears at this teacher and, as a consequence, he is assigned the task of washing all the lunchroom tabletops.

cleaning toilets, using dangerous equipment, or others which carry risks of injury or disease.

References

Adams, A., Carnine, D., & Gersten, R. (1982). Instructional strategies for studying content area texts in the intermediate grades. *Reading Research Quarterly, 18,* 27–55.

Adams, C. D., & Drabman, R. S. (1995). Improving morning interactions: Beat-the-buzzer with a boy having multiple handicaps. *Child and Family Behavior Therapy, 17,* 13–26.

Abramowitz, A. J., & O'Leary, S. G. (1991). Behavioral interventions for the classroom: Implications for students with ADHD. *School Psychology Review, 20,* 220–234.

American Psychiatric Association. (1994). *Diagnostic and statistical manual of mental disorders* (4th ed.). Washington, DC: Author.

Anhalt, K., McNeil, C. B., & Bahl, A. B. (1998). The ADHD classroom kit: A whole-classroom approach for managing disruptive behavior. *Psychology in the Schools, 35,* 67–79.

Arnold, M. E., & Hughes, J. N. (1999). First do no harm: Adverse effects of grouping deviant youth for skills training. *Journal of School Psychology, 37,* 90–115.

Axelrod, S. (1990). Myths that (Mis)guide our profession. In A. Repp., & N. Singh (Eds.), *Perspectives on the use of interventions for persons with developmental disabilities* (pp. 59–72). Illinois: Sycamore Press.

Babyak, A. E., Luze, G. J., & Kamps, D. M. (2000). The good student game: Behavior management for diverse classrooms. *Intervention in School and Clinic, 35,* 216–223.

Baker, S., Gersten, R., & Graham, S. (2003). Teaching expressive writing to students with learning disabilities: Research-based applications and examples. *Journal of Learning Disabilities, 36,* 109–123.

Bandura, A. (1977). *Social learning theory.* Englewood Cliffs, NJ: Prentice-Hall.

Baxendell, B. W. (2003). Consistent, coherent, creative: The 3 C's of graphic organizers. *Teaching Exceptional Children, 35,* 46–53.

Barkley, R. A. (1990). *Attention-deficit hyperactivity disorder: A handbook for diagnosis and treatment.* New York: The Guilford Press.

Boyle, J. R., & Weishaar, M. (2001). The effects of strategic notetaking on the recall and comprehension of lecture information for high school students with learning disabilities. *Learning Disabilities Research, 16,* 133–141.

Brantley, D. C., & Webster, R. E. (1993). Use of an independent group contingency management system in a regular classroom setting. *Psychology in the Schools, 30,* 60–66.

Broussard, C., & Northup, J. (1997). The use of functional analysis to develop peer interventions for disruptive classroom behavior. *School Psychology Quarterly, 12,* 65–76.

Brown, D., & Frank, A. R. (1990). "Let me do it!"—Self monitoring in solving arithmetic problems. *Education and Treatment of Children, 13*, 239–248.

Buehler, R. E., & Patterson, G. R. (1966). The reinforcement of behavior in institutional settings. *Behavior Research and Therapy, 4*, 157–167.

Cameron, J., & Pierce, W. D. (1994). Reinforcement, reward, and intrinsic motivation: A meta-analysis. *Review of Educational Research, 64*, 363–423.

Camp, B. W., Blom, G. E., Herbert, F., & van Doorninck, W. J. (1977). "Think Aloud": A program for developing self-control in young aggressive boys. *Journal of Abnormal Child Psychology, 5*, 157–169.

Carpenter, S. L., & McKee-Higgins, E. (1996). Behavior management in inclusive classrooms. *Remedial and Special Education, 17*, 195–203.

Carr, S. C. (2002). Assessing learning processes: Useful information for teachers and students. *Intervention in School and Clinic, 37*, 156–162.

Cashwell, T. H., Skinner, C. H., & Smith, E. S. (2001). Increasing second-grade students' reports of peers' prosocial behaviors via direct instruction, group reinforcement, and progress feedback: A replication and extension. *Education and Treatment of Children, 24*, 161–175.

Chance, P. (1992). The rewards of learning. *Phi Delta Kappa, 803*, 200–207.

Chess, S., & Thomas, A. (1983). *Evolution of behavior disorders: From infancy to early adult life.* New York: Brunner/Mazel.

Colvin, G., & Lazar, M. (1997). *The effective elementary classroom. Longmont*, CO: Sopris West.

Comings, D. E. (1990). *Tourette Syndrome and human behavior: The genetics of Tourette Syndrome.* Duarte, CA: Hope Press.

Connell, M. C., Carta, J. J., Lutz, S., Randall, C., & Wilson, J. (1993). Building independence during in-class transitions: Teaching in-class transition skills to preschoolers with developmental delays through choral-response-based self-assessment and contingent praise. *Education and Treatment of Children, 16*, 160–174.

Cosden, M., Gannon, C., & Haring, T. G. (1995). Teacher-control versus student-control over choice of task and reinforcement for students with severe behavior problems. *Journal of Behavioral Education, 5*, 11–27.

Davies, S., & Witte, R. (2000). Self-management and peer-monitoring within a group contingency to decrease uncontrolled verbalizations of children with attention-deficit/hyperactivity disorder. *Psychology in the Schools, 37*, 135–147.

Davis, C. A., Brady, M. P., Williams, R. E., & Hamilton, R. (1992). Effects of high probability requests on the acquisition and generalization of responses to requests in young children with behavior disorders. *Journal of Applied Behavior Analysis, 25*, 905–916.

Deaton, A. V. (1990). Behavioral change strategies for children and adolescents with traumatic brain injury. In E. D. Bigler (Ed.), *Traumatic brain injury: Mechanisms of damage, assessment, intervention, and outcome* (pp. 231–249). Austin, TX: Pro-ed.

Deci, E. L., Koestner, R., & Ryan, R. M. (1999). A meta-analytic review of experiments examining the effects of extrinsic rewards intrinsic motivation. *Psychological Bulletin, 125*, 627–668.

Delquadri, J. C., Greenwood, C. R., Stretton, K., & Hall, V. (1983). The peer-tutoring spelling game: A classroom procedure for increasing opportunity to respond and spelling performance. *Education and Treatment of Children, 6*, 225–239.

Dickenson, A. M. (1989). The detrimental effects of extrinsic reinforcement on "intrinsic motivation." *Behavior Analyst, 12*, 1–15.

Dishion, J., McCord, J., & Poulin, F. (1991). When interventions harm: Peer groups and problem behavior. *American Psychologist, 54*, 755–764.

Donnellan, A. M., & LaVigna, G. W. (1990). Myths about punishment. In A. Repp., & N. Singh (Eds.) *Perspectives on the use of interventions for persons with developmental disabilities* (pp. 33–57), Illinois: Sycamore Press.

Doyle, P. D., Jenson, W. R., Clark, E., & Gates, G. (1999). Free time and dots as negative reinforcement to improve academic completion and accuracy for mildly disabled students. *Proven Practice, 2,* 10–15.

Drasgow, E., & Yell, M. L. (2001). Functional behavioral assessment: Legal requirements and challenges. *School Psychology Review, 30,* 239–251.

Eddy, J. M., Reid, J. B., & Fetrow, R. A. (2000). An elementary school-based prevention program targeting modifiable antecedents of youth delinquency and violence: Linking the interests of families and teachers (LIFT). *Journal of Emotional and Behavioral Disorders, 8,* 165–176.

EduSoft Solutions (2001). *Discipline tracker for windows.* Branson, MO: EduSoft Solutions.

Eisenberger, R., & Cameron, J. (1996). Detrimental effects of reward: Reality or myth? *American Psychologist, 51,* 1153–1166.

Eisenberger, R., Pierce, D. W., & Cameron, J. (1999). Effects of reward on intrinsic motivation—negative, neutral, and positive: Comment on Deci, Koestner, and Ryan. (1999). *Psychological Bulletin, 125,* 677–691.

Elliott, S. N. (1988). Acceptability of behavioral treatments: Review of variables that influence treatment selection. *Professional Psychology: Research into Practice, 19,* 68–80.

Engelmann, S., & Carnine, D. W. (1982). *Theory of instruction.* New York: Irvington.

English, K., Goldstein, H., Kaczmarek, L., & Shafer, K. (1996). "Buddy skills" for preschoolers. *Teaching Exceptional Children, 28,* 62–66.

Evans, C., Jenson, W. R., Rhode, G., & Striefel, S. (1990). *LRBI: Least restrictive behavior interventions for students with behavior problems.* Adapted from published, Salt Lake City, UT: Utah State Office of Education.

Evans, S. W., Pelham, W., & Grudberg, M. V. (1995). The efficacy of notetaking to improve behavior and comprehension of adolescents with attention deficit hyperactivity disorder. *Exceptionality, 5,* 1–17.

Fister, S., Conrad, D., & Kemp, K. (1998). *Cool Kids: A Proactive Approach to Social Responsibility,* Longmont, CO: Sopris West.

Flores, D. M., Schloss, P. J., & Alper, S. (1995). The use of a daily calendar to increase responsibilities fulfilled by secondary students with special needs. *Remedial and Special Education, 16,* 38–43.

Forgan, J. W. (2002). Using bibliotherapy to teach problem solving. *Intervention in School and Clinic, 38,* 75–82.

Forness, S. R., Kavale, K. A., Blum, I. M., & Lloyd, J. W. (1997). What works in special education? *Exceptional Children, 29,* 4–9.

Friman, P. C., Jones, M., Smith, G., Daly, D. L., & Larzelere, R. (1997). Decreasing disruptive behavior by adolescent boys in residential care by increasing their positive to negative interactional ratios. *Behavior Modification, 21,* 470–486.

Fueyo, V., & Bushell, D. (1998). Using number line procedures and peer tutoring to improve the mathematics computation of low–performing first graders. *Journal of Applied Behavior Analysis, 31,* 417–430.

Gardner, R., Heward, W. L., & Grossi, T. A. (1994). Effects of response cards on student participation and academic achievement: A systematic replication with inner-city students during whole-class science instruction. *Journal of Applied Behavior Analysis, 27,* 63–71.

Gettinger, M. (1988). Methods of proactive management. *School Psychology Review, 17,* 227–242.

Godt, P., Hutinger, P., Roginson, L., & Schneider, C. (1999). Using a sign-up sheet strategy to encourage emergent literacy skills in young children with disabilities. *Teaching Exceptional Children, 32,* 38–44.

Greene, B. F., Bailey, J. S., & Barber, F. (1981). An analysis and reduction of disruptive behavior on school buses. *Journal of Applied Behavior Analysis, 14,* 177–192.

Gresham, F. M. (2002). *Establishing the technical adequacy of functional behavioral assessment: Conceptual and measurement challenges,* unpublished manuscript.

Gresham, F. M., McIntyre, L. L., Olson-Tinker, H., Dolstra, L., McLaughlin, V., & Van, M. (2002). Relevance of school based studies in *Journal of Applied Behavior Analysis* for functional behavior assessment and positive behavior support. Manuscript submitted for publication.

Gresham, F. M., Watson, T. S., & Skinner, C. H. (2001). Functional behavioral assessment: Principles, procedures, and future directions. *School Psychology Review, 30*, 156–172.

Gronna, S. S., Serna, L. A., Kennedy, C. H., Prater, M. A. (1999). Promoting generalized social interactions using puppets and script training in an integrated preschool. *Behavior Modification, 23*, 419–439.

Gumpel, T. P., & David, S. (2000). Exploring the efficacy of self-regulatory training as a possible alternative to social skills training. *Behavioral Disorders, 25*, 131–141.

Gunter, P. L., Miller, K. A., Venn, M. L., Thomas, K., & House, S. (2002). Self-graphing to success: Computerized data management. *Teaching Exceptional Children, 35*, 30–34.

Heinrichs, R. R. (2003). A whole-school approach to bullying: Special considerations for children with exceptionalities. *Intervention in School and Clinic, 38*, 195–204.

Higgins, J. W., Williams, R. L., & McLaughlin, T. F. (2001). The effects of a token economy employing instructional consequences for a third-grade student with learning disabilities: A data-based case study. *Education and Treatment of Children, 24*, 99–106.

Hughes, C. A., Ruhl, K. L., Schumaker, J. B., & Deshler, D. D. (2002). Effects of instruction in an assignment completion strategy on the homework performance of students with learning disabilities in general education classes. *Learning Disabilities Research and Practice, 17*, 1–18.

Hutchinson, S. W., Murdock, J. Y., Williamson, R. D., & Cronin, M. E. (2000). Self-recording plus encouragement equals improved behavior. *Teaching Exceptional Children, 32*, 54–58.

Jackson, C. W., & Larkin, M. J. (2002). Rubric: Teaching students to use grading rubrics. *Teaching Exceptional Children, 35*, 40–44.

Jenson, W. R., Andrews, D., & Reavis, K. (1994). The "yes" and "no" bag: A practical program for classroom consequences. *The Best Times* (pp. 3–4). Salt Lake City, UT: Utah State Office of Education.

Jenson, W. R., Andrews, D., & Reavis, H. K. (Summer, 1996). Promoting competent behavior of tough kids: Designing classroom rules, *Communique*, 1–6.

Jenson, W. R., Olympia, D., Farley, M., & Clark, E. (in press). Positive psychology and externalizing students in a sea of negativity. *Psychology in the Schools*.

Jenson, W. R., Neville, M., Sloane, H. N., & Morgan, D. (1982). Spinners and chartmoves: A contingency management system for school and home. *Child and Family Behavior Therapy, 4*, 81–85.

Jenson, W. R., & Reavis, H. K. (1996). Using group contingencies to improve academic achievement. In H. Reavis, S. Kukic, W. Jenson, D. Morgan, D. Andrews, & S. Fister (Eds.). *Best practices: Behavioral and educational strategies for teachers* (pp. 77–86). Longmont, CO: Sopris West.

Jenson, W. R., & Reavis, H. K. (1996). Advertising for success: Improving motivation. In H. Reavis, S. Kukic, W. Jenson, D. Morgan, D. Andrews, & S. Fister (Eds.). *Best practices: Behavioral and educational strategies for teachers* (pp. 3–10). Longmont, CO: Sopris West.

Jenson, W. R., Rhode, G., Evans, C., & Morgan, D. (in press). *The tough kid: Principal's Briefcase.* Longmont, CO: Sopris West.

Johns, G. A., Skinner, C. H., & Nail, G. L. (2000). Effects of interspersing briefer mathematics problems on assignment choice in students with learning disabilities. *Journal of Behavioral Education, 10*, 95–106.

Johnson, D. W., Johnson, R., Mitchell, J., Cotton, B., Harris, D., & Louison, S. (1996). Effectiveness of conflict managers in an inner-city elementary school. *The Journal of Educational Research, 89*, 280–285.

Jones, C. B. (1994). *Attention deficit disorder: Strategies for school-age children.* Austin, TX: Communication Skill Builders.

Jones, R. N., Sheridan, S. M., & Binns, W. R. (1993). Schoolwide social skills training: Providing preventive services to students at-risk. *School Psychology Quarterly, 8*, 57–80.

Jones, R. N., Wilson, B. T., Binns, W. R., & Wasden, S. J. (1992, March). A structured recess program: Teaching prosocial skills and decreasing antisocial behaviors. Paper presented at the annual meeting of the Utah Association of School Psychologists, Salt Lake City.

Joseph, L. M. (2002). Helping children link sound to print: Phonics procedures for small-group or whole-class settings. *Intervention in School and Clinic, 37*, 217–221.

Kazdin, A. E. (1977). Assessing the clinical or applied importance of behavior change through social validation. *Behavior Modification, 1*, 427–452.

Kearney, C. A., & Drabman, R. S. (1995). The write-say method for improving spelling accuracy in children with learning disabilities. *Journal of Learning Disabilities, 26*, 52–56.

Keller, C. L. (2002). A new twist on spelling instruction for elementary school teachers. *Intervention in School and Clinic, 38*, 3–7.

Kelley, M. L., & McCain, A. P. (1995). Promoting academic performance in inattentive children: The relative efficacy of school-home notes with and without response cost. *Behavior Modification, 19*, 357–375.

Kellner, M. H., Bry, B. H., & Colletti, L. (2002). Teaching anger management skills to students with severe emotional or behavioral disorders. *Behavioral Disorders, 27*, 400–407.

Kemp, K. Fister, S., & Conrad, D. (1998). *Cool Kids: A Proactive Approach to Social Responsibility*, Longmont: CO, Sopris West.

Kern-Dunlap, L., Dunlap, G., Clarke, S., Childs, K. E., White, R. L., & Stewart, M. P. (1992). Effects of a videotape feedback package on the peer interactions of children with serious behavioral and emotional challenges. *Journal of Applied Behavior Analysis, 25*, 355–364.

Kohn, A. (1999). *Punished by rewards: The trouble with gold stars, incentive plans, A's, praise, and other bribes*. Boston: MA, Houghton Mifflin.

Lalli, E. P., & Shapiro, E. S. (1990). The effects of self-monitoring and contingent reward on sight word acquisition. *Education and Treatment of Children, 13*, 129–141.

Landi, M. A. G. (2001). Helping students with learning disabilities make sense of word problems. *Intervention in School and Clinic, 37*, 13–18, 30.

Lazarus, B. D. (1998). Say cheese! Using personal photographs as prompts. *Teaching Exceptional Children, 30*, 4–7.

Lepper, M. R., Henderlong, J., & Gingras, I. (1999). Uses and abuses of meta-analysis: Comment on Deci, Koestner, and Ryan (1999). *Psychological Bulletin, 125*, 669–676.

Lewis, T. J., & Sugai, G. (1999). Effective behavior support: A systems approach to proactive school-wide management. *Focus on Exceptional Children, 31*, 1–24.

Lewis, T. J., Sugai, G., & Colvin, G. (1998). Reducing problem behavior through a school-wide system of effective behavioral support: Investigation of a school-wide social skills training program and contextual interventions. *School Psychology Review, 27*, 446–459.

Litow, L., & Pumroy, D. K. (1975, Fall). A brief review of classroom group-oriented contingencies. *Journal of Applied Behavior Analysis, 8*, 341–347.

Maag, J. (2001). Rewarded by punishment: Reflection on the disuse of positive reinforcement in education. *Exceptional Children, 67*, 173–186.

Martens, B. K., Ardoin, S. P., Hilt, A. M., Lannie, A. L., Panahon, C. J., & Wolfe, L. A. (2002). Sensitivity of children's behavior to probabilistic reward: Effects of a decreasing-ratio lottery system on math performance. *Journal of Applied Behavior Analysis, 35*, 403–406.

Martin, K. F., & Manno, C. (1995). Use of a check-off system to improve middle school students' story compositions. *Journal of Learning Disabilities, 28*, 139–149.

Mash, E. J., & Wolfe, D. A. (1999). *Abnormal child psychology*. Belmont, CA: Wadsworth.

Mason, L. H., Harris, K. R., & Graham, S. (2002). Every child has a story to tell: Self-regulated strategy development for story writing. *Education and Treatment of Children, 25*, 496–506.

Mastropieri, M. A., Scruggs, T., Mohler, L., Beranek, M., Spencer, V., Boon, R. T., & Talbott, E. (2001). Can middle school students with serious reading difficulties help each other and learn anything? *Learning Disabilities Research and Practice, 16*, 18–27.

Mathes, P. G., & Babyak, A. E. (2001). The effects of peer-assisted literacy strategies for first-grade readers with and without additional mini-skills lessons. *Learning Disabilities Research and Practice, 16*, 28–44.

Mathes, P. G., Fuchs, D., & Fuchs, L. S. (1997). Cooperative story mapping. *Remedial and Special Education, 18*, 20–27.

Mattson, S. N., & Riley, E. P. (1995). Prenatal exposure to alcohol. *Alcohol health and research world, 19*, 56–61.

Maughan, D. (2003). *A meta-analysis of behavioral parent training for externalizing children.* Unpublished doctoral dissertation, University of Utah, Salt Lake City, UT.

McDonnell, J., Thorson, N., Allen, C., & Mathot-Buckner, C. (2000). The effects of partner learning during spelling for students with severe disabilities and their peers. *Journal of Behavioral Education, 10*, 107–121.

McIntosh, R., Vaughn, S., & Bennerson, D. (1995). Fast social skills with a slam and a rap: Providing social skills training for students with learning disabilities. *Teaching Exceptional Children, 28*, 37–41.

Meichenbaum, D. H., & Goodman, J. (1971). Training impulsive children to talk to themselves: A means of developing self-control. *Journal of Abnormal Psychology, 77*, 115–126.

Metzler, C. W., Biglan, A., Rusby, J. C., & Sprague, J. R. (2001). Evaluation of a comprehensive behavior management program to improve school-wide positive behavior support. *Education and Treatment of Children, 24*, 448–479.

Migliore, E. T. (2003). Eliminate bullying in your classroom. *Intervention in School and Clinic, 38*, 172–176.

Miller, A. D., Hall, S. W., & Heward, W. L. (1995). Effects of sequential 1-minute time trials with and without inter-trial feedback and self-correction on general and special education students' fluency with math facts. *Journal of Behavioral Education, 5*, 319–345.

Morgan-D'Atrio, C., Northrup, J., LaFleur, L., & Serpa, S. (1996). Toward prescriptive alternative to suspensions: A preliminary analysis. *Behavior Disorders, 21*, 190–200.

Morin, V. A., & Miller, S. P. (1998). Teaching multiplication to middle school students with mental retardation. *Education and Treatment of Children, 21*, 22–36.

Moroz, K. B., & Jones, K. M. (2002). The effects of positive peer reporting on children's social involvement. *School Psychology Review, 31*, 235–245.

Moxley, R. A., Lutz, P. A., Ahlborn, P., Boley, N., & Armstrong, L. (1995). Self-recorded word counts of freewriting in grades 1–4. *Education and Treatment of Children, 18*, 138–157.

Musser, E. H., Bray, M. A., Kehle, T. J., & Jenson, W. R. (2001). Reducing disruptive behaviors in students with serious emotional disturbance. *School Psychology Review, 30*, 294–304.

Nelson, J. R., & Carr, B. A. (1996). *The think time strategy for schools.* Longmont, CO: Sopris West.

Neatrour, P. E. (1994). Riding by the rules: A practical approach to bus discipline. *Schools in the Middle, 4*, 25–27.

Nelson, J. R., Smith, D. J., & Colvin, G. (1995). The effects of a peer-mediated self-evaluation procedure on the recess behavior of students with behavior problems. *Remedial and Special Education, 16*, 117–126.

Nelson, M. D., Thomas, J. V., & Pierce, K. A. (1995). Inside-outside: A classroom discussion model for conflict resolution. *The School Counselor, 42*, 399–404.

Neville, M. H., & Jenson, W. R. (1984). Precision commands and the "sure I will" program: A quick and efficient compliance training sequence. *Child and Family Behavior Therapy, 6*, 61–65.

Nicholas, P. M. (1998). *Teachers' and school psychologists' selection and use of classroom interventions for reducing behavioral excesses.* Unpublished doctoral dissertation, University of Utah, Department of Educational Psychology, Salt Lake City, UT.

Ninness, H. A. C., Ellis, J., Miller, W. B., Baker, D., & Rutherford, R. (1995). The effect of a self-management training package on the transfer of aggression control procedures in the absence of supervision. *Behavior Modification, 19,* 464–490.

Olympia, D. E., Sheridan, S. M., Jenson, W. R., & Andrews, D. (1994). Using student-managed interventions to increase homework completion and accuracy. *Journal of Applied Behavior Analysis, 27,* 85–99.

Painter, L. T., Cook, J. W., & Silverman, P. S. (1999). The effects of therapeutic storytelling and behavioral parent training on noncompliant behavior in young boys. *Child and Family Behavior Therapy, 21,* 47–66.

Peine, H. A., Darvish, R., Blakelock, H., Osborne, J. G., & Jenson, W. R. (1998). Non-aversive reduction of cigarette smoking in two adult men in a residential setting. *Journal of Behavior Therapy and Experimental Psychiatry, 29,* 55–65.

Patterson, G. R. (1976). The aggressive child: Victim and architect of a coercive system. In E. J. Mash, L. A. Hamerlynck, & L. C. Handy (Eds.), *Behavior modification and families, Vol. 1: Theory and research* (pp. 267–316). New York: Brunner/Mazel.

Patterson, G. R., Reid, J. B., & Dishion, T. J. (1992). *Antisocial boys.* Eugene, OR: Castalia Publishing Co.

Patterson, G. R., Reid, J. B., & Snyder, J. J. (2002). *Antisocial behavior in children and adolescents: A developmental analysis and the Oregon model for intervention.* Washington D.C: American Psychological Association.

Pfiffner, L. J., Rosen, L. A., & O'Learn, S. G. (1985). The efficacy of an all-positive approach to classroom management. *Journal of Applied Behavior Analysis, 18,* 257–261.

Porte, L. K. (2001). Cut and paste 101: New strategies for note taking and review. *Teaching Exceptional Children, 34,* 14–20.

Proctor, M. A., & Morgan, D. (1991). Effectiveness of a response cost raffle procedure on the disruptive classroom behavior of adolescents with behavior problems. *School Psychology Review, 20,* 97–109.

Quinn, M. M., Kavale, K. A., Mathur, S. R., Rutherford, R. B., & Forness, S. R. (1999). A meta-analysis of social skills interventions for students with emotional or behavior disorders. *Journal of Emotional and Behavior Disorders, 7,* 54–64.

Rademacher, J. A. (2000). Involving students in assignment evaluation. *Intervention in School and Clinic, 35,* 151–156.

Raffaele, L. M. (2000). *An analysis of out-of-school suspensions in Hillsborough County,* Tampa, FL: University of South Florida.

Rhode, G., Jenson, W. R., & Reavis, H. K. (1993). *The tough kid book.* Longmont, CO: Sopris West.

Reavis, H. K., Jenson, W. R., Kukic, S., & Morgan, D. (1993). *Utah's BEST Project: Behavioral and educational strategies for teachers.* Utah State Office of Education, Salt Lake City, UT.

Reitman, D. (1997). *The real and imagined harmful effects of rewards: Implications for clinical practice.* Paper presented at the meeting of the Association for Behavior Analysis, Chicago, IL.

Reitman, D., & Drabman, R. S. (1996). Read my fingertips: A procedure for enhancing the effectiveness of time-out with argumentative children. *Child and Family Behavior Therapy, 18,* 35–40.

Rinaldi, L., Sells, D., & McLaughlin, T. F. (1997). The effects of reading racetracks on the sight word acquisition and fluency of elementary students. *Journal of Behavioral Education, 7,* 219–233.

Rivera, M. O., Koorland, M. A., & Fueyo, V. (2002). Pupil-made pictorial prompts and fading for teaching sight words to a student with learning disabilities. *Education and Treatment of Children, 25,* 197–207.

Roderick, C., Pitchford, M., & Miller, A. (1997). Reducing aggressive playground behavior by means of a school-wide raffle. *Educational Psychology in Practice, 13,* 57–63.

Rosen, L. A., O'Leary, S. G., Joyce, S. A., Conway, G., & Pfiffner, L. J. (1984). The importance of prudent negative consequences for maintaining the appropriate behavior of hyperactive students. *Journal of Abnormal Child Psychology, 12,* 581–604.

Rosenthal-Malek, A. L., (1997). Stop and think: Using metacognitive strategies to teach students social skills. *Teaching Exceptional Children, 29*, 29–31.

Rutherford, R. B., Mathur, S. R., & Quinn, M. M. (1998). Promoting social communication skills through cooperative learning and direct instruction. *Education and Treatment of Children, 21*, 354–369.

Salend, S. J., Tintle, L., & Balber, H. (1988). The effects of a student-managed response-cost system on the behavior of two mainstreamed students. *The Elementary School Journal, 89*, 89–97.

Sansone, C., & Harachkiewiez, J. (2002). *Intrinsic and extrinsic motivation: The search for optimal motivation and performance.* San Diego, CA: Academic Press.

Schermerhorn, P. K., & McLaughlin, T. F. (1997). Effects of the add-a-word spelling program on test accuracy, grades, and retention of spelling words with fifth and sixth grade regular education students. *Child and Family Behavior Therapy, 19*, 23–35.

Schirmer, B. R., & Bailey, J. (2000). Writing assessment rubric: An instructional approach with struggling writers. *Teaching Exceptional Children, 33*, 52–58.

Schmid, R. E. (1998). Three steps to self-discipline. *Teaching Exceptional Children, 30*, 36–39.

Schwartz, I. S., & Baer, D. M. (1991). Social validity assessments: Is current practice state of the art? *Journal of Applied Behavior Analysis, 24*, 189–204.

Seidenberg, M., & Berent, S. (1992). Childhood epilepsy and the role of psychology. *American Psychologist, 47*, 1130–1133.

Serna, L., Nielsen, E., Lambros, K., & Forness, S. (2000). Primary prevention with children at risk for emotional or behavioral disorders: Dada on a universal intervention for head start classrooms. *Behavioral Disorders, 26*, 70–84.

Shapiro, E. S. (1988). Preventing academic failure. *School Psychology Review, 17*, 601–613.

Sheridan, S. M. (1995). *The Tough Kid Social Skills Book*, Longmont: CO, Sopris West.

Spohn, J. R., Timko, T. C., & Sainato, D. M. (1999). Increasing the social interactions of preschool children with disabilities during mealtimes: The effects of an interactive placemat game. *Education and Treatment of Children, 22*, 1–18.

Sprick, R. S. (1995). *Cafeteria Discipline: Positive Techniques for Lunchroom Supervision*, Eugene: OR, Teaching Strategies, Inc.

Sprick, R., Sprick, M., & Garrison, M. (1992). *Foundations: Developing positive school-wide discipline policies.* Longmont, CO: Sopris West.

Sprute, K. A., Williams, R. L., & McLaughlin, T. F., (1990). Effects of a group response cost contingency procedure on the rate of classroom interruptions with emotionally disturbed secondary students. *Child and Family Behavior Therapy, 12*, 1–12.

Stage, S. A., & Quiroz, D. R. (1997). A meta-analysis of interventions to decrease disruptive classroom behavior in public education settings. *School Psychology Review, 26*, 333–368.

Sterling, H. E., Robinson, S. L., & Skinner, C. H. (1997). The effects of two taped-words interventions on sight-word reading in students with mental retardation. *Journal of Behavioral Education, 7*, 25–32.

Stormont, M. (2002). Externalizing behavior problems in young children: Contributing factors and early intervention. *Psychology in the Schools, 39*, 127–138.

Sugai, G., & Colvin, G. (1997). Debriefing: A transition step for promoting acceptable behavior. *Education and Treatment of Children, 20*, 209–221.

Sutherland, K. S., & Wehby, J. H. (2001). Exploring the relationship between increased opportunities to respond to academic requests and the academic and behavioral outcomes of students with EBD. *Remedial and Special Education, 22*, 113–121.

Taylor-Greene, S., Brown, D., Nelson, L., Longton, J., Gassman, T., Cohen, J., Swartz, J., Horner, R. H., Sugai, G., Hall, S. (1997). School-wide behavioral support: Starting the year off right. *Journal of Behavioral Education, 7*, 99–112.

Theodore, L. A., Bray, M. A., Kehle, T. J., & Jenson, W. R. (2001). Randomization of group contingencies and reinforcers to reduce classroom disruptive behavior. *Journal of School Psychology, 39*, 267–277.

Thomas, A., & Chess, S. (1977). *Temperament and development.* New York: Brunner/Mazel.

Todd, A., Haugen, L., Anderson, K., & Spriggs, M. (2002). Teaching recess: Low-cost efforts producing effective results. *Journal of Positive Behavior Interventions, 4*, 46–52.

Trammel, D. L., Schloss, P. J., & Alper, S. (1994). Using self-recording, evaluation, and graphing to increase completion of homework assignments. *Journal of Learning Disabilities, 27*, 75–81.

Troia, G. A., & Graham, S. (2002). The effectiveness of a highly explicit, teacher-directed strategy instruction routine: Changing the writing performance of students with learning disabilities. *Journal of Learning Disabilities, 35*, 290–305.

Uberti, H. Z., Scruggs, T. E., & Mastropieri, M. A. (2003). Keywords make the difference: Mnemonic instruction in inclusive classrooms. *Teaching Exceptional Children, 35*, 56–61.

Van Houten, R. (1980). *How to use reprimands.* Austin, TX: Pro-ed.

Walker, C. (1993). Predicting outcome after cerebral insult. *Headlines, September/October*, 4–11.

Walker, H. M., Colvin, G., & Ramsey, E. (1995). *Antisocial behavior in school: Strategies and best practices.* Pacific Grove, CA: Brooks/Cole Publishing Company.

Weiss, B., Catron, T., Harris, V., & Phung, T. M. (1999). The effectiveness of traditional child psychotherapy. *Journal of Consulting and Clinical Psychology, 67*, 82–94.

Weisz, J. R., Weiss, B., Alicke, M. D., & Klotz, M. L. (1987). Effectiveness of psychotherapy with children and adolescents: A meta-analysis for clinicians. *Journal of Consulting and Clinical Psychology, 55*, 542–549.

White, R., Algozzine, B., Audette, R., Marr, M. B., & Ellis, E. D. (2001). Unified discipline: A school-wide approach for managing problem behavior. *Intervention in School and Clinic, 37*, 3–8.

Williams, V. I., & Cartledge, G. (1997). Passing notes to parents. *Teaching Exceptional Children, 30*, 30–34.

Wolf, M. M. (1978). Social validity: The case for subjective measurement *or* how applied behavior analysis is finding its' heart. *Journal of Applied Behavior Analysis, 11*, 203–214.

Wolf, M. M., Hanley, E. L., King, L. A., Lachowicz, J., & Giles, D. K. (1970). The timer game: A variable interval contingency for the management of out-of-seat behavior. *Exceptional Children, 37*, 113–117.

Yeager, C., & McLaughlin, T. F. (1995). The use of a time-out ribbon and precision requests to improve child compliance in the classroom: A case study. *Child and Family Behavior Therapy, 17*, 1–9.

Index